S0-DXE-719

FINANCIAL
REFORM
IN THE 1980s

FINANCIAL REFORM IN THE 1980s

Thomas F. Cargill/Gillian G. Garcia

New York

HOOVER INSTITUTION PRESS
Stanford University/Stanford/California

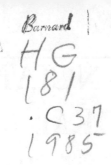

The Hoover Institution on War, Revolution and Peace, founded at Stanford University in 1919 by the late President Herbert Hoover, is an interdisciplinary research center for advanced study on domestic and international affairs in the twentieth century. The views expressed in its publications are entirely those of the authors and do not necessarily reflect the views of the staff, officers, or Board of Overseers of the Hoover Institution.

Hoover Press Publication 313

First printing, 1985
Manufactured in the United States of America
89 88 87 86 85   9 8 7 6 5 4 3 2 1

Library of Congress Cataloging in Publication Data
Cargill, Thomas F.
  Financial reform in the 1980s.

  Bibliography: p.
  Includes index.
  1. Finance—United States. 2. Banks and banking—United States. 3. Monetary policy—United States.
4. Finance—Law and legislation—United States.
5. Banking law—United States. I. Garcia, G. G.
II. Title.
HG181.C37 1985   332'.0973   84-25301
ISBN 0-8179-8131-4
ISBN 0-8179-8132-2   (pbk.)

CONTENTS

TABLES

FIGURES

PREFACE

Since 1979 the financial system and the conduct of monetary policy have undergone significant reform and restructuring. The most important reforms in regulation, procedures, or legislation include the October 1979 Federal Reserve announcement of changed operating strategy, the February 1980 redefinitions of the money supply, the Depository Institutions Deregulation and Monetary Control Act (DIDMCA) of 1980, and the Garn–St Germain Depository Institutions Act of 1982. These reforms are as sweeping as those of the Great Depression in terms of restructuring the financial system and the conduct of monetary policy. This study places these reforms in an historical context, discusses their major features, and assesses the additional reforms that will be required to achieve a stable financial and monetary environment for the 1980s. While the financial reform process has broad and international dimensions, this study focuses on the domestic implications, and on depository institutions.

Of course, financial reform is a continuing process and, as such, no study can be final. In 1982, the Hoover Institution published an earlier study by the authors (Cargill and Garcia, 1982) that focused on the 1980 act and its related policy events. We prepared that study only a short time after the legislation was enacted, and thus we could undertake only a preliminary analysis of a complex effort at financial reform. In the preface of that study, completed in late 1981, we acknowledged the difficulty of the task:

> Assessing the act's effects posed major difficulties, given that, at the time of writing, only slightly more than one year had elapsed since its passage. Much

x   *Preface*

will change in the next few years, and much depends on new legislative efforts to further pursue the act's objectives. [Cargill and Garcia, 1982, p. xi.]

Events since that time amply illustrate the relevance of this statement. Because many of the events forecast in our early study have occurred, it is now time to reassess the progress that has been made toward financial reform. Our present study takes a second and a more reflective examination of the financial reform process in the 1980s. Of course, this study cannot be any more complete than our previous study, for the reform process remains unfinished.

The authors would like to express appreciation to John Dobra, George Kaufman, Robert Laurent, and Larry Mote for reading manuscript material or serving as a sounding board for many of the issues discussed in this study. Gillian Garcia is grateful to the research division of the Federal Reserve Bank of Chicago and to Karl Scheld and Harvey Rosenblum, in particular, for encouragement and support in this undertaking. Appreciation is extended both to members of the Hoover Institution who provided valuable input in a variety of ways and to the Hoover Institution for providing facilities necessary for the completion of this study. The authors were Visiting Scholars at the Hoover Institution during the fall of 1983 when the major portion of this project was completed. We also extend our appreciation to Annie McMahon, Gus Backer, Dean Callison, Robin Beth Liggat and James Newman, who provided research assistance.

As in the previous study, the listing of authors is alphabetical, and both authors assume all responsibility for the content of the study.

1 THE 1980s: A DECADE OF CHANGE IN THE U.S. ECONOMY

The first year of the current decade, 1980, marked the fiftieth anniversary of the Great Depression. The Depression significantly changed attitudes not only about the benefits of unregulated markets but also about the role of government in a market-oriented economic system. In the decades following the Depression, government was regarded as having the right, indeed, the responsibility to undertake a wide spectrum of actions to insure satisfactory market performance and achieve overall economic stabilization. To many, the events of the early 1930s demonstrated that unregulated and competitive markets could not always insure socially desirable outcomes.

As a result of this attitude, the five decades following the start of the Great Depression witnessed significant growth of government regulation, supervision, and general involvement in the economy. The financial system, more than any other sector, was the focus of this government regulation and control. By the 1970s, the flow of funds in the U.S. economy was, to a high degree, regulated, supervised, and controlled. However, in the 1970s, growing concern was voiced by the public, economists, and policymakers about the extent of government regulation and influence in the economy. Many observers argued that high and fluctuating inflation rates, high and fluctuating interest rates, and slow growth in real income and labor productivity were in large part the result of inappropriate government involvement in the economy. The financial system, in particular, was the focus of this concern. As early as 1971, *The Report of the President's Commission on Financial Structure and Regulation* (1971) (also known as the Hunt Report) recommended a complete revision or removal of many of the government regulations over the financial system that had been enacted in the years following the onset of the Great Depression.

The decade of the 1980s resembles the 1930s in being a crucial watershed for determining the structure of the economy and the role of government. But now the emphasis is different. The current decade questions the very ability of government regulation, supervision, and stabilization policy to achieve smoothly functioning markets and general economic stability. The 1980 landslide victory of Ronald Reagan over Jimmy Carter was interpreted as a mandate to reverse the role of government in the U.S. economy initiated by the Great Depression. The new economic recovery program introduced by President Reagan in March of 1981 was a radical departure from previous conceptions of how government should function in the economy. The basic premise of the Reagan program was that extensive government regulation, supervision, and active stabilization policy were, in fact, the primary cause of the poor economic performance in the 1970s. A major component of the new program was government deregulation of major sectors of the U.S. economy. Deregulation would allow competitive forces to increase supply, reduce prices, and stimulate productivity.

The Reagan administration cannot be credited for initiating the deregulation process since deregulation in the financial system, airline industry, and trucking industry was well on its way by the end of 1980. Nevertheless, the Reagan administration has continually emphasized, as an important element of its policies, the need to reverse the trend of government involvement started in the 1930s. One may argue over the extent to which this reversal has been achieved since 1981; however, the Reagan administration is the first administration since the Great Depression to publicly call for a return to the pre-1930s faith in competitive and deregulated markets.

The financial system has been at the center stage of government involvement, both in the 1930s and in the current decade. As in the 1930s, the current financial system of the 1980s is experiencing significant structural change. This study is concerned with those forces and events that have generated current efforts to deregulate the intermediary sector of the financial system (and commercial banks and thrift institutions, in particular). Specifically, this study focuses on the complex set of changes that have recently occurred both in the financial system and in the conduct of monetary policy by the Federal Reserve. These two interrelated events can be collectively referred to as financial reform.

THE CONCEPT OF FINANCIAL REFORM

The meaning of financial reform can be illustrated by considering two aspects of the concept. First, the concept must be defined in broad enough terms to reflect the changing structure of the financial and monetary framework of the economy. In this regard, the close interrelationship between the financial system and the conduct of the monetary authority requires a concept of financial reform broader than mere regulation and supervision of financial institutions and markets.

The financial system is the market in which ultimate lenders and ultimate borrowers exchange funds for financial obligations, either via direct channels in money and capital markets or via indirect channels that utilize financial intermediaries or institutions. The monetary authority has responsibility for maintaining an adequate growth of credit and money to support real economic growth at stable prices. The financial system is the conduit through which monetary policy attempts to achieve its objectives. As such, the structure of the financial system influences the formulation, execution, and even the goals of monetary policy, while the financial system, in turn, is sensitive to changes in monetary policy. Thus the concept of financial reform must recognize this interrelationship. With this in mind, financial reform is defined as describing changes in the structure of the financial system and/or the formulation, execution, and goals of the monetary authority. Financial reform often, but not always, involves a complex interaction between changes in the financial system and the conduct of monetary policy. This is definitely the case with regard to financial reform in both the 1930s and 1980s.

Next, we can consider a second aspect of the concept of financial reform. There are two channels through which financial reform is introduced: government and the market. Government-initiated reform is evidenced by explicit changes in financial legislation or in regulations regarding the flow of funds or the conduct of the monetary authority. Reforms initiated at the governmental level, either through legislation or regulation, are hereafter referred to as regulator financial reforms.[1] Examples of regulator-initiated reform include the Federal Reserve Act of 1913, the Banking Acts of 1933 and 1935, and, more recently, changes in operating procedures announced by the Federal Reserve in October 1979, the February 1980 redefinitions of the money supply, the Depository Institutions Deregulation and Monetary Control Act of 1980 (DIDMCA), and the Garn–St Germain Depository Institutions Act of 1982. Hereafter, the last two legislative reforms are referred to as the 1980 and 1982 act, respectively.

Market-initiated reforms have been equally as important as government reforms, if not more important, on occasion, in the process of financial reform. Market reform occurs in response to profit opportunities that have been created by the failure of government either to address inefficiencies in the flow of funds or to recognize that conflicts exist between the legal/regulatory structure of the financial system and the given economic environment.

The existence of these two reform channels raises additional considerations: What is the appropriate use of the phrase "financial innovation"; and

What is the nature of the interaction between government and market reforms?

The phrase "financial innovation" is frequently used to describe the introduction of new financial assets and services by either the market or government; however, it seems more appropriate to confine the phrase to market-initiated reform. This usage is based on the following observations: Market reform often precedes regulator reform, and the process of innovation is more a market than a government phenomenon. The market is "innovative"; the government is "defensive and reactive." Thus the phrase "financial innovation" will be used to describe reforms initiated by the market in search of profit opportunities. To separate these actions from government-initiated reforms, the latter will be referred to as "regulatory financial innovations."

The interaction between market and regulator reform is an important part of the reform process in the United States, and one must keep the interaction in mind when reviewing the major changes in the financial system and the conduct of monetary policy in the past decade. This interaction provides insight into why financial reform occurs and what direction reform will take in the future. Edward Kane (1977, 1981) has suggested an interesting framework to analyze the interaction.

Kane suggests a framework relevant for a financial system that is subject to a variety of constraints and regulations that limit profit opportunity under certain economic conditions. The interplay of market and regulation commences when economic pressures render regulatory constraints so binding that the market attempts to circumvent the binding regulations to enhance profit. Economic pressures that render existing regulation binding limit profit opportunities and induce financial innovations on the part of the market. For example, when Regulation Q (which set upper bounds on the interest rates payable by banks and thrifts on many accounts) became binding after 1965, institutions and markets responded by introducing new financial instruments.[2] In response to these innovations, regulators responded in two contradictory ways. Regulators, in some instances, changed the regulations to enforce Regulation Q, such as restricting the form and magnitude of implicit interest payments, extending reserve requirements to certain liabilities being used to circumvent the ceilings, and extending Regulation Q ceilings to thrifts[3] in 1966. At the same time, regulators sometimes changed the regulations to relax the more serious constraints. For example, in 1978 regulators introduced the $10,000 money market certificate. This six-month time certificate was not subject to Regulation Q but was still constrained by the six-month Treasury bill yield. According to Kane and others, government-induced financial reform that is designed to constrain financial innovation either exacerbates the existing pressure on the financial system in the presence of other constraints or induces further innovation that partially nullifies the regulation. The response to this is again more government regulation. Kane has summarized this regulatory dialectic in the following way:

> Market institutions and politically imposed restraints reshape themselves in a Hegelian manner, simultaneously resolving and renewing an endless series of conflicts between economic and political power. The approach envisions repeating stages of regulatory avoidance (or "loophole mining") and re-regulation, with stationary equilibrium virtually impossible. [Kane, 1981, p. 355.]

The unstable equilibrium character of Kane's regulatory dialectic may not be realistic except under special conditions; however, there is no doubt that the interplay highlighted by Kane between market and regulatory innovations has played an important part in the recent reforms. As such, it helps one to understand financial reform in the 1980s.

RATIONALE FOR FINANCIAL REFORM: THE FINANCIAL SYSTEM

Financial reform occurs when the functions of the financial system are not satisfactorily fulfilled. There are three basic functions or objectives of the financial system. First, it should provide an efficient transfer of funds from surplus units (ultimate lenders) to deficit units (ultimate borrowers), so that, on the one hand, each participant in the financial system has access to a wide variety of channels to transfer funds, and, on the other, financial services are priced at competitive levels. Second, the financial system needs to be adaptable to the changing requirements of economic growth. Third, it should be stable in the presence of adverse economic events, such as inflation or recession. Other objectives of the financial system could be enumerated, but these three are considered the most important.

Two considerations have been raised regarding these objectives of the financial system. First, while the first two concepts of efficiency and adaptability are fairly clear, the third concept of soundness is much less clear. Can a sound financial system be said to exist when even a very few markets or institutions fail to remain economically viable? This was the interpretation of soundness that emerged from the Great Depression period. The interpretation was based on the importance of public confidence in the viability of the financial system. In a fractional reserve system, the failure of even a small number of institutions or markets can generate significant loss of public confidence and render the entire system unstable.

Another view of the financial system's soundness argues that the failure of small numbers of institutions or markets is still compatible with a sound system, provided that their failure is perceived as reflecting only the particular characteristics of the institution or market rather than those of the entire economy. Unfortunately, this approach offers no guidelines as to what is a small and permissible number of failures, short of the high failure rates of the Great Depression period.

As to the second consideration, the financial system's three objectives of efficiency, adaptability, and soundness are not necessarily compatible with each other. Efficiency and adaptability are, in general, complementary; however, efforts to improve soundness can conflict with efficiency and adaptability if soundness is interpreted in the strict sense of preventing even a small number of failures. Other interpretations of soundness may be more compatible with efficiency and adaptability.

As a minimum, financial reform directed toward the financial system must consider the following factors: (1) the existence and magnitude of trade-offs that exist between the objectives of efficiency, adaptability, and soundness; (2) the point at which the public loses confidence in the viability of financial institutions and markets; and (3) the role played by the monetary authority in influencing the public's perception of the viability of the entire financial system in the face of individual institutional or market failures.

RATIONALE FOR FINANCIAL REFORM: THE MONETARY AUTHORITY

The monetary authority has both a short- and long-run objective with regard to control over the amount of credit and money in the economic system. In the short run, the monetary authority is responsible for altering the amount of credit and money to offset cyclical swings in the demand function for money. In the long run, the authority is responsible for maintaining an adequate growth of credit and money to accommodate economic growth in a noninflationary environment. There is considerable debate over the extent to which the monetary authority can be held responsible for short-run economic performance. There is, however, general agreement that the long-run growth path of real output is determined by the economy's resource base and that the monetary authority is capable of determining the long-run value of money or the rate of inflation. There are several possible performance indicators to judge the monetary authority, but unstable rates of inflation that consistently average above 2 or 3 percent per year are clear evidence of the monetary authority's failure to achieve its most basic responsibility.

In addition to its short- and long-run credit and monetary objectives, the monetary authority must also function as a lender of last resort. Monetary standards evolve toward systems that are based on fractional reserves because they are resource efficient and provide a flexible credit mechanism to support changes in real economic activity. A fractional reserve system exists when depository institutions hold less than a 100 percent reserve behind deposit liabilities. Fractional reserve systems, however, expose institutions to potential liquidity problems. Unexpected and large deposit withdrawals that cannot be satisfied by existing reserve balances can force an institution into default. To prevent the failure of individual institutions that could easily spread to other institutions as the public lost faith in the ability of institutions to meet deposit withdrawals, the monetary authority can function as a lender of last resort. Since the monetary authority has the power to create reserves, lender-of-last-resort activities are an important responsibility of the monetary authority. Failure to successfully perform this responsibility has also been a reason, in the past, for reform of the monetary authority.

Unlike financial reform directed toward the financial system, reform directed toward the monetary authority is almost always channeled through government. In fact, the monetary authority itself is frequently the agent of such reform.

INITIATION OF FINANCIAL REFORM IN THE 1980s

The structure of the financial system established by the reform measures of the 1930s persisted until the late 1970s. This structure was characterized by a variety of constraints on competitive market behavior such as portfolio constraints, interest rate ceilings, extensive federal and state regulation and supervision over financial institutions and markets, and pervasive influence by the Federal Reserve in money and capital markets to target interest rates.

By the late 1970s this structure of the financial system and monetary authority became increasingly unable to provide a stable financial and monetary framework for the U.S. economy. High and unstable inflation and interest rates clearly indicated a failure on the part of the Federal Reserve to achieve effective monetary control, and a series of credit crunches in 1966, 1969, 1974–1975, and 1979–1980 indicated serious malfunctioning on the part of the financial system.

The following chapters will present a detailed discussion of the specific problems in the financial system, the conduct of monetary policy, the interaction between monetary control and the financial system, and the reforms that were introduced to deal with these issues. For the present, however, there are three important considerations to keep in mind.

First, the failure of the monetary authority and of the financial system to achieve their respective objectives during the 1970s initiated the extensive regulatory reform effort begun in October 1979. This reform effort is continuing at present and will continue throughout the decade. Second, the financial reform process deals with problems of both the structure of the financial system and the conduct of monetary policy. Third, the financial reforms of the 1980s are the most significant restructuring of the financial and monetary framework since those of the 1930s; however, the emphasis is markedly different. The current reforms are designed to increase the degree of competitive behavior, primarily among depository institutions, whereas the reforms of the 1930s were designed to limit competition. Likewise, the role of the monetary authority is substantially different during the reform process of the 1980s compared with that in the early period. During the 1930s, the monetary authority was restructured; however, it was not expected to play a significant role in stabilization policy. During the 1980s, the monetary authority is recognized as a key element in the stabilization process.

The reforms directed toward the financial system in general and specifically toward the depository institutions are intended to provide a more competitive environment for the flow of funds. The intended benefits of a more competitive and flexible financial system include: (1) greater efficiency and the provision of a wider range of financial services to lenders and borrowers; (2) greater equity for the small saver, who will be able to earn market rates of interest on small deposits; (3) encouragement of higher saving rates by offering market-determined rates that will allocate funds to those in the economy who demonstrate the greatest demand; (4) increased earning power for thrift institutions, especially savings and loan associations (S&Ls), to improve their viability and soundness; and (5) an environment more conducive to monetary policy.

The reforms directed toward the Federal Reserve are being undertaken to achieve greater control over the money supply. The benefits of more effective monetary control include: (1) long-run price stability and hence, interest rate stability; (2) a financial environment that will encourage increased private investment, productivity, and economic growth; (3) a stabler international value for the dollar; and (4) a stabler financial system in general.

OUTLINE OF THE STUDY

Our objectives in this study are to summarize the major U.S. policy events since 1979 that have been directed toward restructuring the financial system and the conduct of monetary policy, to provide a historical perspective on these events, to analyze their current and probable future impacts, and, finally, to assess the probable direction of financial reform in the 1980s.

Although financial reform is a dynamic process, the forces of change are fairly clear in the present context and define the general path that financial reform will take in the 1980s. At the same time, one cannot be sure about the specifics of the adjustment path since a number of significant issues remain to be resolved.

The objectives of this study are carried out in the following seven chapters. Chapter 2 discusses the rationale for government regulation and involvement in the financial and monetary framework of a competitive economy and reviews the available theories that account for the extensive regulatory involvement of government.

Chapter 3 reviews the major financial reforms introduced in the United States from immediately after the Revolutionary War up to the Interest Rate Control Act of 1966. In addition, this chapter presents a summary of the characteristics of financial reform in the United States.

Chapters 4 and 5 discuss the major efforts to achieve financial reform starting in 1979. Chapter 4 deals with the inability of the financial system and monetary authority to achieve their respective objectives during the 1970s, the policy events of 1979 and 1980, and how these policy events were designed to deal with the financial problems of the U.S. economy. Chapter 5 deals with the failures of the 1979 and 1980 reforms and with the 1982 act as a continuation of the reform effort. The 1982 act is extensively discussed in this chapter.

Chapters 6 and 7 deal with two major issues regarding the financial reform process of the 1980s. Chapter 6 reviews the so-called thrift problem, the role of the thrift industry in the reform process, and the impact of financial reform on housing finance. Chapter 7 discusses a number of issues raised by the reform process for the conduct of monetary policy.

Chapter 8 summarizes the major issues that remain unresolved and whose resolution is necessary if the objective of a stable financial and monetary framework is to be achieved.

This introductory chapter has already introduced a variety of terms and concepts, some of which may be unfamiliar to the reader. To aid in the discussion of the financial reform process, a glossary has been included in the study to briefly define the more important terms and concepts used in this and the remaining chapters.

2 PURSUIT OF A STABLE FINANCIAL AND MONETARY FRAMEWORK: THE ROLE OF GOVERNMENT REGULATION

THE RATIONALE FOR FINANCIAL REFORM

The financial system and monetary authority frequently failed to achieve their respective objectives at various times during the development of the U.S. economy. In fact, the United States did not have an identifiable monetary authority that was specifically responsible for monetary control and lender-of-last-resort functions until the establishment of the Federal Reserve System in 1913. Before 1913 the functions of the monetary authority were performed by various governmental and private institutions, often in a less than satisfactory manner.

Failure of the financial system or monetary authority to achieve its objectives has more than once seriously disrupted the level of economic activity. To recognize this fact does not depend on one's monetarist or nonmonetarist views, but is based on historical study of the financial system, economic theory, and econometric analyses. The important issue at this juncture is to recognize the key role that government, primarily at the federal level, plays in the reform process. The major regulatory reforms in the United States have been in response to a failure of the existing structure of the financial system or of the monetary authority to achieve a stable financial and monetary framework. It may well be that government reacts rather than initiates, that government action is partially offset by financial innovation, and that government action takes a myopic rather than a general equilibrium view of the reform process. Even granting this, one cannot deny the important role government has played in structuring the financial system and the monetary authority. This involvement has been motivated by the desire to establish an environment that permits a rate of economic growth consistent with the resource base of the economy at stable and low inflation rates. Despite the current deregulation terminology, government regulation will continue to play an important role in the financial reform process.

The general objective of a stable financial and monetary framework has been pursued by a variety of government regulatory efforts aiming to achieve several specific objectives. Some efforts have been successful, whereas others have been less than successful. These various efforts will be reviewed in the next chapter. At this point, however, we will survey the objectives of government regulation along with the available regulatory theories that may shed some light on the evolution of financial regulation.

SPECIFIC OBJECTIVES OF
FINANCIAL AND MONETARY REGULATION

The development of government regulation throughout the financial history of the United States suggests at least four specific objectives. First, regulation has been designed to achieve monetary control in order to support steady economic growth at stable prices. Second, regulation has been intended to insure the soundness and viability of financial institutions, especially those institutions whose liabilities function as money. Third, regulation has aimed at protecting deposit holders. Fourth, regulation has sought to improve the efficiency of the flow of funds in the financial system.

These objectives of government regulation are based on the view that financial and monetary arrangements cannot be left to the market, even in the case of an Adam Smith world of competition. Minimal government regulation is based on three considerations. First, financial flows between deficit (net borrowing) and surplus (net lending) units as well as the behavior of the total amount of credit and money are critically important to the overall performance of the economy. Second, monetary systems historically develop toward structures that incorporate fiduciary elements, fractional reserves, incentives for institutions to create excessive deposits, and externality or third-party effects. Third, institutions whose liabilities function as money are fundamentally different from nonfinancial firms since the value of their debt liabilities is fixed in nominal value, whereas the value of their assets is sensitive to interest rate changes. The asymmetrical response of the value of each side of the balance sheet to interest rate changes exposes financial institutions to unique risks not faced by other firms.

THE EVOLUTION OF MONETARY STANDARDS

The historical evolution of monetary standards shows that money develops from commodity to fiduciary forms. This development provides the primary rationale for a minimal degree of government regulation to insure effective noninflationary monetary control. Other specific objectives of government regulation also derive from the natural evolution of monetary standards.

The evolution of monetary standards and the need for regulation has been summarized by Milton Friedman (1959). According to Friedman, a pure commodity standard can provide basic financial and monetary services without government regulation; however, these services are provided in an inefficient manner. The supply of the commodity used as money depends on its relative cost of production, so that changes in supply reflect the commodity's value relative to other goods. Economic systems in the past have adopted a variety of commodity standards such as gold, silver, or bimetalic standards, with either no or only minimal government regulation in the form of providing minting services and insuring weight and purity of the commodity money.

Pure commodity systems provide monetary services in a less than satisfactory manner. The scarce supply of the commodity and the randomness associated with finding new supplies make it unlikely that supply will respond in a smooth fashion to the monetary needs of the economy. Considerable resources are necessary to insure the supply of the commodity money, and the commodity itself has an opportunity cost when used as money. Thus there is an incentive for the market to adopt other forms of money that are less resource-using and more responsive to the changing needs of the economy.

The market finds it advantageous to introduce fiduciary elements into the commodity standard by issuing promises to pay backed by the commodity money. Promises to pay are more efficient since they are less resource-using to produce and are subject to either zero or small opportunity cost. In time, the issuers of promises to pay find that as long as they are generally acceptable as a medium of exchange, reserves in the form of commodity money can be less than the outstanding promises to pay. Thus issuers discover that they can continue to function by maintaining a fractional reserve of the commodity money to satisfy net claims among different issuers or satisfy the needs of those individuals who wish to convert promises to pay into commodity money.

Thus the historical evolution of monetary standards, such as in the United States, reveals two important financial innovations introduced by the market to improve efficiency: the creation of promises to pay and the establishment of the fractional reserve system. The institutional framework of the United States can be related to this framework simply by calling promises to pay "deposits" and issuers of promises to pay "banks."

These financial innovations, however, introduce significant third-party or externality considerations into the operation of individual banks and the banking system. Deposits provide basic monetary and financial services only as long as they are generally accepted as a medium of exchange. This depends on the ease with which they can be converted into the basic commodity money. Fractional reserves economize the commodity money and are sufficient to satisfy limited conversion; however, any event arousing the fear among deposit holders that any one issuer will be unable to convert deposits into reserves will work externality effects on other issuers. The fractional reserve system can not accommodate the conversion of large amounts of outstanding deposits into reserves. Thus the failure of even a small number of issuers can generate the fear that deposits are not convertible and, in turn, generate "runs" on all issuers as the public tries in vain to convert deposits (promises to pay) into reserves (commodity money).

The evolution of monetary standards from pure commodity to fiduciary, the establishment of fractional reserves, and the introduction of third-party effects serves to rationalize a variety of government regulations even in the context of a competitive market. These regulations were intended (1) to insure effective monetary control, (2) to insure the soundness and viability of financial institutions, and (3) to protect deposit holders. A fourth aim, improving the efficiency of the financial system, has also been a related objective of regulation. Each of these objectives will be discussed in turn.

MONETARY CONTROL

The evolution of monetary standards and financial innovation raises an important macroeconomic issue for an unregulated and competitive financial system. Milton Friedman (1959), John Gurley and Edward Shaw (1960), Harry G. Johnson (1968), Don Patinkin (1961), Boris Pesek and Thomas R. Saving (1967), and others have argued that the price level will generally be undetermined if the private market is allowed to provide all of the financial and monetary arrangements for the economy. There is no guarantee that the market will generate an optimal monetary growth path sufficient to meet the requirements of economic growth at stable and low rates of inflation. It is more likely that banks will be under constant pressure to issue promissory deposits, minimize reserve/deposit ratios, and thus generate unstable and excessive monetary growth. As a result, some degree of government regulation is required to insure effective monetary control and, consequently, a stable price level. While there has been little disagreement about this generalization, it leaves considerable room for debate over how extensive government involvement should be and what form that involvement should take. Many ways exist by which government can control the money supply, involving various degrees of influence over the portfolio decisions and operations of banks, other financial institutions, and financial markets.

Historically, in the United States, government has sought to control the money supply by imposing legal reserve requirements on banks and by varying the supply of the reserve asset permitted to satisfy the reserve requirement. This framework of monetary control is illustrated in any standard monetary economics textbook. But legal reserve requirements are neither necessary nor sufficient to achieve effective monetary control and, hence, stable prices.

SOUNDNESS OF THE FINANCIAL SYSTEM

In addition to the objective of monetary control, government regulation is also designed to maintain the soundness and viability of financial institutions and markets. Although this objective encompasses the entire financial system, our focus is again on those institutions whose liabilities provide monetary services.

Deposit money and the fractional reserve system economize on resources and permit a more responsive money supply to the needs of economic growth. But, at the same time, these devices expose individual banks to unique types of risk. First, bank balance sheets are asymmetrically sensitive to changes in the interest rate; second, individual banks and the banking system cannot convert large amounts of promissory deposits into reserves without risking mass failures. Once the public doubts the convertibility of deposits into reserves, deposits will no longer be an acceptable medium of exchange, and the public will attempt to convert their deposit holdings. Runs on the banking system will quickly spill over into other institutions and markets, and a general financial panic will ensue. Thus the soundness of the banking system is essential to the overall stability of the financial system.

The soundness and stability of the financial system is a necessary, but not sufficient, condition for steady economic growth. As such, government regulation has recognized that the soundness of the financial system is an important regulatory objective. Even a cursory review of the financial history of the United States reveals the importance of a sound and stable institutional framework for the flow of funds. On a more fundamental level, however, Ben S. Bernanke (1983) has recently proposed a useful framework for understanding the role that the financial system plays in determining the level of economic activity.

Bernanke's framework is important because it offers an alternative view of how disruptions in the financial system impact on the overall level of economic activity, in contrast to the well-known views of Milton Friedman and Anna J. Schwartz (1963) and Clark Warburton (1966).[1] For their part, Friedman, Schwartz, Warburton, and others focus attention on changes in the money supply that result from disruptions in the financial system, primarily bank failures, and the desire of existing banks to increase reserve/deposit ratios. In contrast, Bernanke focuses on factors that interfere with the basic function performed by intermediaries, which may or may not influence the money supply.

Bernanke argues that financial intermediation involves significant market-making and information-gathering services. The basic service performed by banks and other financial institutions is the ability to differentiate between "good" and "bad" borrowers, that is, productive and nonproductive uses of loaned funds. The cost of supplying credit intermediation consists of the resources devoted to screening, monitoring, administration, and the expected losses from "bad" loans in attempting to channel funds from surplus units (ultimate lenders) to "good" borrowers. Significant increases in the cost of credit intermediation can reduce the effectiveness of the financial system and reduce the funds available to all borrowers, including "good" borrowers. Shocks to the economy as well as policy mistakes also tend to increase the cost of credit intermediation. These factors, in turn, reduce credit availability, with corresponding adverse impacts on aggregate demand and real economic performance.

Thus disruptions in the financial system, whether through unstable changes in the money supply or through reduced opportunities for borrowers, have serious implications for economic activity. It is apparent, then, that the soundness of the financial system is an important component of the goal of maintaining a stable financial and monetary framework. Government regulation has attempted to enhance this soundness in a wide variety of ways. A partial listing of government efforts to maintain a sound financial system would include imposition of legal reserve requirements, portfolio constraints to limit risk taking, deposit insurance to maintain public confidence in deposit money in the face of failures of individual banks, and lender-of-last-resort services provided by the monetary authority.

PROTECTION OF DEPOSIT HOLDERS

Deposit money has historically evolved as a more efficient means of payment in comparison with other forms of money. Its general acceptability, however, depends on the public perception that deposits can be converted into reserves. The public will hold deposit money and continue to use it as a medium of exchange only as long as deposit debt is perceived as having low or zero default risk. Deposit holders are not concerned with interest rate risk since the nominal or face value of deposits remains constant despite changes in interest rates.

Any perceived increase in the default risk of deposits will induce the public to convert their deposits into reserve money. In the United States, this tendency has been demonstrated by significant increases in the currency/deposit ratio during major financial panics, especially during the 1930–1933 period of the Great Depression.

Thus the protection of deposit holders has been an important objective of government regulation. It is a means both to insure the general acceptability of deposit money and to maintain a stable and sound financial system. The forms of government regulation designed to protect deposits are generally the same as those used to insure the soundness of the financial system. In fact, the objectives of soundness and protection of depositors are closely interrelated.

EFFICIENCY OF THE FINANCIAL SYSTEM

The market for financial claims is subject to a variety of nontrivial transaction and information costs. In the case of direct financial markets, the transfer of funds from surplus to deficit units is constrained by the need to achieve a coincidence of amount, the need to achieve a coincidence of maturity, and the need to incorporate the risk preferences of the surplus unit (ultimate lender). Intermediation markets represent an innovation designed to reduce the importance of these constraints and to lower the cost of credit intermediation.

Thus, changes in the financial system that facilitate the flow of funds between surplus (net lender) and deficit (net borrower) units will have a positive impact on the overall level of economic activity. As such, government regulation has often been designed to improve efficiency. For example, reducing entry restrictions to banking, standardizing bank note issues, issuing Federal Reserve notes, and establishing a national check-clearing facility have all been regulatory efforts to improve efficiency.

At the same time, the individual objectives of efficiency and soundness may conflict, depending on how soundness is interpreted. The major distinction between the financial reforms of the 1930s and those of the 1980s centers precisely on what interpretation is given to soundness and what regulatory framework is most conducive to a sound financial system. If soundness means preventing the failure of even a very small number of financial institutions and protecting all depositors, then soundness and efficiency objectives will necessarily conflict. This point poses another issue relevant to the possible conflicts among the specific objectives of government regulation that has recently been raised by Eugene Fama (1980).

IS REGULATION NECESSARY FOR
EFFECTIVE MONETARY CONTROL?

Monetary control constitutes the basic foundation of financial regulation in the United States and in most other market-oriented economies. Many writers have argued that an optimal money supply cannot be guaranteed by the market and that government must in some manner regulate the banking system to insure optimal monetary growth.

This view has been challenged by Eugene Fama (1980). He bases his analysis on the concept of competitive and efficient markets and a banking framework suggested by James Tobin (1963). Fama argues that the price-level control problem is separate and distinct from regulation of either the banking system or of any group of issuers of promises to pay that function as money. Fama contends that the concern expressed by Friedman and others over the need to regulate the banking system in some minimal fashion is incorrect and based on a confusion between money and deposits. According to Fama, deposits represent merely one of many ways of holding and transferring wealth. Since deposits permit only a more efficient wealth transfer, their limit is determined by the wealth opportunities available to the economy. A wide range of financial assets and institutions could provide this service. Trying to control a group of assets via regulation of the issuers of those assets in order to achieve a stable price level makes no more sense than trying to control the amount of bonds and stocks and regulate corporations in order to achieve a stable price level.

We can expand Fama's argument by identifying his three major ideas. First, government does have a responsibility to determine a stable price level. This cannot be accomplished by the market. Second, government regulation of the banking system is not necessary to achieve price control since other methods of price control are available in the context of competitive markets. Third, government banking regulation actually interferes with the efficiency of the financial system and thus interferes with the legitimate responsibility of government to control the price level.

According to Fama's argument there is no need to regulate the banks to limit their issuance of deposits since deposits have nothing to do with the determination of the price level in a competitive system. Fama summarizes the analysis in the following terms.

To achieve a stable price level, Fama reasons, government is required to control only the supply of some numeraire good for which there exists a well-defined demand function. Deposits do not have a well-defined demand function since deposits are only a means of accounting and there exists a wide range of substitutes that can provide the same function.

Currency could, but presently does not, meet the minimal requirements to act as the numeraire good. Currency performs a valuable service to society as an efficient medium of exchange, especially for small transactions. Currency can serve as a unit of account because the prices of goods and services are expressed in terms of the principal unit of currency, the dollar. Thus the determination of the price level could result from the interplay between the demand and supply for currency. The public's demand for currency is well-defined, and its supply could be regulated by the monetary authority. Although currency could, therefore, fulfill the role of numeraire, it does not because the authorities do not now attempt to limit its supply. Rather, they provide whatever amount is demanded.

At present, the Federal Reserve is popularly believed to determine the price level through its control over the quantity of money. The problems attendant to this approach are discussed further in Chapter 7. However, it is already clear that such a method conflicts with Fama's requirements for adequate price control and an efficient banking system. Such an approach to control does not separate the numeraire function of price level determination from the portfolio allocation, or wealth-holding attributes, of deposits.

Using Fama's analysis, it might be argued that the Federal Reserve is, in effect, trying to control the price level via depository institution reserves (or alternatively, via the monetary base, which includes both reserves and currency). The monetary authority establishes a reasonably predictable demand for reserves by imposing reserve requirements on a given set of depository institution liabilities. It is the sole supplier of the needed reserves, and it carefully limits their quantity. Currently then, the relationship between the demand for and the supply of reserves determines the price level.

Fama, however, argues that this is not an efficient procedure. Financial regulation of the banking system is not necessary and may not be sufficient to achieve price control. First, it is not necessary since other means are available. Second, such regulation imposes a cost on society in the form of an inefficient allocation of resources. Third, regulation of the banking system may not be sufficient, since it will induce financial innovation as institutions shift from more regulated to unregulated, or less regulated, financial activities. In this process, institutions continually introduce new and unregulated forms of money. This process is an illustration of the regulatory dialectic process described by Edward Kane and discussed above.

In short, Fama regards controlling the price level where reserves are the numeraire as unsatisfactory because it generates an inherent conflict between the desire to establish an efficient and competitive financial system on the one hand and the need to maintain a stable price system on the other. The second objective requires control only over the supply and demand for a numeraire good and has no direct relationship to the first objective.

SIGNIFICANCE OF FAMA'S FRAMEWORK

The argument advanced by Fama is correct within the context of complete or efficient markets. In this regard it represents an alternative view to the traditional argument advanced by Friedman and others. In its defense, however, the traditional argument was never expressed in the context of the type of world employed by Fama. The traditional argument was rooted as much in history as in economic theory.

The complete and efficient market world of Fama is inappropriate for the current structure of the economy and is not likely to become relevant for some time. Fama's framework is based essentially on the efficient market hypothesis in which markets incorporate all available and useful information, transaction costs are ignored, and systematic errors do not persist. In its favor, the efficient market hypothesis has generated insights into the operation of individual markets and has even been applied to macroeconomic issues in the form of rational expectations. But, by itself, it is a weak reed on which to base financial reform issues that impact on the entire economy. Even for the most competitive financial markets, the efficient market hypothesis has not found consistent support (Sheffrin, 1983, chapter 4). Moreover, Fama's framework reveals nothing about the actual historical evolution of financial institutions. Rather than start from the theoretical assumption of efficient markets and then go on to question the role of banks, one might more profitably follow John Wood's (1981) suggestion and start from an assumption of inefficient markets and then go on to question how financial intermediaries evolve to make these markets more efficient. It seems more reasonable to emphasize the existence of markets characterized by varying degrees of efficiency, significant costs of information acquisition, and transaction costs, such as Bernanke discusses. In fact, Bernanke (1983, p. 263) points out that the contraction of the banking system from 1930 to 1933, together with its impact on the real performance of the economy, could not have occurred in the Fama world of efficient markets!

Although one can be critical of the Fama framework for analyzing financial reform issues of the 1980s, it does provide useful insights. Monetary control via regulation of the banking system will induce financial innovation as institutions shift from reserved to nonreserved liabilities under the present system of noninterest-earning and high-reserve requirements. Advances in computer technology lower the level of the interest rate necessary to induce this shift. Merely extending reserve requirements beyond the banking system as was done in the 1980 act will, in time, stimulate offsetting innovations.

On a more fundamental level, the Fama framework suggests that price control objectives may require a complete re-evaluation as computer technology and financial innovation increase the substitutes for deposits (Klitgaard, 1983). Unless there is complete synchronization between expenditures and receipts, some medium of exchange will be required in the future. Historically, currency and bank deposits have satisfied the public's need to bridge the gap between expenditures and receipts. Deposits have been and remain more than a mere accounting system that can be duplicated by others; however, financial reform has blurred the distinction between traditional deposit money and other financial assets. Every passing year, it becomes more difficult to define a stable set of financial assets to serve as money. As a result, it may be necessary to completely re-evaluate the methods used to achieve price control in the United States. Currently, the monetary authority focuses on targeting the growth of a well-defined measure of money based on a structure of reserve requirements imposed on depository institutions.

DEVELOPMENT OF REGULATORY POLICY

Government financial regulation has constantly expanded throughout the history of the U.S. economy. This regulatory growth has not, however, proceeded in a continual or consistent manner in terms of objectives or methods to achieve those objectives. The most dramatic shift in government regulation occurred during the Great Depression. This and other efforts to achieve a stable financial and monetary framework will be reviewed in the next chapter. At this point, however, it will be useful to discuss the present state of the theory of regulatory policy. That is, does there exist a theoretical framework that provides insight into why regulation exists, the relationship between the regulator and the regulated, and how regulation changes over time?

Historically, government financial regulation has been rationalized on the basis of public interest or market failure considerations. But serious questions arise as to how realistic this view is in the present context of extensive regulation. The public interest or market failure perspective may indeed shed light on the initial efforts to regulate some sector of the economy, but this perspective does not account for the evolution of regulation since the Great Depression.

Financial institutions, especially depository institutions, are subject to significant government regulation and supervision. In fact, the recent efforts toward deregulation do not imply that depository institutions will thereafter function in an unregulated environment. The regulatory agencies have become a permanent part of government, and, as such, regulation is the last function regulators wish to cease performing! The term *deregulation* must be interpreted more narrowly. The current (as of early 1984) "deregulation" effort is focused on removing only a small number of key competitive constraints on depository institutions. Some institutions in fact will be subject to increased regulation. This has led some writers (Kane, 1982) to refer to the Depository Institutions Deregulation and Monetary Control Act (DIDMCA) of 1980 as the "re-regulation" act of 1980. Thus, despite the current efforts at deregulating, the role of regulation in the financial system will remain a permanent part of our financial structure.

One would think that given the role of regulation in the U.S. economy, a substantial body of regulatory theory would have been developed. Unfortunately, the large volume of work done on regulatory policy has serious limitations, especially when applied to financial regulation. Before discussing the implications of current regulatory theory for financial reform, we need to briefly summarize the major approaches.

The theory of regulation has been surveyed by Robert J. Mackay and Joseph D. Reid, Jr. (1979), Richard Posner (1974), and Sam Peltzman (1976). According to Mackay and Reid,[2] there are four discernible views: (1) the "public interest," "market failure," or "general welfare" theory; (2) the "capture" or "special interest" theory; (3) the "many interests" theory; and (4) the "public choice" theory.

The public interest theory suggests that regulation is a collective request by market participants for government to correct inefficient markets. This view provides the primary rationale for the extensive regulatory reforms introduced during the 1930s, which were designed to correct inefficient and unstable financial markets and institutions and to restore public confidence in the nation's depository institutions and money. Government is here viewed as an exogenous entity that establishes regulation to improve the "general welfare" by rectifying market failures.

The public interest view suggests that regulation benefits a broad public base and that the costs of regulation will be born by a much smaller and narrower part of the public. To illustrate this, the regulators rationalized deposit interest rate ceilings by arguing that the benefits would be distributed to a much larger group than the group that was to bear the costs of regulation. The public, they contended, benefited by removing an incentive for banks to assume risky loan and investment portfolios. In addition, interest rate ceilings on deposits were expected to generate lower interest rates on loans by constraining the cost of funds. The benefits of Regulation Q were seen as substantial and widespread, whereas the cost to deposit holders in the form of forgone interest income were judged small in comparison. The Securities and Exchange Commission provides another example of the public interest rationale for regulation. The commission requires companies whose stock is traded on organized securities markets to provide accurate and standardized financial information to the public. Such regulation is based on the rationalization that no single investor or group of investors would find it profitable to obtain the financial information since they never purchase a significant portion of the outstanding shares. Thus investors as a group do not have access to meaningful financial information. Government regulation designed to provide standard-ized financial information benefits a large group (investment community and general public), while imposing the costs on a smaller group (companies wishing to trade their stock on organized exchanges).

Public interest theory was the first rationalization of government regula-tion to receive serious consideration since it provided the foundation for much of the regulation that was introduced by the reforms of the Great Depression. In fact, as discussed above, the public interest theory provides the rationale for a minimal degree of government regulation in a competitive economy. Public interest, however, is not regarded as a very useful framework to explain the current structure of regulation. Imperfections in the political system make it highly unlikely that the public interest can easily be identified or, even if identified, that government would place the public interest above the special interest. George Stigler (1971) was the first to formally argue that regulation, as a rule, is designed and operated primarily for the benefit of the regulated activity or industry.

The failure of the public interest view to account for the existence and evolution of regulatory policies led first to the "special interest" and then to the "many interests" theories (Stigler, 1971; and Pelzman, 1976). These views suggest that government regulation protects one or several special interest groups who "capture" the regulatory institution.[3]

Building on the special interest approach, public choice theory broadens the theory of regulation in order to incorporate the evolution of the regulatory agency over various phases. The special interest theories view government as a supplier of regulation and various special interests as demanders of that regulation. Government is viewed as rather passive in responding to the special interest, sometimes responding to narrow interests or, on occasion, to more broadly based interests. Mackay and Reid (1979, p. 105) point out, however, that the public market differs significantly from the goods market, and one cannot easily analyze regulation in terms of supply and demand. Outcomes are subject to coercion in the political environment. Even when regulation is influenced by market-type forces, the time lags of the regulatory response are considerably longer than those that exist in the goods market.

Public choice theory starts with the premise that government bureaucrats and regulatory agencies have their own independent existence; they do not merely respond in a passive manner to the demand for regulation by any one group. Regulators seek an independent existence. They desire and hold discretionary power, and they operate to maximize their own objective function. The parameters of this function include the regulated industry or activity, the consumers of the goods and services produced by the regulated industry, and the regulator's concept of what promotes the general welfare. Public choice theory is dynamic in the sense that it can explain the evolution of a regulatory agency throughout its stages of growth: from its initial creation, which might be the result of some market failure (the collapse of the banking system in the 1930s), through the stage where the regulatory agency reflects the wishes of the regulated industry, to the stage where the agency becomes self-sustaining and independent.

PRESENT STATE OF REGULATORY THEORY

Despite the large volume of writing on regulatory theory and policy, there is no generally accepted framework. Even more significantly for our purposes, much of the available regulatory theory is not directly applicable to financial regulation.

The major developments in regulatory theory have focused on nonfinancial industries such as transportation, communications, and energy. Despite some work on the Securities and Exchange Commission, the regulatory framework of the financial system has not been extensively investigated. What accounts for this lack of treatment? The financial system differs from other sectors of the economy in at least two respects that make it difficult to apply existing regulatory frameworks. First, financial institutions, in general, and depository institutions, in particular, are subject to special risks that influence the objectives, form, and potential usefulness of regulatory policy. To illustrate, deposit liabilities of banks and other similar institutions are fixed in nominal value despite significant changes in interest rates; however, the value of the assets are sensitive to interest rate changes. Thus the different response of the two sides of the balance sheet to interest rate movements exposes financial institutions to unique types of risk. In addition, there are other types of risk special to the financial system. Second, the advances in computer technology have and will continue to revolutionize the flow of funds, invalidating the concept of an identifiable "industry" grouping in the financial system. Regulation requires the ability to isolate some group to regulate, such as banks or S&Ls; however, financial innovation aided by advances in computer technology makes it difficult to identify stable components of the financial system that can be regulated. In fact, the experience of the 1970s has demonstrated dramatically the ability of the market to innovate and circumvent regulation.

Whereas technological change is generally held constant in the existing theories of regulation, this is an unrealistic assumption in the context of financial reform in the 1980s.

But, in a more general sense, there remains a basic problem with existing regulation theory. In order to be realistic, such theory must, as a minimum, specify two elements: (1) the special interest(s) served by the regulator and (2) the objective function of the regulator. The variations implied in these elements multiply rapidly, and once the value judgments of the regulator are incorporated it becomes exceedingly difficult to use the theory as a predictive tool. It is easier to use existing regulatory theory to account for ex post (hindsight) regulation; however, it is much more difficult to account for ex ante (predictive) behavior. Combined with the problems of applying existing theory to the intermediary sector of the financial system, a formidable task awaits those who would establish a viable theory of financial regulation.

3 FINANCIAL REFORM IN THE UNITED STATES, 1791–1966

IMPORTANCE OF A HISTORICAL PERSPECTIVE

A review of the major legislative and regulatory changes in the financial and monetary arrangements of the U.S. economy is necessary for understanding financial reform in the 1980s. Such a review allows us to place the current reform process in perspective and to understand the general characteristics of reform in the United States. The objectives and efforts of past financial reforms will provide a better vantage point for comprehending the financial reform process in the 1980s.

A review of U.S. financial history would suggest that the following reforms are the most important: (1) the First and Second Banks of the United States; (2) the reforms introduced by the private and state-government sectors from 1836 to the Civil War; (3) the National Bank Act of 1864 and associated market innovations; (4) the Federal Reserve Act of 1913; (5) the McFadden Act of 1927; (6) the reforms introduced in the wake of the banking collapse of the Great Depression of the 1930s; (7) the Bank Holding Company Act of 1956, the Bank Merger Act of 1960, and the respective amendments to each act; and (8) the Interest Rate Control Act of 1966.

This review does not pretend to be exhaustive, nor does it represent all of the efforts to influence the financial system or the monetary authority. Two standards were used to construct our list. First, each reform had to have a significant impact on the financial and monetary framework of the economy; second, an understanding of the major issues related to each action had to contribute, in turn, to a better understanding of the current efforts toward financial reform.

Our discussion is divided into three parts. First, the content and objectives of the major reforms through the late 1920s are reviewed. Second, the reforms from the Great Depression through 1966 are summarized. Third, the major characteristics of financial reform are indicated that continue to influence the reform process in the United States.

FINANCIAL REFORM PRIOR TO THE GREAT DEPRESSION PERIOD

THE FIRST AND SECOND BANKS OF THE UNITED STATES

The development of U.S. banking started shortly after the Revolutionary War when several states began chartering commercial banking establishments for the purposes of holding deposits and making short-term loans, principally by issuing bank notes. Bank charters were provided via legislative act at the state level; yet, aside from chartering there was only limited banking regulation at the state level and none at the federal level. The Constitution of 1789 authorized the federal government to issue money and regulate its value. Almost a century would pass, however, before the federal government became a chartering agency on a regular basis. There are two notable exceptions to this lack of federal involvement.

In 1791, at the urging of Alexander Hamilton and based on the new powers provided by the Constitution, Congress chartered the Bank of the United States for a twenty-year period. The Bank differed from existing state-chartered banks in several respects: (1) one-fifth of the Bank's stock was owned by the U.S. Treasury; (2) the Bank held deposits of the federal government and in general acted as fiscal agent for the government; (3) the Bank was much larger than existing state banks and took upon itself the responsibility of disciplining state banks that overissued their promises to pay; and (4) the Bank acted as a lender of last resort in several cases by making temporary loans to state banks.

The Bank provided a stable and efficient component to the emerging financial system and served as an effective fiscal agent for the federal government (Hughs, 1983; and Klebaner, 1974). At the same time, the Bank stirred up much controversy. Arguments arose over the appropriateness of partial federal ownership, foreign ownership of a portion of the remaining shares, and the general issue of how far the Constitution allowed the federal government to extend itself in the financial affairs of the private sector. All these debates played a key role in the controversy of whether to extend the Bank's charter in 1811. As a result, Congress declined to renew the charter.

The performance of the financial system deteriorated after this failure to recharter the Bank. As a result of removing restraints on note issues, together with a rapid increase in state banks and state bank notes,[1] the War of 1812, and the associated war shortages, the United States experienced a severe inflation over the period 1812–1815. In addition, conditions were aggravated because the federal government had embarked on a war effort without a well-defined fiscal agent. These factors account for the renewed interest by Congress to charter the Second Bank of the United States in 1816, so soon after failing to recharter the First Bank.

The Second Bank was chartered on a basis similar to that of the First Bank. Like the First Bank, it adopted regulatory and lender-of-last-resort functions and performed as a stabilizing and efficient component of the financial system. The Second Bank provoked the same controversies as the First Bank, and, just as with the First Bank, political considerations account for the failure to recharter the Second Bank. The famous "Bank War" over rechartering, waged between Nicholas Biddle (the Bank president since 1823) and Andrew Jackson, has been the subject of much historical and economic study. Jackson vetoed the early recharter effort by Biddle in 1832, and in 1833 he withdrew federal deposits from the Bank, placing them in selected state banks, referred to as "pet banks." The state bank depositories provided unsatisfactory fiscal agent services compared with either the First or the Second Bank.

The period that followed the failure to recharter the Second Bank was one of unstable financial markets and turbulent economic conditions. The price level and money supply increased rapidly in 1835, and a severe bank panic broke out in 1837. After a brief recovery from 1838 to 1839, the economy again declined rapidly to 1843. The severity of this contraction has been compared to the Great Contraction during the period 1929–1933 by Bray Hammond (1957), Douglas C. North (1966), and Milton Friedman and Anna J. Schwartz (1963).

Two major issues are related to the failure to recharter the Second Bank. First, the traditional view of the period attributes the post-1835 inflation to the absence of the Bank's restraining influence on state bank expansion. However, this view has been successfully challenged by Peter Temin (1969), and Temin's challenge has been substantiated by others (Rockoff, 1971). They concede that the money supply did indeed expand rapidly, but they point out that this expansion of the money supply occurred for reasons unrelated to the Bank War.

The second issue is related to the first. The Second Bank and, to a lesser extent, the First Bank have traditionally been regarded as the first efforts to establish a monetary authority. No doubt both institutions provided effective fiscal agent services for the federal government, and on their own initiative both pursued some monetary authority functions. Countering this view, however, Temin (1969, p. 56) has concluded that the Second Bank gets higher marks for its aspirations to be a central bank than for its accomplishments. Despite the traditional interpretation that the First and Second Banks functioned as central banks, neither can be so regarded. The United States would not establish a central monetary authority until 1913, after almost 125 years of substantial economic growth.

FINANCIAL REFORM AT THE MARKET AND STATE LEVEL, 1836–1864

Serious efforts at the federal level to influence the financial system ended with the failure to recharter the Second Bank of the United States. The few subsequent incursions[2] by the federal government after 1832 have been judged (Temin, 1969; and Milton Friedman, 1959) to have been, on balance, destabilizing and of minor significance to the long-run development of the financial system. During the 1836–1864 period, it was the private and state-government sectors that initiated the most significant reforms.

The Suffolk System of Boston represents a major market innovation, starting in 1825 and continuing until 1857. Banks located outside of the Boston area, called country banks, frequently overissued bank notes and maintained insufficient reserves. Country bank notes would thus circulate at a discount in Boston and drive out of circulation the more valued bank notes issued by the Boston banks. In retaliation, the Boston banks, led by the Suffolk Bank, coordinated their actions to collect bank notes of selected country banks and to present them en masse for redemption. The Boston banks agreed to accept country bank notes at par and refrain from disciplining action only if the country banks maintained reserves at the Boston banks. As a result, the number of bank note issues declined in the Boston and surrounding areas, and Boston bank and country bank notes circulated at par. Although the Suffolk System was replaced in the late 1850s by other private initiated institutions, it had a lasting impact on the financial system and served as a partial model for the Federal Reserve Act of 1913.

Bank clearing houses represent another important market reform. Clearing houses were established by private banks to settle net claims among bank groups. For example, the clearing house provided a facility for the banks to present their claims on each other in the form of bank notes. Bank A, which had collected bank notes issued by Banks B and C, would use the house to present claims on Banks B and C. Likewise, Banks B and C might present bank notes issued by Bank A. The clearing house significantly reduced the number of transactions among banks in settling their respective claims on each other. The clearing house also imposed a degree of self-discipline and regulation on its members, thereby encouraging conservative banking practices.

Reforms were also introduced by state governments. These reforms reflected a variety of approaches to achieving a stable financial framework. Several states actively sponsored or owned state banks whose functions resembled the federal government's role in the First and Second Banks of the United States. A number of states also imposed reporting requirements on state banks, reserve requirements for deposits and bank notes, and deposit insurance schemes.

The concept of free banking introduced by New York in 1838 represents a major financial reform. Prior to that time, banks received their charters by special legislative act, and thus entry was limited and subject to special privilege. The Free Banking Act of 1838 allowed any group to form a business for the purpose of banking as long as it registered and satisfied those general conditions established by the state of New York. The concept of free banking spread rapidly, becoming a basic element of financial intermediation until the 1930s.

THE NATIONAL BANKING SYSTEM

The National Currency Act of 1863, which was amended in 1864 as the National Bank Act, is of significance for the evolution of the U.S. financial system for two reasons. First, it represents the beginning of the federal government's extensive and continuous involvement in the structure of the financial system. Second, it introduced the concept of dualism in the U.S. financial system, though the dual concept was not the original intention of the act.

The National Bank Act was designed, first of all, to solve the financing needs of the federal government. Second, the act sought to improve the efficiency and stability of the financial system. The federal government found that the existing financial system was insufficient to finance its needs at the outbreak of war with the Confederacy. Direct financial markets had not yet developed to a sufficient stage to easily absorb large amounts of government debt. To satisfy its financial needs and, at the same time, to improve the efficiency of the banking system, the government decided to restructure the financial system. Judged from the degree of economic growth during this period, the unregulated banking system did not seriously constrain long-term growth. Nevertheless, the system exhibited characteristics of inefficiency and instability throughout the period. Although not as inefficient or as unstable as once judged by historians, who emphasized "wildcat banking" practices, the financial system was capable of considerable improvement. For example, the variety and number of bank note issues contributed to an inefficient and unreliable medium of exchange. Some estimates indicate that by 1860 there were 10,000 different types of bank notes in circulation with varying degrees of value (Hughs, 1983, p. 379). Bank note directories were frequently published to inform the public as to what were the different types of notes, whether the notes were accepted at par or discount, which were fraudulent notes, and what were notes of banks no longer in existence. In addition, there were many bank failures. According to Klebaner (1974, p. 48), of the 2,500 banks organized over the period 1781 and 1861, almost two-fifths had closed within ten years of their establishment.

The National Bank Act, as noted above, attempted to satisfy the government's need to finance the war effort and improve the efficiency and soundness of the banking system. The most important features of the act and its subsequent amendments were the following: (1) national charters would be available to private banks through a new office of the U.S. Treasury, the Comptroller of the Currency; (2) the newly-created national bank notes would serve as a unified currency and could be offered only by nationally chartered banks; (3) national bank notes were backed by government debt since for each $100 in national bank notes issued by a bank, $90 in federal government bonds had to be deposited with the Comptroller; (4) national banks were subject to minimum capital and reserve requirements.

IMPACT OF THE NATIONAL BANKING SYSTEM

The national banking system was initially successful through 1870 in replacing state banks because of a special 10 percent tax placed on state bank note issues. In 1869, 90 percent of total bank assets were held by national banks; however, by 1900 this percentage had declined to 43 percent (U.S. Department of Commerce, 1975). The re-emergence of state banks was the result of three factors. First, and most important, demand deposits rapidly replaced bank notes as the medium of exchange; second, state banking regulations were often less restrictive than those imposed by the Comptroller; and third, the yield on government bonds declined during part of the period, making national bank notes less attractive to national banks.

In many ways, the national banking system significantly improved U.S. banking. The uniform currency and the elimination of the large number of state bank notes contributed to a more efficient financial system. Despite these improvements, however, the new system contained serious structural defects. It did not achieve the goal of a stable financial framework for four reasons.

First, although the introduction of a uniform currency was a major improvement, there was no mechanism to provide for orderly changes in currency to satisfy seasonal and longer-term changes in the public's demand for currency. Currency in circulation was responsive not to the economic needs of the country, but to the demand and supply for government debt suitable for national bank note backing.

Second, the national banking system underestimated the role that deposits would come to play as the nation's medium of exchange. The increasing use of demand deposits by state banks prevented the national banking system from forcing state banks out of existence. In addition, the act did not provide a nationwide check-clearing mechanism. Check clearing was accomplished through a complicated system of correspondent banks. A check drawn on a bank in the same town might travel through several correspondent banks and over great distances before it cleared, unless the receiving bank had a correspondent relationship with the bank on which the check was drawn.

Third, the imposition of uniform deposit reserve requirements for all national banks was an improvement compared with the heterogeneous system of reserve requirements imposed at the state level. On the other hand, this reserve requirement structure created an unstable financial environment because of reserve pyramiding. Reserve requirements were set according to the reserve classification of a national bank: central reserve city bank, reserve city bank, or country bank. Country banks could keep part of their reserve in a reserve city bank, which, in turn, could keep part of its reserve in a central reserve city bank. The pyramided reserve structure was responsible for seasonal strains on the financial system. On several occasions this contributed to severe financial difficulties when country banks called on their correspondent reserve balances at reserve city banks, which, in turn, placed pressure on central reserve city banks. The final result would often be high interest rates as well as bank failures when individual banks searched for liquidity.

There was a fourth reason why national banking did not achieve a stable financial framework. The National Bank Act did not establish central bank functions to provide lender-of-last-resort services and steady long-term growth in the money supply. The frequent bank failures and financial panics of 1873, 1893, and 1907 were the combined result of structural defects in the national banking system and the absence of a central bank. Especially severe was the panic of 1907, which called the nation's attention to the difficulties of a monetary and financial framework that was inefficient, inflexible, and unstable.

THE FEDERAL RESERVE ACT OF 1913

As a result of the panic of 1907, the National Monetary Commission was established to suggest ways to achieve a stable financial and monetary framework. The commission recommended the establishment of a central bank, and, after much debate, the Federal Reserve Act was passed in 1913. This act established the first true central bank in the United States.

The Federal Reserve Act, as part of the evolution of financial reform in the United States, is prominent in many respects. It represents the first major reform directed toward the establishment of a monetary authority and issues of monetary control. The act also dealt with issues of the financial system and, to some extent, recognized the interrelationships between the structure of the financial system and monetary control. The major objective of the act was to remove the inefficient and unstable elements of the national banking system and establish a central bank responsible for orderly changes in currency in circulation and lender-of-last-resort services.

At the same time, one should not read too much widom into the act in terms of its recognizing the interrelationships between the financial system and monetary authority responsibilities. The major emphasis of the act was to improve the structure of the financial system and, almost as an afterthought, to recognize that the central bank had other functions. Today, these other functions dominate Federal Reserve policy.

The details of the Federal Reserve Act are reviewed in other places (West, 1977). For purposes of this present survey, several observations are important. First, to ease concerns that were once raised about the First and Second Banks of the United States, the federal government would not own shares in the central bank. Instead, the central bank would be owned by private member banks. Member banks (national banks had to belong, and state banks were permitted to join) were required to purchase Federal Reserve stock; however, this stock provided only limited ownership rights.

Second, to ease fears that the federal government would dominate the central bank, a decentralized central bank was established. The country was divided into twelve Federal Reserve districts, each with its own reserve bank. Private banks in each district dealt directly with the regional reserve bank. A Federal Reserve Board located in Washington, D.C., provided an administrative head for the system. The primary functions of the central bank, however, were carried out at the district level.

Third, the establishment of a monetary authority was a long overdue reform and placed the U.S. financial system on a more mature level of development. At the same time, the monetary control functions of the Federal Reserve were conditioned more by a set of rules than subject to the discretionary control that characterizes current Federal Reserve actions. This original design was consistent with the then-current view that government should provide a stable financial and monetary environment, but allow as much freedom as possible for competitive markets to function. The economy was viewed as basically stable and was expected to grow along a path consistent with its resource base without active government involvement. Thus the monetary control functions of the Federal Reserve were structured to respond in automatic rather than in discretionary ways. This was accomplished through adherence to rules of the gold standard, strict eligibility requirements for the discounting of commercial paper, and the real bills doctrine.

THE McFADDEN ACT OF 1927

The national banking system never achieved the dominance over banking that its originators had expected. After 1870, the state banking system re-emerged and continued to expand. In 1869, 90 percent of total bank assets were held by national banks. This percentage declined to 39 percent by 1927. There was general concern about both the future of the national banking system and the threat to Federal Reserve membership. The McFadden Act of 1927 was the outcome of a complex debate[3] and was designed in part to place national banks on a more competitive level with state banks.

National banks had not been permitted to set up branch banks, even in those states that allowed branching. The National Bank Act made no mention of within-state branching, though branching had been practiced since the first banks were established. Subsequent Comptrollers interpreted this omission as a prohibition against branching. State banks in many states were not so constrained.

The McFadden Act expanded the lending and deposit powers of national banks, explicitly prohibited interstate branching for all banks unless agreed to by the states themselves, and provided some limited branching powers to national banks to branch within their home cities, if state law so permitted. The Banking Act of 1933 expanded branching powers for national banks to equal those of state banks.

The McFadden Act played an important role in establishing the structure of banking by explicitly prohibiting interstate branching and reaffirming the concept of dual banking.

SUMMARY OF FINANCIAL REFORM
PRIOR TO THE GREAT DEPRESSION

The Great Depression stands as a significant watershed for the U.S. economy with respect to the role played by government regulation, supervision, and stabilization policies. During the Depression the financial and monetary framework was the object of unprecedented legislative and regulatory reform. The resulting structure constituted the financial and monetary environment of the U.S. economy until the current reform efforts of the 1980s. To appreciate the significance of the reforms of the 1930s requires that we summarize the structure of the financial system and monetary authority before we discuss the Great Depression period.

As of the late 1920s, the financial system was, by present standards, essentially unregulated and competitive. Government regulation had sought to achieve a sound and efficient banking system in several ways: by establishing reserve requirements for banks, by providing a uniform currency and a national check-clearing facility, and also by imposing minimal portfolio constraints to limit bank risk. The federal government had emerged as a major regulatory body along with state government, and the dual banking structure was to remain a permanent part of the financial system. At the same time, there were few competitive constraints on bank operations. There were no meaningful interest rate constraints, entry restrictions into banking were minimal, and, in general, the portfolio operations of banks were unconstrained. Hence, government, primarily at the federal level, had assumed the responsibility to regulate the financial system to some degree; however, this involvement was tempered by the general faith in competitive and unregulated markets.

The United States did not establish a monetary authority until 1913, and the Federal Reserve did not even begin to function as a central bank until the early 1920s. During its first few years the Federal Reserve devoted itself to organization and to the financing of World War I. The establishment of the Federal Reserve was largely based on the desire to enhance the soundness and efficiency of the banking system by providing Federal Reserve notes, national check-clearing facilities, and lender-of-last-resort functions. Monetary policy designed to influence economic activity was not judged to be a primary function of the central bank, and, in any event, monetary policy actions were constrained by rules derived from the gold standard and real bills doctrine.

THE FINANCIAL REFORMS OF THE GREAT DEPRESSION PERIOD THROUGH 1966

The reforms that emerged in the wake of the collapse of the financial system were the most significant in all respects of the reforms introduced by government up to this time. The Banking Acts of 1933 and 1935, the Securities Act of 1933, the Securities and Exchange Act of 1934, the amendments to the Federal Reserve and National Bank acts, and other policy events brought about dramatic changes. These reforms significantly altered the structure of the financial system, the conduct of the monetary authority, and, in general, the future role that the federal government would play in achieving the objective of a stable financial and monetary framework.

These reforms are both numerous and complex. They dealt with both the structure of the financial system and the conduct of the monetary authority and, more than ever, recognized the interrelationships between financial and monetary arrangements. The reforms can be summarized according to the following topics: (1) interest rate ceilings on deposits, (2) portfolio constraints, (3) deposit insurance, (4) regulation and supervision of financial markets and institutions, (5) limits on entry, (6) centralization and concentration of Federal Reserve power.

Interest Rate Ceilings.   Deposits of banks were subjected to interest rate ceilings. Banks were prohibited from paying explicit interest on demand deposits. In addition, Regulation Q imposed nonzero ceilings on savings and time deposits. The Federal Reserve could not remove the zero ceiling on demand deposits; however, it did have discretion over the ceilings applied to savings and time deposits. Prior to September 1966, Regulation Q ceilings applied only to federally insured savings and time deposits held by banks.

Portfolio Constraints.   Banks and other financial institutions were subjected to a variety of constraints on their portfolios. This area of financial reform was most significant in regard to the uses of bank funds. Banks were prohibited from speculative lending and investing. For example, banks were prohibited from purchasing stock for their own portfolios and were limited in their ability to purchase corporate debt. In addition, loans collateralized by stock or convertible bonds were subject to margin requirements administered by the Federal Reserve. The major objective of these and other regulations was to establish a sharp separation between commercial and investment banking.

Deposit Insurance.   To restore public confidence in banks and in deposits as a medium of exchange, federal insurance was made available to banks, mutual savings banks, and S&Ls. The Federal Deposit Insurance Corporation (FDIC) was established in 1934 to provide federal insurance for banks and mutual savings banks. In the same year, the Federal Savings and Loan Insurance Corporation (FSLIC) was established to provide deposit insurance for S&Ls. Many writers consider federal deposit insurance as one of the most fundamental and important reforms of the 1930s. Deposit insurance made it less likely that the failure of individual banks would generate the massive runs on other banks that had been experienced during the period from 1930 through 1933.

Regulation and Supervision.   The reforms created an extensive framework of federal regulation and supervision of financial markets and institutions. The Securities and Exchange Commission, FDIC, FSLIC, Federal Home Loan Bank Board (FHLBB), Federal Bureau of Credit Unions, the Comptroller of the Currency, and the Federal Reserve became major agents of regulation and supervision. Financial regulation and supervision were also correspondingly increased at the state level. But, overall, there was a definite shift in power from the state to the federal level via the incentives of federal deposit insurance. Most state-chartered institutions did, in fact, subscribe to federal deposit insurance.

Limits on Entry. The national banking system incorporated the concept of free banking. But in the 1930s, the concept was significantly altered. Regulatory agencies adopted criteria that both emphasized the needs of the community for additional banking services and that inquired whether the existing banks and new banks could both earn adequate rates of return on capital. Thus banking became a protected industry. The same limits to entry were also applied to nonbank institutions as these increased in importance after World War II.

Centralization and Concentration of Federal Reserve Power. The Federal Reserve was equipped with new or revised instruments of monetary policy and was provided with a more centralized framework for formulating and executing policy. Several new or revised instruments of monetary policy were created, including margin requirements over loans used to finance the purchase of equities, the ability to change reserve requirements within a wide range, Regulation Q ceilings, flexible discounting eligibility requirements, and enhanced open market operation powers. In addition, the system was restructured to shift responsibility from the Reserve Banks to the newly reorganized Board of Governors (previously called the Federal Reserve Board). These reforms were designed to establish a centralized central bank as opposed to the previous regionalization of monetary policy.

*BANK HOLDING COMPANY ACT OF 1956
AND BANK MERGER ACT OF 1960*

Bank holding companies emerged in the early 1900s and grew fairly rapidly after World War II. Despite their growth, they were almost completely neglected at the federal level and received little attention from state regulatory agencies until 1956. The Bank Holding Company Act of 1956 was an attempt to regulate and supervise bank holding company activities. It required a bank holding company, defined as comprising two or more banks, to register with the Board of Governors, prohibited the acquisition of banks in other states unless state law specifically permitted such acquisitions, and required Board approval for acquisition of any bank or nonbanking interest. Moreover, the Board was to use caution in allowing bank holding companies to acquire nonbanking interests, and such interests had to be "closely related to the business of banking."

The 1956 act left a significant loophole since it defined a bank holding company as an organization of two or more banks. Thus single bank holding companies, escaping the act's restrictions, expanded significantly after 1956. The act was amended in 1970 to authorize the Board to regulate one-bank holding companies. In addition, the nonbanking interests of either multi- or single-bank companies were more narrowly defined.

The Bank Merger Act of 1960 together with its 1966 amendments gave regulatory authorities responsibility over bank expansion through mergers. The Bank Holding Company and Bank Merger acts required regulatory agencies to consider the competitive effects of acquisitions and mergers. The 1963 Supreme Court decision in the case of Philadelphia National Bank was particularly important in establishing the interpretations of these legislative actions regarding bank expansion (Rhoades, 1980).

INTEREST RATE CONTROL ACT OF 1966

This was the last significant reform initiated by government prior to current efforts at financial reform. It is fitting that this is the last reform to be discussed because in many ways its rationale and impact reflect the conflicts between the structure of the financial system and the inflationary environment of the late 1970s.

Short-term interest rates increased rapidly in the mid-1960s (see Figure 6.2), and for the first time in several decades the yield curve was downward-sloping in 1966. Short-term interest rates were frequently higher than long-term rates. This created severe problems for thrifts, which traditionally had obtained their funds from savings and time deposits and allocated these funds to long-term, fixed-rate residential mortgages. Regulation largely explains the limited portfolio choices of the S&L industry (Thygerson, 1983) and, to some extent, the mutual savings bank industry. In addition, both types of depository institutions were provided with tax incentives to allocate a major portion of their uses of funds to mortgages.

Unexpectedly high short-term interest rates lowered thrift profits and threatened their viability. Congress responded by passing the Interest Rate Control Act of 1966, which extended Regulation Q ceilings to S&Ls, mutual savings banks, and uninsured banks. The thrift ceilings were set at a level above those applied to banks to provide them with more flexibility to compete for deposits, given their role in providing mortgage credit.

The 1966 act represents a significant point in the reform process since it marked the extension of deposit ceilings to all major depository institutions and set the stage for considerable disruption in the flow of funds between direct and indirect markets.

CHARACTERISTICS OF FINANCIAL REFORM IN THE UNITED STATES

At this point, it will be useful to summarize several generalizations that can be made about financial reform in the United States.

First, reform has frequently been crisis-oriented. Despite an awareness of the structural defects in the financial system or in the monetary authority, little effort is directed toward reform until a crisis has occurred or is about to occur. The inefficiencies of the state banking system were readily apparent by the late 1840s; yet, it was not until 1863 that the national banking system was established. In addition, a primary reason for establishing the national banking system was unrelated to improving the financial system, but related rather to the short-run needs of financing government expenditures. The problems of the national banking system were readily apparent; however, it took a severe financial panic in 1907 to arouse enough interest to restructure the system and seriously consider establishing a central bank. The significant reforms of the 1930s were in direct response to a major malfunction of the financial system. The crisis orientation of financial reform in the United States remains an important characteristic.

Second, related to the crisis orientation of reform, financial reform is frequently myopic and backward-looking. It is designed to deal in *ad hoc* fashion with an immediate set of problems, usually within a specific sector of the financial system. Seldom does such reform take a general equilibrium view of the type of financial system and monetary authority that will provide a stable environment for the economy over the long run. This reflects the U.S. political framework, which is prone to deal with only the most immediate problem and to focus on short-run rather than long-run implications of any action. As a result, the financial system and monetary authority have not developed in a smooth and orderly fashion, but rather have been influenced by major events like the panic of 1907 or the Great Depression. The consequences of such crisis-oriented financial reform have been a series of disjointed attempts to restructure the financial system and the monetary authority. Such attempts often fail to achieve their objectives over the long run.

Third, financial reform has been increasingly directed toward improving the soundness of the financial system and public confidence in depository institutions. Although these are important goals they have been pursued by at least two different approaches. Until the reforms of the 1930s, regulation of the financial system was tempered by the notion that competition was beneficial. While it was never expressed in clear terms, the implicit assumption was that a competitive financial system would be efficient and adaptable, if not the most stable. The uneven development of banking and bank failures were regarded as the natural outcome of competition. Government regulation was adopted only with reluctance and was designed to deal with only the most serious problems. Following the reforms of the 1930s, however, a new approach was employed. The benefits of competitive financial markets were questioned, and the emphasis shifted to limiting competition as a way to insure public confidence in the nation's financial institutions and money supply.

Fourth, such considerations as crisis orientation, concern with soundness of the financial system, and efforts to improve the efficiency of the flow of funds highlight the fact that regulator-induced financial reform has been a reaction to perceived market failure. Regulation has almost always been designed to improve the public welfare in those areas where the market is unable to provide a stable financial and monetary framework. The Great Depression, however, represents a major shift in the importance and emphasis on market failure as the foundation of regulation.

Fifth, reform prior to 1913 was directed toward the financial system, while devoting little attention to the monetary authority. The establishment of the Federal Reserve marked the beginning of the need to consider financial reform in a broader context. The reforms of the 1930s, as well as those in process today, deal with both the structure of the financial system and the conduct of the monetary authority.

Sixth, the responsibility for reform has shifted increasingly from the state to the federal level. The national banking system represents the first significant effort of the federal government to take responsibility on a continuing basis. This trend continued with the establishment of the Federal Reserve, and it accelerated with the introduction of federal deposit insurance in 1934. It continues in the 1980s.

Seventh, the most significant reforms have been initiated by government; however, the market has also played an important role in the process. In the absence of governmental influence, the private sector has frequently devised methods to improve the functioning of the financial system. The Suffolk System, clearing houses, and the coordinated efforts to suspend conversions of deposits into reserves by large banks during financial panics are well-known examples of financial reforms introduced by the private sector. At other times, the market sought ways to avoid regulation. State-chartered banks avoided the 10 percent tax by shifting to demand deposits as the major source of funds. The emergence of bank holding companies after World War II reflected responses to the binding constraints on geographic expansion imposed by the McFadden

Act and state restrictions on branching. The ability of the private sector to introduce its own reforms and offset prior government efforts to constrain the system has accelerated over time.

Eighth, regulation has adopted different approaches toward the intermediary and direct components of the financial system. Banks and other depository institutions have been the subject of more regulation than direct markets because of their role in the payments mechanism, the use of reserve requirements to control the money supply, and the invariance of debt values to interest rate changes that expose intermediaries to special types of risk.

4 THE 1970s: UNSTABLE FINANCIAL AND MONETARY ENVIRONMENT

FINANCIAL REFORM AND THE GREAT DEPRESSION

The Great Depression represents an important period in the development of financial reform and the role of government in the U.S. economy. The financial system and Federal Reserve failed to provide a stable financial and monetary framework during the early 1930s. As a result, extensive and unique financial reforms were introduced that established the structure of the financial system and Federal Reserve until the late 1970s. At that time it became apparent again that the existing structures were unable to achieve their respective functions.

Almost any description of the Great Depression understates the depth of the decline and the extent of the influence that this period has had on the role of government regulation. The Great Contraction of 1929–1933 was characterized by an unemployment rate of 25 percent, almost a 50 percent decline in nominal GNP, a 30 percent decline in real GNP, the collapse of the banking and financial system, and mass destruction of financial assets. The lower turning point of the depression was reached in March 1933; however, the entire decade was depressed. In 1939, the unemployment rate still stood at 17 percent.

The financial reforms of the 1980s cannot be fully understood unless a closer review of the significance of the Great Depression is provided. It is mandatory to grasp the significance and uniqueness of the Great Depression period because it accounts for the major expansion in government regulation, which in many respects has come to be recognized as a failure. The financial regulatory structure would become incompatible with economic activity in the 1970s, fail to achieve a stable financial and monetary framework, and require significant reform.

THE GREAT DEPRESSION AND THE FINANCIAL SYSTEM

The financial reforms introduced in the mid-1930s reflect several of the characteristics of previous financial reforms. They were crisis-oriented, designed to improve the soundness of financial institutions and markets, and intended to restore and sustain the public's confidence in the acceptability of demand deposits as a medium of exchange.

There are several aspects of these reforms that require special emphasis. First, the reforms imposed a variety of competitive constraints on bank portfolios, limited entry to bank markets, established deposit insurance, imposed interest rate ceilings, and increased bank supervision and regulation at the federal level. Banks were the primary focus of these reforms because their demand deposit liabilities represented three-fourths of the nation's money supply. It was the widespread bank failures over the 1930–1933 period that were the most destructive aspect of the collapse of the financial system. Moreover, banks constituted the largest component of the intermediary market at that time.

Second, the competitive constraints were also applied to nonbank depository institutions to limit competition within and between the major classes of depository institutions. S&Ls, mutual savings banks, and credit unions constituted a relatively small part of the financial system in the 1930s; however, they would later become the focal point of financial reform in the 1980s. Regulation thus established artificial heterogeneity among depository institutions. More than any other institution, S&Ls were constrained by regulation to function in a restricted market for the flow of funds.

Third, the direct and indirect components of the financial system were treated in an asymmetrical manner. The limits on competitive behavior centered on the intermediary component, and, within this component, to depository institutions. This is especially true with respect to deposit ceilings. In addition, a number of state governments subjected specific types of intermediary credit to usury limits. In contrast, direct markets were not subjected to the same type of constraints. Regulation focused primarily on improved disclosure of financial information, standardized accounting conventions for reporting financial information, and the separation of commercial banking from investment banking activities. Interest rates on direct market instruments were left unregulated.

Fourth, constraints on competition, increased regulation, and increased supervision by the federal government were consistent with the new economic philosophy that emerged during the Great Depression. The new view emphasized the inherent instability of a competitive system and the need for government to assume a significant role in achieving goals of economic stabilization (Cargill, 1980). The attitude shifted from faith in competitive and unregulated markets to doubt about the ability of these markets to achieve socially desirable outcomes. In the case where competitive markets failed to achieve socially desired outcomes and where significant third-party effects were present, government regulation was appropriate and required to rectify market failure. Regulation of the financial system, more than any other sector of the economy, reflected the new philosophy.

Thus the Great Depression and the financial reforms introduced during the Depression radically changed the structure of the financial system from one that was competitive to one subject to constraints on competition.

THE GREAT DEPRESSION
AND THE FEDERAL RESERVE

The reforms of the 1930s differed from earlier regulator-initiated reforms in many respects. One important distinction was the explicit incorporation of the monetary authority in the reform process. As was the case with the financial system, the Great Depression reforms that were directed toward the Federal Reserve established a structure that persisted until the late 1970s. The Federal Reserve was influenced by these reforms in two important ways.

First, the Federal Reserve was restructured and provided with new powers that would allow it to function as a true central bank. At the start of the Great Depression, the Federal Reserve had been in existence for less than two decades. The economic conditions of the 1920s had called for little active central bank action, and the decentralized structure of the system in the early 1930s had limited central formulation and execution of monetary policy. The view commonly held during the 1930s (Goldenweiser, 1951) attributed the Federal Reserve's failure to prevent or shorten the Great Depression to several limitations: to the lack of experience, to the lack of effective instruments of monetary policy, to the decentralized structure, and, most important, to the dominance of nonmonetary forces that generated and maintained the Depression.

Thus the ensuing financial reform was directed to remedy those limitations: centralizing the formulation and execution of monetary policy, revising existing instruments (open market operations and discount policy), and providing the Federal Reserve with new instruments (changes in reserve requirements, margin requirements, and Regulation Q). In addition, monetary policy was to function more according to discretionary action by the Board and the Open Market Committee rather than relying on automatic responses to gold flows or conducting discount policy according to rigid definitions of eligibility.

Second, the role of monetary policy in the government's general stabilization efforts was revised by the events of the Great Depression. The Quantity Theory of Money was replaced by the Keynesian view of demand management. The Keynesian view argued that the Depression was the result of insufficient aggregate demand by the private sector and that the gap could be filled either directly by increasing government spending and/or reducing taxation or indirectly by influencing the cost and availability of credit by monetary policy. Theoretically, fiscal and monetary policy were equally effective stabilization instruments in the Keynesian framework. Nevertheless, what elevated the role of fiscal policy at the expense of monetary policy was the failure of the Federal Reserve to prevent or reduce the severity of the Great Depression, together with statements by the Federal Reserve that easy monetary policy had been maintained throughout most of the decline. Keynesian-oriented writers, such as Alvin Hansen (1941), formalized and popularized the notion that monetary policy was not an effective instrument of stabilization.[1] These authors argued that either the demand function for money was highly interest-elastic or the investment function was highly interest-inelastic to such an extent that expansionary monetary policy was equivalent to "pushing on a string."

EVOLUTION OF GOVERNMENT REGULATION AFTER THE GREAT DEPRESSION

The Great Depression was a major turning point in the degree and form of regulation. Developments in regulation since then suggest several important observations.

First, the regulatory structure became compartmentalized to a high degree in that separate agencies began to deal with different sectors of the financial system. It is difficult to rationalize the existence of the Comptroller of the Currency, FDIC, FHLBB (Federal Home Loan Bank Board), Federal Reserve, National Credit Union Administration, and the wide variety of state regulatory agencies on grounds other than states' rights or historical and political considerations. The compartmentalization obstructed unified regulatory policies and encouraged interagency conflicts. It also contributed to maintaining an artificial heterogeneity among financial institutions that were more similar than different. This was artificial in the sense that different depository institutions would be willing and able to compete directly in the same market if they were not prevented from doing so. The existence of different regulatory agencies for each major type of institution insured that regulations would differ among depository institutions. In addition, the self-interest of the regulator would insure that differences would be maintained among classes of institutions. Thus the structure of regulation influences the type of regulations imposed on the financial system.

Second, although much of the regulatory structure was initially erected on the grounds of market failure or the public interest perspective, regulatory agencies adopted new perspectives as the agencies developed over time. They often became an advocate for the very group they were required to regulate and supervise. This is most clearly illustrated by the policies of the National Credit Union Administration and the FHLBB, which on numerous occasions advocated expanded or protected status for credit unions and the S&L industry, respectively. There was little concern that these positions might adversely affect the remainder of the financial system. Nor did this contribute to consistent policy. For example, the National Credit Union Administration established deposit insurance and advocated broadened common bond criteria; however, at the same time, it defended the tax-free status of credit unions. Likewise, the FHLBB was concerned more with maintaining both the dominance of S&Ls in the flow of mortgage credit and continued public policy support of the housing industry than it was with assuring the soundness of the financial system.

Third, the Federal Reserve was burdened with supervisory and regulatory responsibilities over banks, holding-company acquisitions, and mergers, while at the same time it was responsible for conducting monetary policy. Monetary policy was not regarded as an important stabilization instrument for several decades following the Great Depression; however, having the same agency responsible for monetary control and regulation further complicated the regulatory structure and may have contributed to less effective monetary control.

Fourth, regulation became contradictory in how it treated depository institutions, especially banks. On the one hand, regulatory policy clearly restrained competition. At the same time, regulatory policy toward mergers, holding-company acquisitions, and entry has often been concerned with their impact on restricting competition. The 1960 Bank Merger Act specifically required federal regulators to consider adverse effects on competition when ruling on requests for mergers and related matters. The simultaneous pursuit of regulations that both restrain and promote competition testifies to the lack of a clear regulatory focus. In addition, much of the regulatory policy that applied to mergers and related matters relied on the structure-performance framework. This framework had been developed in the context of the industrial organization of nonfinancial firms. The fact that it was relied on to such an extent underlines again the lack of a clear focus of the regulatory process. According to the structure-performance framework, there is a measurable relationship between structure (concentration) and performance (price, profit, etc.) of an industry. In the 1960s when considerations about the effects on competition were incorporated into merger and related decisions, the structure-performance framework was applied to the banking industry by Arnold Heggestad (1979) and others. Empirical evidence was often used to demonstrate that increased bank concentration in the market area was associated with higher loan rates, lower deposit rates, and higher bank profits. There exists a variety of standard econometric and theoretical problems with this literature (Gilbert, 1984). But, in addition, the use of empirical relationships derived from highly constrained markets to infer impacts of changes in market structure on performance was dubious at best.

Fifth, since regulation has been designed to deal with a static financial system, it has frequently failed to recognize the dynamic nature of the system to evolve over time as its environment changes. The result of this myopic view is that regulations soon become ineffective or destabilizing. Kane (1981) has been the most articulate proponent of the view that regulation fails to keep abreast of advances in the technology of financial transactions.

In summary, the regulatory structure that emerged from the Great Depression period lacked a unified or consistent perspective of how to achieve a stable financial and monetary framework. This regulatory structure was based on arguments and assumptions that significant market failure had occurred in the 1930s, that regulated financial markets and institutions were more stable and sound than unregulated ones, and that more, rather than less, regulation was preferable over time. In many ways, these views were based on a misinterpretation of the events in the 1930s, and as events unfolded in the 1970s, the failures of the existing regulatory structure became apparent. In addition, views about the conduct of the Federal Reserve through the 1970s were, in a similar manner, based on a misinterpretation of the Great Depression.

The forces of instability arose in the mid-1960s and continued to increase in a cumulative manner, reaching a stage where major reform was mandatory. This process can be described according to three issues: (1) the re-evaluation of the Great Depression period, (2) the incompatibility of the intermediary sector of the financial system with economic conditions in the 1970s, and (3) the role of monetary policy in the 1970s. Each issue will be discussed in turn.

THE INTELLECTUAL PREREQUISITES
FOR FINANCIAL REFORM:
THE GREAT DEPRESSION REINTERPRETED

The financial reforms of the 1980s were preceded by changes in attitude about the causes of the Great Depression. The re-evaluation of the Great Depression has significantly influenced views as to what is the appropriate structure of the financial system and the appropriate role for monetary policy.

Many observers recognized by the 1970s that a number of competitive constraints that were placed on the intermediary sector during the 1930s exposed the financial system to instability in an environment where high interest rates rendered the constraints binding. In response, the market innovated to circumvent these constraints by seeking out profit opportunities. This circumvention, however, was never complete, often inefficient, inequitable to low-income groups, and frequently exposed the financial system to greater instability. Attitudes shifted toward the view that removing the constraints would allow greater flexibility, adaptability, and stability for the financial system. In part, this changed view could only have resulted from a re-evaluation of the collapse of the banking system in the early 1930s. Close study of the period suggested that the unconstrained payment of interest on demand deposits was not responsible for riskier loan and investment portfolios (Benston, 1964). Also, it was discovered that the collapse of the banking system was the result of more fundamental problems, which could only have been effectively dealt with by a vigorous monetary authority (Milton Friedman and Anna J. Schwartz, 1963; and Warburton, 1966). There is no doubt that structural problems existed in the financial system; however, the collapse of the banking system is more appropriately seen as the result of the inability or unwillingness of the Federal Reserve to act as lender of last resort.

In the 1970s, monetary policy was elevated to the role of the primary instrument of economic stabilization. In part, this was the result of the growing recognition that inflation was a monetary phenomenon. But, just as important, it was seen that monetary policy had the potential to stimulate or slow economic activity significantly. This second view resulted from a re-evaluation of the Federal Reserve's conduct during the Great Depression.

This re-evaluation was one of the more important outcomes of the monetarist-Keynesian debate (Mayer, 1978b) of the late 1960s. The debate was initiated by Friedman and Schwartz (1963), who argued that the Great Depression was the result of inappropriate monetary policy, that the collapse of the banking system was the result of the failure to act as lender of last resort, and that the period cannot be used to support the hypothesis that the market was inherently unstable. This, as expected, generated a lively debate that has reached a sort of consensus, as recently summarized by Robert J. Gordon and James A. Wilcox (1981). They categorize the views into four groups: hard-line monetarism, hard-line nonmonetarism or Keynesian, soft-line monetarism, and soft-line nonmonetarism. Evidence rejects the two hard-line views, while it is difficult to distinguish between two soft-line views. Soft-line monetarism places emphasis on the monetary forces and actions of the Federal Reserve; however, this view recognizes that nonmonetary forces contributed to the depressed period, especially in accounting for the turning point in August of 1929. Soft-line nonmonetarism, for its part, emphasizes nonmonetary forces such as shifts in consumption and investment functions, but it also places importance on the policies of the Federal Reserve as contributing to the contraction phase and collapse of the banking system.

Thus the two soft-line views recognize that the Great Depression cannot be used to argue that monetary policy was impotent. By implication, these two views also recognize that the Great Depression period cannot be used to argue that the market is inherently unstable or that regulated markets are preferable to unregulated markets in the majority of cases. This latter point is perhaps best summarized by Thomas Mayer:

> This leaves the third question, whether the Great Depression teaches us anything about the stability of the private sector. The answer to this question is a simple no. We know already what the system is unstable if we have a fractional reserve banking system with no adequate provision for control of the quantity of money via a central bank that acts as a lender of last resort . . . The relevant question is whether the system is unstable if we *do* have a central bank that prevents large erratic shifts in the quantity of money. And there is little the Great Depression can tell us about this because the stock of money did decline drastically. [Mayer, 1978a, p. 143.]

The re-evaluation of the Great Depression has significantly influenced the financial reform process of the 1980s. Monetary policy can significantly influence economic activity. Unregulated markets in general and financial markets in particular are not necessarily unstable. The view that monetary policy is a potent instrument of stabilization policy has also been substantiated by a variety of other approaches besides the re-evaluation of the Federal Reserve during the Great Depression. Historical study of major changes in the money supply such as during the 1930s, econometric studies on the relationship between money and economic activity, econometric studies of the interest-elasticity of the demand functions for money and investment, and simulations of large and small econometric models all support the view that economic activity is greatly influenced by past and current changes in the money supply.

With the re-evaluation of the Great Depression in mind, attention can now be directed to the events of the 1970s. These clearly indicated failure on the part of the financial system and of the monetary authority to achieve their combined objective of a stable financial and monetary framework. These events can be placed into two categories: (1) the structural incompatibility of the intermediary sector of the financial system with high and fluctuating interest rates and (2) the role of the Federal Reserve in the inflationary process that eventually generated inflation rates of almost 20 percent per year by 1980.

STRUCTURAL INCOMPATIBILITY OF THE INTERMEDIARY SECTOR IN THE 1970s

Many of the constraints that were placed on depository institutions by the reforms of the Great Depression became binding after 1965. In this regard, the most significant factor was the historically high levels achieved by short- and long-term interest rates, which rendered Regulation Q interest rate and other interest rate ceilings binding (see Figure 6.2). Prior to 1965, interest rate ceilings were not binding since market forces dictated rates less than the ceilings. Once the ceilings became binding, however, they significantly affected the behavior of depository institutions, while rendering the financial system unstable in four ways.

First, interest rates on money and capital market instruments induced disintermediation as depositors transferred funds from deposits subject to ceilings to financial assets in direct markets not subject to ceilings. Banks, S&Ls, mutual savings banks, and credit unions all experienced disintermediation in varying degrees. Even nonbank nondepository institutions experienced disintermediation. For example, life insurance companies lost reserves to the direct market as the insured took advantage of their policies to borrow at low interest rates against accumulated cash value. Disintermediation was enhanced by the rapid growth of Money Market Mutual Funds (MMMFs) after 1971. MMMFs grew from $3.7 billion in 1975 to $45.2 billion by the end of 1979. They competed aggressively with depository institutions. MMMF shares could be purchased in denominations as low as $100. They provided transaction services subject to minimum amounts per draft and earned money market interest rates, less a small management fee. Despite the lack of deposit insurance, deposit holders obviously regarded MMMFs as close substitutes for demand, savings, and time deposit accounts. Not all the funds that were transferred to MMMFs, however, represented disintermediation to money markets since MMMF portfolios contained significant amounts of large certificates of deposit (CDs) issued by commercial banks. This still created difficulties, though, because funds were being distributed from a wide-range of depository institutions to a small number of large commercial banks.

Second, the disintermediation process was especially destabilizing during periods when market interest rates rose significantly above Regulation Q ceilings, such as in 1966, 1969, 1974–1975, and 1979–1980. These periods are referred to as "credit crunch" periods because they were characterized by a significant reduction in the flow of funds into consumer and mortgage credit. Depository institutions are the important suppliers of consumer and mortgage credit.

Third, depository institutions introduced a number of innovations to circumvent Regulation Q and prevent disintermediation. Commercial banks aggressively used unregulated sources of funds such as bank holding company–related commercial paper, repurchase agreements, or Eurodollar deposits. They also adopted new management strategies of liability management. At the same time, these practices exposed banks to increased risk. Even though banks held the most diversified portfolio of assets compared with other financial institutions, their reliance on unregulated sources of funds exposed banks to a duration or maturity problem. Their shift toward short-run sources of funds sensitive to market interest rates placed banks in a situation where the duration of the uses exceeded the sources of funds. S&Ls and mutual savings banks in the eastern part of the country introduced NOW (negotiated order of withdrawal) deposits to broaden the base of their source of funds. NOW accounts were subjected to Regulation Q; however, they provided interest-earning transaction services.

Fourth, and last, regulators also introduced innovations to deal with the disintermediation process, usually at the request of the depository institutions. These reforms were not well conceived and, in many instances, aggravated the severity of the problem. At the request of the S&L industry, Regulation Q was extended to S&Ls and mutual savings banks to contain the cost of funds; however, this merely had the effect of increasing the degree of disintermediation. In 1973, large CDs issued by banks were exempted from Regulation Q, but this served only to introduce a liquid unregulated asset in the financial system that provided greater opportunities to disintermediate. In 1978, the six-month $10,000 time certificate was introduced. This time deposit was not subject to Regulation Q but rather paid a rate tied to the six-month Treasury bill rate. While these deposits were immediately successful in slowing down disintermediation, they exposed S&Ls and mutual savings banks to greater interest rate risk.

THE FEDERAL RESERVE AND
MONETARY POLICY IN THE 1970s

The Federal Reserve System also failed to achieve the objectives of a stable monetary framework during this period. The Federal Reserve was increasingly criticized for excessive and unstable monetary growth from 1965 on. The Federal Reserve was blamed because of its willingness to monetize the growing federal debt, its adherence to a strategy that focused on short-run money market conditions, and its willingness to achieve interest rate targets at the expense of monetary aggregate targets. Whatever the reason, the Federal Reserve allowed excessive monetary growth to occur during the 1970s. This was ultimately the root cause of the problems in the financial system. This excessive monetary growth generated inflation, and through the Fisherian mechanism[2] it increased market interest rates and made Regulation Q binding. By the late 1970s, the Federal Reserve made some attempt to achieve a noninflationary monetary growth; however, financial innovations initiated by the market circumvented the efforts of the Federal Reserve. Increasing numbers of banks withdrew from the System to operate under a more liberal reserve requirement system imposed by state governments. High interest rates had significantly increased the cost of Federal Reserve membership without a corresponding increase in the perceived benefits. By 1979 the Federal Reserve had indication that 600 to 900 banks were planning to withdraw from the system. In 1970 member banks held 80 percent of total bank deposits; however, by 1979, the percentage of member bank deposits decreased to 71 percent. The declining membership problem constrained the Federal Reserve against slowing the monetary growth rate for fear that a tighter monetary policy would induce further loss in membership. In addition, a number of financial innovations broadened the concept of money beyond coin, currency, and demand deposits at banks. NOW accounts, credit union share drafts, ATS (automatic transfer service) accounts, and MMMF shares all fulfilled the basic functions of money. Although they were not perfect substitutes for demand deposits, they were close enough in function to be regarded as an important part of the money supply. The Federal Reserve did not have direct influence over nonbank depository institutions to control the new demand deposit substitutes. Although the Federal Reserve could ultimately influence their behavior, such aggressive tight monetary policy would increase the severity of the membership problem. Thus by the late 1970s, the Federal Reserve accepted the responsibility for excessive monetary growth, but felt constrained by the membership problem to impose tighter monetary policy. In any event, the new substitutes for demand deposits offered by nonbank depository institutions limited the effectiveness of monetary control efforts.

5   FINANCIAL REFORM IN 1979, 1980, AND 1982

EFFORTS TO REFORM THE
FINANCIAL SYSTEM PRIOR TO 1979

As is characteristic of financial reform in the United States, the recent reforms are crisis-oriented. The problems discussed in Chapter 4 had evolved in a fairly clear manner, starting from the mid-1960s. Disintermediation seriously interrupted the flow of consumer and mortgage credit as early as 1966 when Regulation Q first became binding. Similar credit crunch periods occurred in 1969, 1974–1975, and 1979–1980.

In December 1971, the Hunt Commission (see Report on the President's Commission, 1971) released its analysis and made a number of wide-ranging recommendations that would have removed several key constraints on competitive behavior among depository institutions. It took several more years of instability in the financial system, along with increasing inflation rates, before attention was also directed to the Federal Reserve.

A brief review of the initial reform efforts will serve as an introduction to the financial reforms of 1979, 1980, and 1982. The initial efforts, though not successful in many ways, set the tone and direction for the reforms that were eventually put into place.

The discussion in Chapter 4 emphasized the interrelationship between the structural problems of the intermediary sector and the monetary control problems of the Federal Reserve. By 1979 that interrelationship was clearly apparent to most observers and thus required reforms that dealt with the interrelationship; however, the structural problems of the intermediary sector were the first to receive attention.

The Hunt Commission called for significant financial reform of depository institutions. Its recommendations included removal of Regulation Q rate ceilings on savings and time deposits, broader powers in acquiring and using funds for nonbank depository institutions, the removal of geographic restrictions, and other changes that would have increased the competitive environment of the intermediary sector. The commission did not deal with monetary control issues to any great extent, since the Federal Reserve had not yet experienced a significant loss in membership (membership had declined only slightly from 1950 through 1970), and the relationship between monetary growth, inflation, and interest rates was not yet widely demonstrated or accepted by policymakers and economists. The commission argued that a more competitive and less constrained intermediary sector would contribute toward establishing a stable financial and monetary framework.

The Financial Institutions Act of 1973 incorporated a number of key recommendations of the Hunt Commission; however, the lack of a clear financial crisis and the Watergate scandal of the Nixon administration prevented the proposed legislation from receiving serious consideration. Failure to pass the proposed 1973 act and increased disintermediation in 1974–1975 led to a congressional study of the financial system in 1975. The Financial Institutions and the Nation's Economy (FINE) Report reached the same conclusions as the Hunt Report and made similar recommendations. Like the Hunt Report, the FINE Report devoted relatively little attention to monetary control issues. The Financial Institutions Act of 1975, based on the FINE Report, also did not find a receptive Congress and failed to become law.

The Hunt and FINE reports share many similarities as well as some significant differences. In any event, both failed to produce structural change in the financial system. The problems in the financial system had not yet reached crisis proportions. As is typical throughout the financial history of the United States, although recommendations to correct those problems can be discussed and put forth, financial reform will not take place until an actual or threatened crisis emerges.

EFFORTS TO REFORM
MONETARY POLICY PRIOR TO 1979

The first significant discussion of the monetary control problems of the Federal Reserve at the policymaking level occurred in 1975, when the Senate Banking Committee conducted hearings on monetary policy. The Hunt and FINE reports had considered issues related to the Federal Reserve. But these studies had focused mainly on reorganization changes to shift regulatory and supervisory control over banks to other federal agencies rather than considering appropriate monetary policy. The Senate Banking Committee focused primarily on the latter issue. The chair, Senator William Proxmire (D., Wisc.) was strongly influenced by the monetarist arguments that the Federal Reserve had followed inappropriate policies during the late 1960s and early 1970s (Burns, 1973; and Milton Friedman, 1974). Critics of the Federal Reserve charged that attempts to vary the money supply countercyclically generated more instability than stability because of long lags and uncertainty about the channels through which money influenced economic activity. They further claimed that the focus on interest rates and short-run money market conditions generated excessive and unstable monetary growth rates and that the lack of clear intermediate and ultimate goals prevented an objective assessment of Federal Reserve performance.

Concurrent Resolution 133 was the outcome of these hearings. This resolution was designed to make the Federal Reserve more accountable for monetary growth by requiring the Board to consult with congressional committees on a quarterly basis about monetary aggregate targets. The Federal Reserve was required to announce monetary aggregate targets for twelve-month periods and to explain why past deviations from target occurred. Concurrent Resolution 133 was a significant step toward focusing attention on the money supply rather than on interest rates; however, its impact was disappointing (Weintraub, 1978; James Pierce, 1978).

The resolution failed to provide a satisfactory basis for evaluating the performance of the Federal Reserve because of the unique manner in which monetary growth rates were reported and targets established at each quarter. The Federal Reserve used a new base each quarter, resulting in base drift that made it difficult to evaluate performance. By shifting the base each quarter, the Federal Reserve could average over excessive monetary growth and make it appear the monetary targets were being achieved in any one quarter. This also provided a forgiveness factor to past failure of the Federal Reserve to achieve announced monetary targets.

The next attempt to reform the Federal Reserve occurred in 1978 when the Humphrey-Hawkins Act (or Full Employment and Balanced Growth Act) was passed. The act established explicit, though somewhat unrealistic, goals of economic stabilization: full employment (4 percent unemployment), price stability (3 percent annual rise), economic growth, and balance of payments equilibrium. The explicit goal of price stability distinguishes this act from previous announcements by government regarding its role in achieving economic stability, such as the Employment Act of 1946. The act elevated inflation to the same level of concern as unemployment and economic growth. As part of the pursuit of these goals, the Federal Reserve was required both to establish calendar-year growth ranges for the monetary aggregates in February of each year and to use the same base during the year, although the ranges could be altered. Preliminary targets were to be reported to Congress in July for the following year, and final targets were to be reported in February of that year. This is the current reporting framework used by the Federal Reserve. The July and February presentations provide a focal point of public discussion and comment about monetary policy.

Both Concurrent Resolution 133 and the Humphrey-Hawkins Act contributed to a greater awareness of the role of the Federal Reserve in the inflationary process. They also focused attention on the need to shift emphasis from interest rate to monetary aggregate control as well as on the need to establish and achieve growth rate targets longer than several months. Despite these efforts to reform the conduct of monetary policy, they must be judged unsuccessful. After 1978, the Federal Reserve still directed attention to interest rate targeting, almost always achieving interest rate targets and almost always exceeding monetary aggregate targets. The last two years of the decade witnessed some of the most unstable economic conditions since the Great Depression. The unwillingness or inability of the Federal Reserve to achieve noninflationary monetary control contributed to the unstable conditions.

THE CRISIS ENVIRONMENT OF 1979 AND 1980

The unsettled financial environment by the end of the 1970s provided the needed inducement for financial reform. The performance of the financial system as well as the general economy created a sense of crisis. The economic environment in late 1979 was characterized by several ominous developments: historically high interest rates; inflation rates approaching 20 percent per year; intense disintermediation; rapid growth of MMMFs and the corresponding deposit drain from banks, S&Ls, mutual savings banks, and credit unions; speculative developments in silver and gold markets; declining value of the dollar on foreign exchange markets; and prospects of the failure of Chrysler Corporation as well as several large banks. Ironically, 1979 was the fiftieth anniversary of the Great Depression, which had begun in August of 1929. Such an ominous coincidence did not go unnoticed by policymakers.

Other conditions were also conducive to major financial reform. The constraints on depository institutions, especially interest rate ceilings, were clearly recognized as destabilizing when effective, and at the same time these constraints were becoming less effective as market- and regulator-initiated innovations circumvented the ceilings. High interest rates were also clearly recognized as the reflection of the high inflation rates, which were generated by excessive monetary growth. By 1979, inflation had become identified as the major economic problem, and monetary policy was viewed as the only effective instrument capable of reducing long-run inflation. This, however, required more effective monetary control.

On a more intellectual level, the re-evaluation of the Great Depression fundamentally altered attitudes about the rationale and desirability of regulated financial institutions and markets. At the same time, this reassessment focused attention on the power of monetary policy to influence economic activity.

The poor performance of the economy and other forces created an environment conducive to financial reform. Starting in October of 1979, a series of policy events were introduced that significantly changed the structure of the intermediary sector of the financial system and the structure of the Federal Reserve. These were the most extensive set of financial reforms introduced since the Great Depression. Like the reforms of the Great Depression period, they were crisis-oriented, with the major objective of establishing a sound and stable financial and monetary framework. Unlike the earlier reforms, however, they were designed to remove key constraints imposed during the 1930s, with the objective of increasing the competitive environment in the financial system.

In order to bring the discussion up to the time of this writing (early 1984), we will discuss the financial reforms in three parts: (1) the policy events of 1979 and 1980; (2) the reform process during the period from March 1980 through October 1982; and (3) the Garn–St Germain Depository Institutions Act of 1982.

MAJOR FINANCIAL REFORM IN 1979 AND 1980

There were three major policy events starting in late 1979 that initiated the financial reform process: (1) the October 1979 announcement by the Federal Reserve of a shift in its operating strategy from targeting interest rates to targeting the monetary aggregates, (2) new measures of the money supply introduced by the Federal Reserve in February of 1980, and (3) the Depository Institutions Deregulation and Monetary Control Act (DIDMCA) of March 1980.

ACTIONS TAKEN BY THE FEDERAL RESERVE

The October 1979 announcement was a dramatic shift in policy. Prior to this, the Federal Reserve had consistently focused on interest rates. In the 1950s and 1960s, when the Federal Reserve lacked a formal monetary policy framework, policy instruments were concerned with conditions in the money and capital markets as reflected by short-term interest rate movements. Scant attention was paid to money supply behavior. By the late 1960s, however, the lack of a formal framework was criticized by many economists, and the Federal Reserve responded by developing a more formal framework that incorporated both interest rates and the money supply. By the mid-1970s, interest rate and monetary aggregate targets were formally announced; however, the Federal Reserve consistently focused on achieving interest rate targets at the expense of monetary aggregate targets. Excessive monetary growth generated inflation, which, in turn, generated higher interest rates and eventually forced the Federal Reserve to further expand money to achieve interest rate targets that were inconsistent with noninflationary monetary growth. Excessive monetary growth had, of course, other causes. But the Federal Reserve's reliance on a mechanism that placed greater importance on achieving interest rate targets contributed significantly to the excessive monetary growth.

The Federal Reserve revised the official measures of money in February of 1980. The new measures departed from the traditional focus on banks and demand deposits by incorporating financial assets such as NOW accounts, ATS accounts, repurchase agreements, MMMF shares, credit union share drafts, traveler's checks, and Eurodollar deposits. These new forms of money were the outcome of innovations designed to circumvent binding regulation. The basic measure of money (M1) was defined as transaction accounts offered by any depository institution, traveler's checks, currency, and coin. Although banks and demand deposits still dominated the money supply process in 1980, demand deposit substitutes and nonbank institutions were becoming increasingly important.

The October 1979 and February 1980 policy events were directed toward the conduct of monetary policy; however, the 1980 act was more general and directed both toward the structure of the intermediary sector of the financial system and toward monetary policy.

THE 1980 ACT: DEREGULATION COMPONENT

The deregulation component of the act was designed to increase the degree of competition in the financial system by (1) removing or modifying existing interest rate constraints, (2) increasing the sources of funds for depository institutions, and (3) expanding the uses of funds and other powers for S&Ls. Although the term deregulation is used to describe these actions, for reasons argued above, the term is an exaggeration of the actual content of the reform process.

INTEREST RATE CEILINGS

Both interest rate ceilings on deposits and a variety of state-imposed usury limits on credit were binding from the mid-1960s throughout the 1970s and imposed serious interruptions to the flow of funds. The impact of Regulation Q ceilings had been well-documented in the Hunt and FINE reports, and several other studies (Kane, 1970; Pyle, 1978; and Taggart, 1978) had clearly documented the adverse effects of binding Q ceilings, as well as the adverse effects of binding usury ceilings at the state level (Nathan, 1980). Thus a major objective of the 1980 act was to modify or remove interest rate ceilings.

1. There was to be an orderly phaseout by March 31, 1986, of Regulation Q ceilings on time and savings deposits for all depository institutions subject to Regulation Q; however, the zero ceiling on demand deposits was to remain in force.

2. The authority to oversee the phaseout of Regulation Q ceilings and other matters related to the deregulation process was vested in a newly established Depository Institutions Deregulation Committee (DIDC). The DIDC membership was composed of the secretary of the Treasury, the chairman of the Board of Governors of the Federal Reserve, and the heads of the FDIC, Comptroller of the Currency, FHLBB, and National Credit Union Administration. The DIDC was given wide latitude to achieve the phaseout, ranging from increasing ceilings on existing accounts to introducing new accounts not subject to ceilings. The DIDC, however, was required to consider the soundness and safety of depository institutions.

3. The DIDC would cease to exist as of March 1986.

4. State-imposed usury ceilings for first-lien residential mortgage loans (including mobile-home loans) were permanently eliminated; however, a state could reject the federal override if it specifically reinstated the usury limit by April 1, 1983.

5. Business and agricultural loans in excess of $25,000 would not be subject to a state-imposed usury limit if the usury limit was less than 5 percentage points above the Federal Reserve discount rate plus any surcharge. As in the case of mortgage loans, a state could reject the federal override by April 1, 1983.

6. Other loans made by insured institutions would not be subject to a state-imposed usury ceiling if that ceiling was less than 1 percentage point above the discount rate. A state could reject the federal override by April 1, 1983.

7. Any existing state restrictions on deposit interest rates for insured institutions were eliminated.

8. The loan ceiling for federal credit unions was raised from 12 to 15 percent and could be raised above 15 percent under certain conditions.

Thus the 1980 act significantly altered the structure of interest rate restrictions in the intermediary sector of the financial system; however, one major ceiling was left in place. Demand deposits were still subject to a zero ceiling.

EXPANDED SOURCES OF FUNDS FOR DEPOSITORY INSTITUTIONS

The 1980 act significantly increased the ability of depository institutions to attract funds to compete more effectively with each other and broaden their sources of funds, especially for thrifts.

1. Banks, S&Ls, and mutual savings banks were permitted, as of January 1, 1981, to issue NOW accounts; however, NOW accounts could only be held by natural persons or nonprofit organizations organized primarily for religious, philanthropic, charitable, educational, or similar purposes. NOW accounts would be subject to Regulation Q until the ceilings were phased out.
2. Credit unions were permitted to issue share draft accounts that were essentially NOW accounts.
3. Insured banks were provided with authority to offer ATS (automatic transfer service) accounts, and S&Ls were permitted to maintain remote service units.
4. Federal deposit insurance was increased from $40,000 to $100,000 per account.

The authorization to offer interest-earning transaction deposits significantly increased the potential for competition in the intermediary sector. Although banks still retained a virtual monopoly over commercial transaction accounts, nonbank depository institutions were provided with significant powers to compete more directly with the banking system.

EXPANDED USES OF FUNDS FOR S&Ls

The 1980 act expanded the uses of funds for depository institutions; however, this feature of the act was directed primarily toward the S&L industry. It was designed to provide S&Ls with increased diversification powers and allow them an opportunity to reduce dependence on mortgage loans.

1. A number of S&L loan categories would not be subject to percentage-of-asset limits. These included account loans, single- and multi-family mort-

gage loans, U.S. government securities, home-improvement loans, mobile-home loans, etc. Percentage-of-asset limitations had previously been imposed on some categories of assets.

2. S&Ls were authorized to make single- and multi-family mortgage loans up to 90 percent of appraised value.

3. S&Ls were authorized to make commercial real estate loans and consumer loans and to invest in, sell, or hold commercial paper and corporate debt up to 20 percent of assets.

4. S&Ls were authorized to issue credit cards and offer consumer credit associated with credit card activity.

5. S&Ls were authorized to apply for special permission from the Board to offer trustee, executor, administrator, of other fiduciary services, unless restricted by state law.

6. Mutual savings banks were permitted to make commercial, corporate, and business loans up to 5 percent of assets within the state where the institution was located or within 75 miles of the bank's home office.

THE 1980 ACT:
THE MONETARY CONTROL COMPONENT

The monetary control component of the act was designed to increase Federal Reserve control over the monetary aggregates by (1) extending reserve requirements to nommember banks and nonbank depository institutions, (2) extending certain other Federal Reserve controls to nonmember banks and to nonbank depository institutions, and (3) redefining the relationship between the Federal Reserve and member/nonmember institutions.

EXTENSION OF RESERVE REQUIREMENTS

There were two separate structures of reserve requirements prior to March 1980 that were administered by the Federal Reserve and state banking regulatory agencies. The declining-membership problem was the result of more restrictive requirements imposed by the Federal Reserve compared with many state agencies (Prestopino, 1976). The 1980 act introduced a new and more uniform reserve requirement structure that would be completely phased in by the late 1980s.

1. Each depository institution would be required to maintain a reserve requirement to be established by the Board. Reserve requirements were to be uniform for all institutions, irrespective of size, location, type, or charter.

2. Only two categories of deposits would be subject to reserve require-ments. Transaction deposits (an account on which the holder is permitted to make withdrawals by check, telephone, or preauthorized transfers to a third party) were initially subject to a 12 percent reserve requirement that could be altered by the Board within the range of 8 to 14 percent. The 12 percent requirement applied only to deposit amounts above $25 million (as of March 1980), whereas deposit amounts of $25 million or less would be subject to a 3 percent reserve. Nonpersonal deposits (large CDs or Eurodollar deposits) were initially subject to a 3 percent requirement that could be altered by the Board within the range of 0 to 9 percent. In addition, the Board could impose supplemental reserve requirements under certain conditions.

3. Foreign branches, subsidiaries, and international banking facilities of nonmember depository institutions would be required to meet the same reserve requirements imposed on the foreign facilities of member institutions.

4. Reserve requirements would not earn interest; however, the Federal Reserve may pay interest on supplement requirements if these were imposed under certain conditions. Reserve requirements can be satisfied by deposits at the Federal Reserve Bank, vault cash, or deposits with another institution on a pass-through arrangement approved by the Board.

This feature of the 1980 act significantly expanded the control of the Federal Reserve and simplified the structure of reserve requirements. The new structure represents another major transfer of regulatory responsibility from the state to the federal level.

EXTENDED GENERAL INFLUENCE OF THE FEDERAL RESERVE

The extension of reserve requirements to nonmember banks and nonbank depository institutions is merely the most obvious reflection of increased Federal Reserve influence; however, the 1980 act increases the power of the Federal Reserve in other ways. For example, any depository institution that is subject to the reserve requirements imposed by the Federal Reserve will be required to provide reports of its liabilities and assets to the Board at pre-scribed intervals.

RELATIONSHIP BETWEEN THE FEDERAL RESERVE
AND DEPOSITORY INSTITUTIONS

The 1980 act redefines the relationship between the Federal Reserve and the banking system. Prior to March 1980, the Federal Reserve interacted only with the banking system and, within the banking system, only with member banks. Member banks were permitted to use Federal Reserve services such as check clearing without charge and could request funds from the discount window. After the 1980 act, the relationship included all depository institutions, and services were no longer available without charge to any institution.

1. All depository institutions subject to reserve requirements would be entitled to the same discount and borrowing privileges as member banks.

2. All Federal Reserve services that were covered by a fee schedule would be available to nonmember depository institutions. These services will be priced at the same rates for member and nonmember institutions.

The declining membership problem was eliminated by the 1980 act. In essence, it was eliminated by making all depository institutions de facto members of the Federal Reserve.

INTERRELATIONSHIP OF
THE THREE POLICY EVENTS

There is a close relationship among the three policy events. First, implementation of monetary-aggregate targeting would increase interest rate fluctuations, at least in the short run. Second, the February 1980 redefinitions were designed to provide the Federal Reserve with realistic measures of the monetary aggregates. Third, the removal of interest rate ceilings permitted the Federal Reserve to pursue monetary-aggregate targeting more aggressively since fluctuating interest rates would not conflict with ceilings. The removal of interest rate ceilings would also end periods of disintermediation and increase the efficiency of the financial system. Fourth, the monetary control component of the 1980 act would simplify and enhance the Federal Reserve's control over the monetary aggregates.

THE PROCESS OF FINANCIAL REFORM:
MARCH 1980 TO OCTOBER 1982

There was considerable optimism among policymakers and some economists about the effect of the three policy events; however, the two-and-a-half-year period following the passage of the 1980 act showed that the objective of a stable financial and monetary framework was far from achieved by the combined efforts of the October announcement, the February redefinitions, and the 1980 act. There are several considerations that support this judgment.

First, despite a decline in interest rates for several months after passage of the 1980 act, by June they had increased to levels much higher than in late 1979 and early 1980 (see Figure 6.2). This prevented an aggressive phaseout of Regulation Q ceilings. The payment of the higher market interest rates on deposits that were subject to ceilings prior to the 1980 act would, at a minimum, impose significant adjustment burdens on a wide range of depository institutions. S&Ls and mutual savings banks were especially sensitive in this regard. Regulators and the DIDC felt that these institutions could not withstand the sudden and dramatic increase in the cost of funds that would result from a rapid phaseout of Regulation Q in a financial environment of high interest rates. S&Ls were already experiencing an increase in the cost of their loanable funds as depositors shifted from low-interest passbook savings accounts to NOW accounts, which were subject to a 12 percent noninterest-earning reserve requirement. In addition, S&Ls had been paying market interest rates on $10,000 money market certificates since 1978. After June 1980, the cost of attracting and retaining these deposits increased significantly. In 1981, the S&L industry operated with a negative interest rate spread between the average return on their mortgage portfolio and the cost of funds.

A second observation also confirms the instability in the wake of the 1980 act. Depository institutions that allocated part or most of their loan portfolio to mortgages were subjected to an additional earnings squeeze, exacerbated by a number of state-imposed restrictions on the due-on-sale clause contained in mortgage contracts. The clause provided the lender of a mortgage loan the option to declare the loan due on sale, if all or part of the property securing the loan was sold or transferred before maturity. Prior to the high interest rate period of the late 1970s, the clause was used primarily to protect the security of the loan in the advent the mortgage was to be assumed by a high-risk borrower. It was common practice for home buyers to assume mortgages at existing terms; however, in an environment of high interest rates, lenders used the clause as a portfolio management tool to adjust upward the return on the mortgage portfolio to current market levels. Thus mortgages could only be assumed at the market interest rate or at whatever terms were offered by the lender. The issue received national attention with the California Supreme Court's 1978 ruling in *Wellenkamp* v. *Bank of America*. The court ruled that the due-on-sale clause unreasonably prevented borrowers from selling their property during periods of high interest rates and that adjustment of the mortgage rate via the clause represented an "unreasonable restraint on alienation." California extended the prohibition against the clause to noninstitutional lenders and explicitly ruled that laws restricting the clause were not superseded by federal regulation. Some sixteen other states also had laws prohibiting enforcement of the clause along lines of the Wellenkamp decision. Such laws were contrary to the deregulation effort and made it more difficult for mortgage lenders to adjust to a high interest rate environment. In the case of California, the interpretation that the restriction on the clause applied to both state- and federally chartered institutions challenged the dominance of the federal regulatory structure.

Third, despite the new demand deposit substitutes, institutions still faced considerable competition from MMMFs. Assets held by MMMFs continued to increase. During the period from the end of 1980 to November 1982, MMMF assets grew from $76.6 billion to $241 billion. Thus, despite the 1980 act's major objective of eliminating disintermediation, the process of transferring deposits from the intermediary sector to money and capital markets continued during this period. The rapid growth of MMMFs reflected the continuation of disintermediation, although the extreme and rapid forms of disintermediation experienced in the 1960s and 1970s were avoided by the ability of depository institutions to pay market rates on some types of instruments. In addition, the ability of S&Ls to offer NOW accounts and of credit unions to offer share drafts reduced, but did not eliminate, the competition from MMMFs. The new, milder form of disintermediation experienced after 1980, however, still had serious and adverse implications for depository institutions. Access to new sources of funds would have allowed institutions to invest in new, higher-yielding assets and would have increased earnings. Instead, the new funds were acquired by the MMMFs, with corresponding slower deposit growth for depository institutions, especially thrifts.

Fourth, the 1980 act failed to provide sufficient powers to enable industry regulators to deal with the increasing failure rate among depository institutions, especially S&Ls. The high failure rate, or the exposure to greater risks of operation for those surviving institutions, resulted from the coincidence of unbalanced deregulation and the general condition of the economy. The absence of sufficient regulatory powers exposed the financial system to the risk that isolated failures might spread, escalating into a crisis. This omission resulted from two factors: first, the overly optimistic view of the nature of the transition process from a constrained to a less constrained or deregulated environment and second, the failure of the 1980 act to address a number of constraints on competitive behavior that interfered with the ability of regulators to deal with troubled institutions. For example, the FDIC might encounter difficulty finding a suitable merger candidate for a troubled bank that would not violate restrictions against cross-industry mergers, geographic constraints, or anti-trust considerations.

Fifth, the 1980 act was a limited, but nonetheless significant, step toward a more competitive intermediary sector of the financial system; however, the act left many constraints in place that interfered with the deregulation process. The 1980 act had adopted the major competitive philosophy of the Hunt

Report, but without adopting the general equilibrium philosophy. The Hunt Commission stressed the need for financial reform to adopt a general equilibrium perspective rather than a partial perspective that only dealt with a portion of the structural problems. The 1980 act, for example, failed to deal with the extensive geographic constraints, which themselves restrained regulators in dealing with troubled institutions after 1980. The 1980 act deregulated the asset portfolios of S&Ls to a much lesser extent than their liability portfolios, with painful consequences.

Sixth, the monetary control objective of the 1980 act also faced considerable difficulty during this period. The Federal Reserve had shifted toward monetary-aggregate intermediate targets, particularly M1; however, monetary-aggregate targeting shortly encountered difficulties. Large and growing federal deficits, the plight of the S&L industry, the depressed conditions in the auto and housing sectors, and the belief that the Federal Reserve was responsible for the high interest rates after March 1980 brought considerable pressure on the Federal Reserve to de-emphasize monetary targeting. In addition, financial innovation, both regulator- and market-induced, blurred the distinction between the various monetary aggregates, thus making the monetary-aggregate-targeting approach more complex to implement. In fact, observers such as James Pierce (1983) emphasize the increasing inability to employ a monetary-aggregate target framework in a deregulated environment. The concept of money was in a constant state of flux as computer technology made it increasingly easier to circumvent regulatory constraints. Others (Battan and Stone, 1983) stressed that the historically sharp decline in the velocity of money in 1982 reflected an unstable demand for money, partly caused by deregulation and market-induced financial innovation.

Seventh, it became increasingly evident to observers that the financial reform issues were not unique to the United States. Much of the environment that produced financial reform in the United States has been shared by other countries.[1] The impact of oil and other energy shocks on the flow of funds, government deficits, high rates of inflation, and correspondingly high and fluctuating interest rates, as well as the advances in computer technology, have all been experienced by other countries in varying degrees. These forces have occurred at the same time that many countries constrained their financial system in a variety of ways. They, like the United States, have sought a variety of financial reforms to make their financial systems or the performance of the monetary authority more compatible with the economic requirements of the 1980s. In several respects, the financial reform process in other countries resembles that in the United States. The conflict between a constrained system and the economic conditions of the 1970s provides the major force for reform. Market innovations play a significant role in the process since existing constraints were often rendered ineffective by innovation, when the market substituted nonregulated for regulated activities. In addition, reform initiated both by the regulator and by the market have had important implications for the conduct of monetary policy.

Thus the period from March 1980 through the end of 1982 was disappointing in terms of achieving the objectives of the 1980 act. The events during this period demonstrated that financial reform was not complete in any sense of the word; further structural change would be required to achieve a stable financial and monetary framework. The delays and difficulties in achieving this objective called for further financial reform effort, and in October of 1982, the Garn–St Germain Depository Institutions Act of 1982 was passed and signed into law by President Reagan. The 1982 act shares a number of important similarities with the 1980 act, but also contains significant differences.

THE CATALYST FOR THE 1982 ACT

Regulator reform often fails to take into account a broad and forward-looking perspective of the requirements for a stable financial and monetary framework because such reform frequently occurs only as an *ad hoc* response to a serious malfunction. As a result, regulation reacts to problems in a myopic manner, focusing only on the most immediate and pressing issues. In many ways, the 1980 act can be criticized for this myopic approach.

At the same time, however, the forces that generated the October 1979 announcement, the February 1980 redefinitions, and the 1980 act were more broadly based than those that generated the 1982 act. The 1982 act is explicitly designed to be a relief measure for the thrift industry. More than any other institution, thrifts have been confined to a narrow part of the flow of funds. Regulation in one form or another has constrained thrifts to borrow short-term and lend long-term. The following chapter is devoted to the unique portfolio problems experienced by thrifts. At this point we need only emphasize that the continued deterioration of thrifts after March 1980—as reflected by continued MMMF growth, slow deposit growth, declining earnings, negative book values, and increasing failure rates—were the primary motivation of the 1982 act.

COMPARISON BETWEEN THE 1980 AND 1982 ACTS

There are several points that should be emphasized in comparing the 1980 and 1982 acts. First, the motivation for the 1982 legislation is more specific and narrower than that for the 1980 act. The 1982 act is a reaction to the deterioration of the thrift and housing industries, especially the S&L

industry. Second, the 1982 act devotes almost no attention to monetary control issues, with the exception of some minor changes in the reserve requirement structure introduced in the 1980 act. Third, despite the narrower focus of the 1982 act, the act contributes to the deregulation process that was initiated in 1980. The provisions of the 1982 act have increased the competition among depository institutions and other sectors of the financial system. In this respect, the 1982 act contributes to the objective of establishing a more competitive financial system.

Although this is true, there is a peculiarity in the 1982 act that strikingly suggests that Congress and the administration do not yet have a clear perspective of the requirements of a stable financial and monetary framework. Support of the thrift and associated housing sector is the stated objective of the 1982 act. One cannot read the text of the act without encountering the word "housing" or related phrases repeatedly. Thus, on the one hand, there are provisions in the act that increase competition; yet, the act simultaneously states that support of housing and the role of thrifts as major suppliers of mortgage credit is paramount. There is no inherent conflict between a competitive financial system and significant flows of credit into housing, as long as this is the result of market forces. In the past, however, the system has been constrained and induced to provide funds to the residential mortgage market at favorable terms.

THE GARN–ST GERMAIN
DEPOSITORY INSTITUTIONS ACT OF 1982

Like the earlier 1980 act, the 1982 act is long and complex. It contains eight titles dealing in detail with a variety of areas of financial reform. The act can be summarized[2] in three parts: (1) the impact on the sources of funds for depository institutions, (2) the uses of funds as well as other powers for thrifts, and (3) emergency powers for federal regulatory agencies that oversee the operations of depository institutions.

EXPANDED SOURCES OF FUNDS FOR DEPOSITORY INSTITUTIONS

The act makes major contributions toward broadening the ability of depository institutions to attract funds and compete with MMMFs.

1. The 1982 act authorizes depository institutions to offer an account "directly equivalent to and competitive" with MMMFs. The new money market deposit account (MMDA) became available as of December 14, 1983. It is insured, has an interest rate restricted only by the discretion of the

depository institution (on an initial and maintained balance of $2,500 or more), and has limited transaction features. The MMDA allows up to six preauthorized, telephone, or automatic transfers of which no more than three may be by check; however, unlimited personal withdrawals are permitted. Personal MMDAs are not subject to a reserve requirement, but a 3 percent reserve requirement is imposed on nonpersonal accounts.

2. Federal, state, and local governmental entities are given permission to hold NOW and Super-NOW(SNOW) accounts.

3. In response to the act, the DIDC acted quickly to authorize another new account that further broadened the sources of funds. As of January 5, 1983, the SNOW account became available. The SNOW account is restricted to the NOW account clientele (natural persons and nonprofit organizations and government units), has a minimum initial and maintained balance of $2,500, has unlimited transaction features, and is not subject to any interest rate restriction. The SNOW account is subject to the transaction reserve requirement.

4. Federally chartered thrifts are permitted to offer demand deposit services to persons or organizations that have a business loan relationship with the institution or that desire to receive payment due from business customers.

5. The DIDC is required to remove as of January 1, 1984, any existing differentials in Regulation Q ceilings between banks and nonbank depository institutions.

EXPANDED USES OF FUNDS AND OTHER POWERS

The 1982 act is first and foremost a reaction to the plight of S&Ls and mutual savings banks. As such, a major part of the act is designed to enhance the powers of thrifts.

1. Federally chartered S&Ls and savings banks are authorized for the first time to (1) make overdraft loans, (2) invest in the accounts of other insured institutions, and, most important, (3) offer commercial loans. In addition, they are provided with enhanced powers to (4) invest in state and local government obligations, (5) make residential and nonresidential real estate loans, and (6) make consumer and educational loans.

2. The act provides a federal override to existing state-imposed restrictions on the enforcement of the due-on-sale clause in mortgage contracts. The override is delayed for certain states during a three-year "window period."

3. Thrifts are given wide powers to alter their charters. They can convert from state to federal charter and conversely, with minimal effort, where state law permits. They may also easily switch between mutual and stock form and between S&L and savings bank designation.

4. State-chartered depository institutions are empowered to offer the same alternative, variable rate mortgage instruments as their federal counterparts.

5. National banks receive some relatively minor adjustments to their powers. For example, the "safety and soundness" limitations placed on the size of loans made to a single borrower are relaxed. At the same time, these limitations will henceforth be applied to loans made to foreign governments and their agencies. Restrictions on bank real estate lending and "insider" loans are relaxed.

6. There are, in the act, several miscellaneous features that influence banking operations. Bank holding companies are prohibited from providing insurance as principals, agents, or brokers; however, a number of exceptions are stated. The act authorizes a broad range of financial transactions between a parent holding company and sister subsidiary banks, with only a few exceptions. Banks are permitted to form service corporations that can render a variety of financial services, such as discount brokerage services.

EMERGENCY POWERS

The Garn–St Germain Act provides federal agencies with enhanced powers to deal with troubled or failing institutions; however, these powers are in force for only three years and expire as of October 1985. Congress will, no doubt, consider extending them.

1. The FDIC and FSLIC can aid institutions (1) that are closed, insolvent, in default, or similarly endangered, or (2) where severe financial conditions exist that threaten the stability of the financial system, or (3) in order to reduce the federal agency's exposure to loss. They are empowered to take six types of actions to aid institutions: (1) issue guarantees, (2) purchase or assume assets or liabilities of institutions, but not their common stock, to preclude nationalization, (3) make loans to, contributions to, or deposits in institutions or companies that will acquire the troubled institution, (4) organize charter conversions, (5) arrange extraordinary mergers and acquisitions, and (6) issue net worth certificates.

2. The FDIC and FSLIC are authorized to arrange emergency acquisitions that in the past would have conflicted with restrictions against cross-industry and cross-state-line acquisitions. Under the new rules the FDIC can organize the acquisition of a large bank (assets over one-half billion dollars) by another federally insured institution, in-state or out-of-state. The FSLIC may exercise such powers without regard to the size of an institution. Further, any qualified purchaser, including out-of-state banks, holding companies, other insured institutions, or any acceptable company, may submit bids for a failed

thrift institution. The federal agencies are instructed to minimize risk of loss subject to the following priorities for selecting bidding candidates: (1) alike, in-state institutions, (2) alike, out-of-state institutions, (3) different, in-state institutions, (4) different, out-of-state institutions, (5) among out-of-state bidders, adjacent-state institutions, and (6) applying to the FSLIC, but not to the FDIC, minority-controlled bidders when a minority-controlled thrift is to be acquired.

IMPLICATIONS OF THE
1982 ACT FOR DEREGULATION

Despite the act's focus on the thrift industry and housing, the major thrust of the act is to enhance those deregulation efforts initiated by the 1980 act. The 1982 act significantly increases the degree of competition within and between classes of depository institutions, and between depository institutions and MMMFs. There are six features of the act that directly enhance competition and accelerate the movement toward a more efficient and flexible intermediary sector.

First, the MMDAs and SNOW accounts measurably enhance the ability of depository institutions to compete with MMMFs. Previously rapid MMMF growth was reversed into declines by the introduction of the new accounts. The new accounts have been an unqualified success. It took only the first two months of 1983 for depository institutions to exceed the level of MMMFs at their height in November 1982 ($241 billion). As a result of the 1980 and 1982 acts, disintermediation is no longer an issue.

Second, S&Ls are authorized to offer demand deposit services under limited conditions. Until the 1982 act, S&Ls were not permitted to offer commercial transaction services. The limited authorization will not pose a significant competitive threat to banks unless it is expanded in the future. The 1982 act, however, does initiate a change that may eventually come to represent a major increase in the competitive environment for depository institutions.

Third, the act contributes to the phaseout of Regulation Q. The MMDAs and SNOW accounts are not subject to interest rate restrictions of any type for initial and maintained amounts above $2,500. SNOW accounts can be held by governmental entities, and MMDAs can be held by business firms. As of January 1, 1984, any differential ceiling between banks and nonbank institutions is removed for those accounts still subject to Regulation Q.

Fourth, thrifts received enhanced asset acquisition powers. These powers significantly improve their ability to diversify and achieve a closer duration between assets and liabilities than in the past. In addition, S&Ls now become more competitive with banks. S&Ls can allocate up to 60 percent of their assets to three types of commercial loans: loans secured by commercial real estate (up to 40 percent of assets), secured or unsecured commercial loans (up to 10 percent of assets), and loans related to leasing operations (up to 10 percent of assets). S&Ls received permission to allocate up to 30 percent of their assets to consumer loans; previously, the 1980 act had permitted only a 20 percent allocation of assets to consumer lending. S&Ls can now invest in a wide range of federal, state, and local obligations. S&Ls received new diversification powers that will provide them with a better chance to remain economically viable in a deregulated environment. At the same time, the diversification powers are still constrained since much of the expanded commercial lending authority is tied to real estate and only limited powers have been granted to make non–real estate loans.

Fifth, the 1982 act provides a federal override of state-imposed restrictions on the due-on-sale clause. Such restrictions had dubious legal foundations at best and were clearly in conflict with a competitive financial system. The ability to include and enforce a due-on-sale clause will help mortgage lenders achieve a more balanced match between liabilities and assets. In addition, the ability to enforce this clause will help in time to remove the backlog of low-yielding mortgages held by institutions.

Sixth, the emergency powers given to federal agencies provide a more realistic appraisal of the transition process from a constrained to a less constrained financial system. Large numbers of depository institutions have remained economically viable because of limits on competition. In a more competitive environment many of these institutions cannot remain in existence. The 1982 act recognizes that a number of institutions will cease to exist either through mergers with, or acquisitions by, stronger institutions. Despite the temporary nature of these powers, the emergency provisions set an important precedent for interstate banking and for eliminating many of the remaining constraints that enforce artificial heterogeneity among different types of depository institutions.

IMPLICATIONS OF THE
1982 ACT FOR MONETARY CONTROL

Unlike the 1980 act, the 1982 act devotes little attention to monetary control issues. This is not a result of the success of the Federal Reserve's effort to achieve stable monetary growth during this period, but a reflection of the absence of a crisis situation in the structure of the monetary authority. Prior to 1980, the declining-membership problem and demand deposit substitutes offered by nonbank institutions were the primary problems facing monetary control, in the opinion of the Federal Reserve. These issues were dealt with by the 1980 act. The 1982 act dealt with the crisis in the thrift industry.

The 1982 act did address one minor issue of monetary control. The earlier legislation imposed reserve requirements on all depository institutions that issued a transaction account or nonpersonal deposit. But reserve requirements imposed hardships on small institutions, mainly credit unions, while at the same time these institutions played an insignificant role in the money supply process. Consequently, the 1982 act provided a zero-reserve requirement for the first $2 million in deposit liabilities of each depository institution. This is of minor importance.

THE REMAINING TASKS

This chapter has summarized the major efforts at financial reform in the United States by analyzing the unique policy events of 1979, 1980, and 1982. We have attempted to place these efforts in a historical framework in order to understand the evolution of financial reform in the United States. We have also pointed out that the recent financial reform process is not unique to this country; similar efforts with similar objectives are being pursued in other countries.

The remainder of our study will concentrate on three issues. First, the reforms have focused on many issues, but, at the same time, many of the reforms are directed toward the thrift industry and are designed to deal with the so-called thrift problem. The effort to constrain a large segment of the financial system to support housing has been a major source of instability in the financial system. Many of the deregulation efforts are designed to deal with the thrift problem; however, the commitment to housing is still a major component of social policy in the United States. The role of housing and thrifts in the U. S. financial system must be understood to determine the possibilities and limitations of financial reform in the 1980s.

Second, we will study how the shift toward monetary-aggregate targeting and the failure to stabilize monetary growth since 1979 have renewed old debates. These controversies revolve around the entire framework of conducting monetary policy via intermediate targets as well as the appropriateness of the money supply as the intermediate target. The discussion has become more intense because the changing structure of the financial system raises a number of new issues about the conduct of monetary policy.

Third, we will consider how financial reform is a continuing process. The 1980 and 1982 acts not only make significant progress toward a more competitive and effective financial system but also contribute to the ability of the Federal Reserve to conduct monetary policy. At the same time, considerable work remains. There are significant issues left unresolved. Unless these are dealt with in a satisfactory manner, the objective of a stable financial and monetary framework will not be realized in the 1980s.

6　THE S&L CRISIS

Political support for the housing industry has been long-standing. Over the years a body of laws and regulations has grown up to foster the development and expansion of the housing industry. To this end, financial institutions that supply funds for housing have also been favored by Congress. Regulations, especially Regulation Q, were established with the intention of providing a stable, low-cost supply of mortgage funds. S&Ls and savings banks were given tax advantages if they specialized in housing finance. Legislation restricted their lending that was unrelated to housing. In short, a social contract was established with the housing and housing-finance industries.

The system of laws and regulations applicable to S&L activities—the system favoring the housing industry—proved profitable for S&Ls during the 1950s and 1960s. As the years went by, however, the confining laws and regulations proved ineffective in fulfilling their objective. By the 1970s the regulatory constraints became binding and began to interfere with S&L profitability. By the beginning of the 1980s, the flow of funds to housing was recognized to be neither stable nor low-cost. Moreover, other priorities were emerging. Other industries and the government itself (faced with funding an escalating deficit) became candidates for financial preference. Consequently, the social contract was modified, but it was not ended. In fact, Congress has exhibited considerable ambivalence in this regard. It has not so far explicitly decided to end its preferences for housing. It has merely added other concerns to those it had marked for preferential treatment, without recognizing the illogicality of trying to give favored treatment to many competing objectives.

Its failure to admit any trade-off among financial preferences has led to internally inconsistent actions.

HOUSING AND THE SOCIAL CONTRACT

We can trace support for the housing-related industries back at least as far as the end of the Second World War. For example, congressional support for the housing industry is stated clearly in the 1949 declaration of national housing policy: to provide "a decent home and suitable living environment for every American family, thus contributing to the development and redevelopment of communities and to the advancement of the growth, wealth, and security of the Nation" (Declaration of National Housing Policy, contained in the *Housing Act of 1949*, Section 2).

As a result of this social commitment, Congress created several federal agencies to provide assistance to the housing and housing-finance industries. Mortgage insurance was offered by the Federal Housing Administration (FHA), and mortgage guarantees by the Veterans Administration (VA); secondary mortgage markets were established by the Federal National Mortgage Association (Fannie Mae), the Government National Mortgage Association (Ginnie Mae), and the Federal Home Loan Mortgage Association (Freddie Mac). In addition, Congress instituted a variety of programs to directly assist (that is, to subsidize) low- and middle-income families in purchasing or renting housing.

Financial regulation, designed to keep mortgage rates low by allowing S&Ls and savings and commercial banks to raise low-interest rate funds, was also an important feature of the housing promotion program. Further, the tax laws provided (and still provide) incentives not only to S&Ls and savings banks to specialize in housing finance but also to homeowners and landlords.

REGULATORY CONSTRAINTS

Consequently, the thrift industry developed in the 1960s and 1970s in an environment of regulatory constraints that were designed to sustain a steady flow of mortgage credit on favorable terms. These constraints did influence behavior because optimizing under constraints, as a rule, produces optimal values different from those when constraints are removed. As time passed and nominal interest rates rose with inflation, and as changing tastes and technologies demanded new ways of conducting financial transactions, the regulatory environment became increasingly confining.

Then, economists, policymakers, regulators, and ultimately even industry participants came to view the constraints as counterproductive. Constraints had failed, for example, to provide a safe and sound financial system, as the S&L crisis of 1981–1983 attests. And they had not assured the intended, sustained flow of mortgage funds to the housing industry. In the early 1980s, "creative financing" techniques prevailed, representing a step backward to primary (owner/financing) rather than intermediary sources of funds. Furthermore, the system of constraints was seen as interfering with the attainment of other goals—goals more recently enunciated, such as providing fair returns to savers and investment funds to other industries.

TYPES OF CONSTRAINT

The constraints imposed in the era between the Great Depression and the financial reforms of the 1980s were of four kinds: (1) some restricted the permitted quantities of assets and liabilities; (2) some restricted the prices charged or the interest rates offered; (3) others limited the range of activities undertaken; (4) and still others circumscribed the geographic location of approved activities.

Asset Constraints: Quantities and Activities.   On the asset side of the balance sheet, quantity restraints were imposed under the Home Owners Equity Act (HOEA) of 1933 on the nonmortgage uses of funds. Two intentions interplayed in the design of the HOEA restrictions. One was to enhance the soundness of S&Ls by forbidding overly risky assets and activities. The other was to provide a supply of funds dedicated to housing. Many of these quantity restraints were relaxed as a result of the 1980 and 1982 acts (see Chapter 5). But a question has arisen as to what extent S&Ls can take advantage of these relaxations to restructure their asset portfolios into potentially more rewarding outlets. Current tax laws impose a second set of quantity constraints on asset composition, and neither of the two thrift restructuring acts has changed these constraints.

Tax Considerations.   The received analysis of the effects of the tax rules under which S&L and savings banks operate holds that it seriously inhibits the institutions' ability to diversify their asset portfolios in response to the asset-side deregulation of the two acts (U.S. Department of the Treasury, 1980; Eisenbeis, 1983; Kaplan, 1983). Associations that hold 82 percent or more of their assets in qualified form are allowed to contribute a proportion of their profits untaxed to a bad-debt reserve. This tax advantage decreases as the percentage of qualified assets declines; it disappears entirely when S&L qualified assets are reduced below 60 percent. (Qualified assets include mortgages, mortgage-backed securities, and government securities.) Consequently, the received analysis contends, diversification into assets permitted by the two acts, such as consumer and commercial loans, will be profitable only for exceptionally advantageous rates on these alternative loans. Such advantageous rates, estimated to be 150 percent of the rate paid on qualified assets, are unlikely to be found in the market. Thus, the diversification needed to promote S&L profitability is effectively prevented by current tax law.

There are, however, four objections to the received analysis. First, most associations have recently been unprofitable; so they may diversify without disadvantage. Second, since both profitable and nonprofitable associations typically have qualified assets in excess of 82 percent, they have room to diversify to some extent before incurring tax disadvantages. Third, the qualified asset limitations imposed on savings banks are less restrictive than those imposed on S&Ls. The Garn–St Germain Act provides for easy charter conversion between S&L and savings bank designation. S&Ls, wishing to diversify, can then convert. For example, savings banks can hold 28 percent of their assets in nonqualified categories before they begin to experience tax disadvantages (Federal Reserve Bank of Chicago, 1983). Fourth, and most important, as Herbert Baer (1983) demonstrates, the received argument overlooks the institutions' ability (given under the 1980 act and increased under the 1982 act) to shelter income, as do commercial banks, by holding tax-exempt state and local government securities.

Thus, despite the tax advantages derived from holding mortgage and mortgage-backed securities, some meaningful diversification may be feasible. State and municipal securities can be used to shelter income, and, at the same time, commercial and consumer loans can be made in an attempt to raise gross earnings. Nevertheless, the existing tax structure, designed to allocate funds to housing, was revised to modestly reduce the bad-debt deduction under the Tax Equity and Fiscal Responsibility Act (TEFRA) of 1982. Nevertheless, it still interferes with the diversification process.

Asset Constraints: Prices.   While the quantity constraints imposed on S&L assets tended to be national in application, price constraints on assets were more frequently imposed at the state level. For example, several states imposed usury ceilings on those loan rates charged by banks and thrifts. These ceilings were variously imposed on mortgages and on other loans, both business and consumer. Such ceilings led to episodes of credit rationing (when interest rate levels rose above the ceilings) and to other distortions and redirections of funds (Nathan, 1980). Ceilings on mortgage loans were largely overridden by the 1980 act; state-imposed restrictions on the due-on-sale clause were overridden by the 1982 act. Although the 1980 act served to raise (unless overridden, by new legislation enacted before April 1983) the ceilings that existed in some states, they sometimes remained fixed and binding on non-mortgage loans.

Asset Constraints: Geographic.   S&Ls and other depository institutions were also restrained as to the geographic location of their assets. In some states, particularly in unit- or limited-branching states, legal restrictions confined the granting of mortgages to an area adjacent to the S&L's office (or head office). Even in less restrictive states, S&L lending did not cross state lines. Apart from legal restrictions, practical reasons exist for the confinement, or at least the decentralization, of S&L activities by area. Mortgage lending involves highly localized expertise in property valuation. Although national or regional data bases are available on the creditworthiness of potential borrowers, no such data are currently available on the value of mortgageable property.[1]

Liability Constraints: Activities and Quantities.   Similarly, in the period of the 1930s–1970s, four kinds of constraints prevailed on the liability side of the balance sheet. In general, S&Ls were permitted to offer only savings and time deposits prior to 1980. However, they can now offer NOW accounts, MMDAs, and SNOW accounts nationwide. All the instruments are fixed in value, that is, their principal and market values do not vary, and are typically insured to $100,000. S&Ls and other depository institutions do not, apart from their equity capital, offer liabilities that can vary in price, as is the case with mutual funds. Nondeposit liabilities, such as repurchase agreements (RPs), are not insured by the federal insurance funds, but, even so, typically they are contractually fixed in nominal value. In recent years large CDs and RPs have come to play an increasingly important role as sources of S&L funds.

Other restrictions, in the form of reserve requirements, also exist. Although they are not imposed directly on the issuable quantities of individual liabilities, they do serve to constrain an S&L's overall size and to influence the composition of its liabilities. Liability composition is influenced because some accounts incur higher reserve ratios than others. Reserve requirements, previously applicable to member banks, were extended to nonmember banks and thrifts under the Monetary Control Act of 1980. They decree that the Federal Reserve, under Regulation D, must impose reserve requirements on transaction accounts and nonpersonal time deposits.

Liability Constraints: Prices.   Price constraints were imposed both by law and by regulation. Colloquially, these restrictions are referred to as Regulation Q. Table 6.1 shows the extension of these restrictions, which were imposed first on member commercial banks under Banking Act amendments to the Federal Reserve Act of 1933. They were next extended to insured nonmember banks (under the Banking Act of 1935) and to S&Ls and mutual savings banks

TABLE 6.1
REGULATION Q RATES FOR PASSBOOK
SAVINGS DEPOSITS

Date	Commercial Banks[a]	S&Ls[a]
November 1933	3.00	
January 1935	2.50	
January 1957	3.00	
January 1962	3.50	
November 1964	4.00	
September 1966	4.00	4.75
January 1970	4.50	5.00
July 1973	5.00	5.25
July 1979	5.25	5.50

[a]Regulation Q was extended to insured nonmember banks in 1935 and to S&Ls in September 1966.
SOURCES: Board of Governors of the Federal Reserve (1971) and (1981); Jones (1979).

in 1966. Table 6.2 records the dates on which Regulation Q was imposed on different institutions, as well as the initiating rate imposed. Since that date, until recently, Regulation Q has restricted the interest rates that could be offered on virtually all S&L liabilities. The movement of Regulation Q ceilings as applied to passbook savings accounts at both banks and thrifts is shown in Table 6.1.

Liability Constraints: Geographic. Geographic restrictions exist on the location of bank and thrift activities. The Federal Reserve defines a commercial bank as one that accepts demand deposits and makes commercial loans. Interstate banking is prohibited by the McFadden Act. However, although S&Ls accept NOW and SNOW deposits, which are very similar to demand deposits, and, since October 1982, have been able to make commercial loans, they are not classified as commercial banks, and thus they are not subject to the McFadden Act.

Manipulation of these geographic restrictions has resulted in a geographically dispersed set of activities that must appear illogical to a visitor from Mars. Commercial banks can own S&Ls in different states. At the time of this writing (early 1984), New York's Citicorp owns an S&L in California (formerly Fidelity Savings and Loan Association of Oakland) and two other large failed associations, one in Illinois and the other in Florida (First Federal S&L of

TABLE 6.2
EXTENDING INTEREST RATE REGULATIONS

Source	Regulation	Original Percentage Rate	Date of Regulation	Regulator
Congress (Banking Act of 1933)	(a) Commercial bank demand deposits: member banks	0	August 1933	Federal Reserve
	(b) Regulation Q: member bank time and savings deposits	3.00[a]	November 1933	Federal Reserve
Congress (Banking Act of 1935)	(a) Insured nonmember bank demand deposits	0	August 1935	FDIC
	(b) Regulation 329: insured nonmember bank savings and time deposits	2.50	August 1935	FDIC
Congress (Federal Home Loan Bank Act Amendment)	S&Ls and savings banks: Regulation Q: savings deposits time deposits	4.75[b] 5.25	September 1966 September 1966	FHLBB FHLBB

[a]In November 1964, passbook and time deposit rates (in accounts held over 90 days) were separated: longer time deposits were allowed to pay up to 4.50 percent.
[b]For adjustments to Regulation Q ceilings after their imposition, see Table 6.1.

Chicago and New Biscayne S&L, respectively). As another example, commercial loans are frequently made out-of-state by commercial bank loan production offices. Credit cards are issued across state lines. Deposits can be accepted from an out-of-state resident if they are sent by mail or delivered in person, but they cannot be sent electronically. Yet the same customer can more readily withdraw money out-of-state—from automatic teller machines, for example. Numerous nonbank banks have grown up that avoid the Federal Reserve's regulatory domain by refraining from the letter of the law governing one or other of the bank-defining activities. Then they can operate interstate (Whitehead, 1983a). Because S&Ls are subject to less restrictive interstate regulations than are commercial banks, they offer an attractive way to effect *de facto* interstate banking.

PROBLEMS ARISING FROM THE REGULATIONS

The various restrictions gave rise to a number of problems for the S&L industry. They will be characterized here under four headings: (1) disintermediation, (2) interest rate risk, (3) credit risk, and (4) unprofitability and failure—the outcome arising from the industry's inability to handle its various risk exposures. Each of these symptoms of industry malaise will be discussed in turn.

DISINTERMEDIATION

Disintermediation, the loss of funds to nondeposit institutions, developed two manifestations in the post-1966 years. During the late 1960s and much of the 1970s, disintermediation was reflected as a sharp reduction in deposit inflows or, on occasion, deposit outflows, when market interest rates rose above the Regulation Q ceiling rates. This phenomenon is represented in Figure 6.1, which shows the monthly changes in S&L deposits from 1960 through 1983. Figure 6.2 shows the relationship between Regulation Q ceilings and market interest rates. These deposit changes, which include both seasonally adjusted inflows of new monies to associations and interest credited to existing accounts, actually declined during eight individual months in the interval between the imposition of Regulation Q and the end of 1983.[2]

After the introduction of the six-month money market certificate in June 1978, the nature of the disintermediation problem changed. Beginning in that month, S&Ls and commercial banks were able to offer Treasury-bill-compatible rates on certificates of $10,000 or more. This facility reduced the sharpness and suddenness of disintermediation. Thereafter, the problem became one of a slower attrition of funds. For example, funds that might have been placed with S&Ls or other depository institutions were siphoned off into money market mutual funds. The value of these money market funds rose from $10.2 billion at the end of 1978 to $241 billion in November 1982, just before the introduction of the money market deposit account in December 1982. By the end of December 1983, these funds had declined to $177.3 billion.

The interpretation used above of disintermediation as a decline in S&L deposits is the one commonly employed. However, while the use of total deposit levels is not as objectionable as it would be for commercial banks, whose large institutions placed greater reliance on managed liabilities (such as large CDs), it is, nevertheless, restrictive. What is more usefully required is some measure of the unexpected decline in deposit levels. Such a measure would take into account the projected rise in deposit levels that result, for example, from increases in the nominal value of income.

To capture this idea, we have constructed a simple model of the growth in deposit levels over time. Our model projects that deposit levels grow at a constant rate over time, by regressing the natural logarithm of the monthly

FIGURE 6.1
CHANGE IN S&L TOTAL DEPOSITS

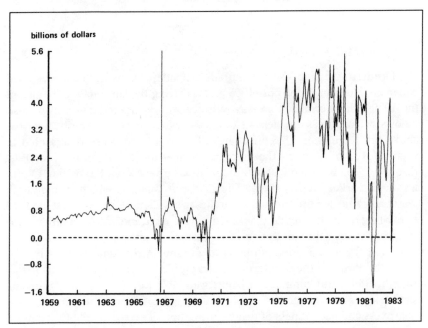

NOTE: The vertical line represents the extension of Regulation Q to S&Ls in September 1966.

FIGURE 6.2
THREE-MONTH TREASURY BILL RATES AND
REGULATION Q CEILINGS

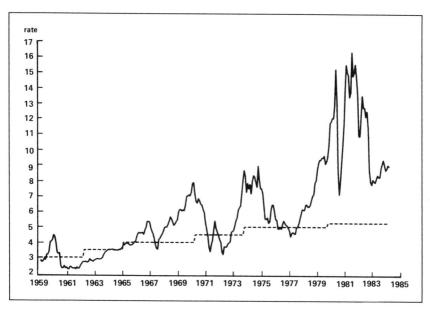

level of S&L total deposits seasonally adjusted $(LSLD)$ on time (t, measured in months). The following regression equation was obtained from data for the period January 1959 through November 1982.

$$LSLD = 3.9078 + 0.0086\,t \qquad (6.1)$$
$$(476.1) \quad (174.5)$$

$R^2 = 0.9907$

The figures in parenthesis are the t values, which, together with the coefficient of determination (R^2), show the significance of regression.

The actual values of S&L deposits and their trend values, as given by the predicted values from the regression equation, are shown in Figure 6.3. Although the figure provides a good indication of disintermediation's incidence, an even clearer representation is given in Figure 6.4. This maps the deviations for the period January 1959 through October 1983 from trend values as estimated from data for 1959 through November 1982. The Garn–St Germain Act gave thrifts broad powers to change their charters. During 1983,

FIGURE 6.3
S&L TOTAL DEPOSITS: ACTUAL AND PREDICTED

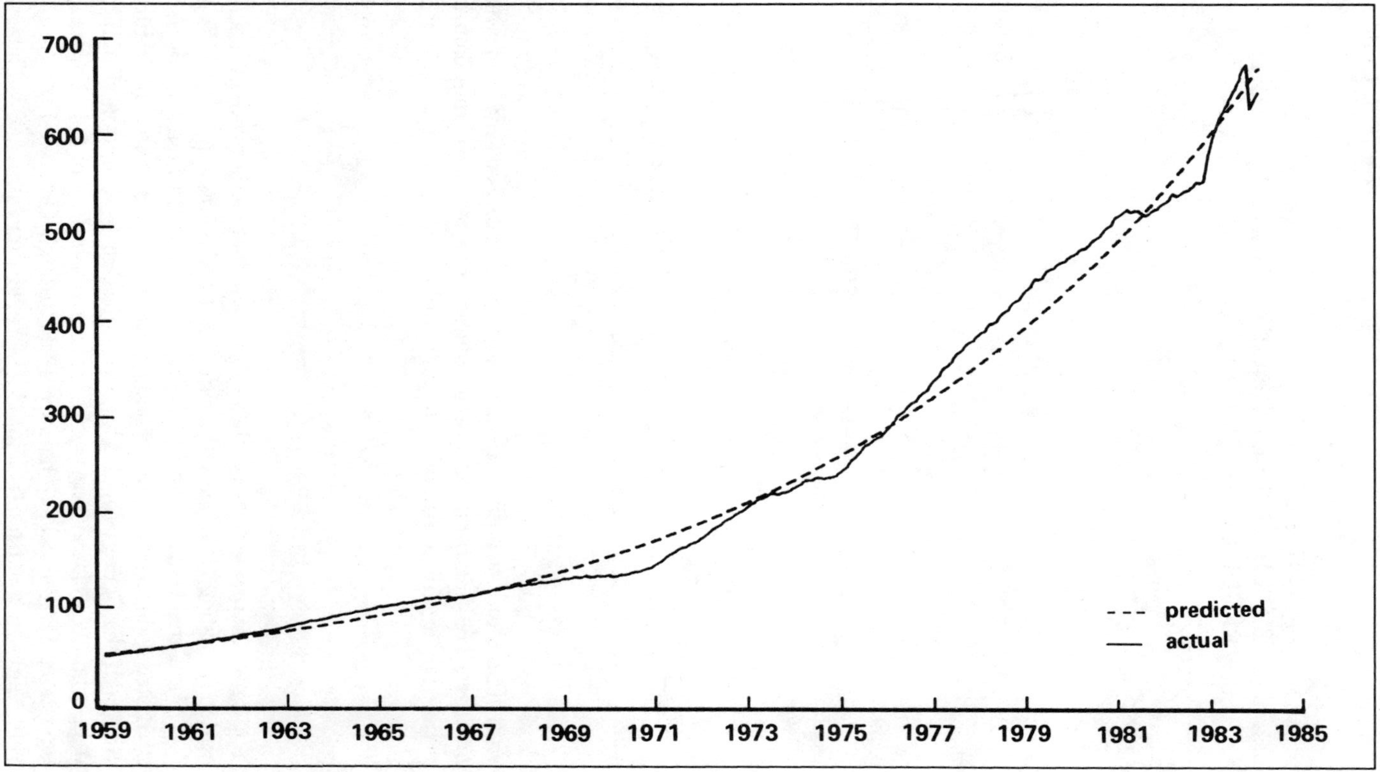

--- predicted
— actual

over a hundred S&Ls switched to the savings bank designation. Consequently, beginning in December 1982, data for savings bank deposits are included together with those for S&Ls in order to avoid a decline in S&L deposits arising from the changes in charter designation.

Ending the regression in November 1982 allows us to estimate the impact on S&L deposit levels of the introduction of the money market deposit account in December 1982 and the SNOW account in January 1983. Extrapolating the trend (estimated on data existing before the introduction of the new accounts) also allows us to compare the deposit levels with those that might have been expected without the new accounts. The regulatory innovations are shown to have had an important impact in reversing, during the first half of 1983, the decline in S&L deposits below their earlier trend. However, the recovered advantage was lost during the second half of 1983. The industry ended the year again below trend. Earlier episodes of disintermediation, occurring in years when the Regulation Q ceilings were most binding, are also highlighted in the figures.

INTEREST RATE RISK

Since the 1930s, S&L mortgages have typically been of the long-maturity and fixed-rate type. Long-term mortgages constituted the bulk of S&L assets into the 1980s. This put the industry in the position of funding long-term assets with short-term liabilities. This presented, of course, no problem when the secular level of interest rates was low. As George Kaufman (1972) demonstrates, and as Figure 6.5 graphically shows, S&Ls can in principle profitably manage cyclical interest rate variability if they can accurately predict the average level of rates and if they set mortgage rates above this average level.

Figure 6.5 shows a stylized interest rate cycle extending over the time interval $t = 0$ to $t = 4$. During the interval, the S&L is profitable because its average earnings substantially exceed its average interest costs.[3]

However, several regulatory and other factors inhibited the profitable response. Usury ceilings restricted rates that could be charged on assets. As market interest rates rose with inflation, these interest rate ceilings became increasingly restrictive. Regulation Q ceilings threatened a disintermediation crisis and forced S&Ls to preserve liquidity by purchasing funds and paying implicit interest. These measures often involved elevated and difficult-to-forecast interest costs. In short, escalating inflation raised interest levels above those generally anticipated, and this rendered illusory any reassurance suggested by Kaufman's analysis.

The data in Table 6.3 show the S&L industry's exposure to interest rate risk. Average deposit rates paid followed a monotonically (or relentlessly) rising trend from 4.25 percent in 1965 to 11.19 percent in 1982. Nevertheless, the speed of increase varied with the business cycle. During the same period, average mortgage rates received did not rise so quickly. Although they rose monotonically, they ultimately failed to keep up with the cost of funds. The spread between the average mortgage rate received and the average rate paid (in Table 6.3 the difference between columns 3 and 2) remained positive through 1980. In fact, it varied cyclically, remained strong, and even reached a peak as late as 1978. But thereafter it declined rapidly and became negative during 1981 and 1982.

While average rates charged on new mortgages rose rapidly over the years, rising from 5.81 percent in 1965 to 14.73 percent in 1982, S&Ls still became unprofitable. The major cause of S&L unprofitability in these years was retarded average mortgage earnings because of the backlog of old mortgages. This backlog did not present a problem initially, when rates on new mortgages were below the average being earned on the existing mortgages. However, the two mortgage rates increasingly diverged over time, as the data in Table 6.3 show. Then, the backlog problem became more serious because, as rates on new mortgages rose to historical highs, homeowners became increasingly reluctant to surrender their old, lower-rate mortgages. The mortgage redemption rate fell as householders refrained from selling their homes or engaged in creative-financing expedients when they did sell.

FIGURE 6.4
S&L TOTAL DEPOSITS: RESIDUAL VALUES

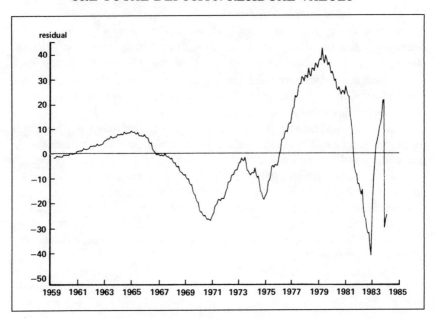

FIGURE 6.5
HANDLING INTEREST RATE RISK

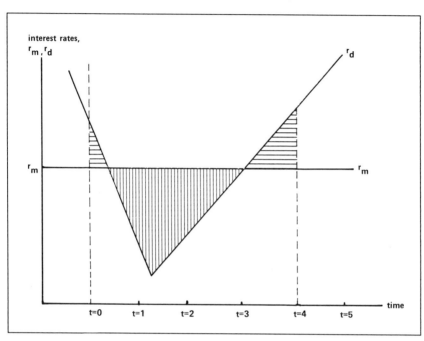

CREDIT RISK

The pronounced disintermediation and substantial interest rate risks can be regarded as risks undertaken beyond the industry's call of duty; they were also risks imposed on S&Ls by the perverse regulatory structure. However, credit risk is part of the inherent business of S&Ls, a business in which management should be expert at all times. In general, the industry has handled this risk reasonably well. Table 6.4 reports the industry's performance in this respect. The data show, as expected, that exposure varied with the business cycle, but, in general, remained at acceptable levels until 1982, when it rose to levels twice those typical in the earlier decade. Nevertheless, research by Brewer and Garcia (1983) shows that poor handling of credit risk contributed to the reduced profitability of some Midwestern S&Ls in 1981, especially the most unprofitable S&Ls.

S&L UNPROFITABILITY

These problems took their toll. The industry surmounted the smaller problem (disintermediation) only to be entrapped by its successor (interest

TABLE 6.3

S&L EXPOSURE TO INTEREST RATE RISK

Col. 1	Col. 2	Col.3	Col. 4	Col. 5	Col. 6
Year	Average Effective Interest Rate Paid	Average Interest Return on Mortgages	Spread Col. (3)– Col. (2)	Conventional Mortgage Rate on New Loans	Backlog Penalty Col. (5)– Col. (3)
1965	4.25	5.93	1.68	5.81	−0.12
1966	4.48	5.94	1.46	6.25	0.31
1967	4.68	6.01	1.33	6.46	0.45
1968	4.71	6.13	1.42	6.97	0.84
1969	4.81	6.32	1.51	7.81	1.49
1970	5.14	6.56	1.42	8.45	1.89
1971	5.30	6.81	1.51	7.74	0.93
1972	5.37	7.03	1.66	7.60	0.57
1973	5.51	7.22	1.71	7.95	0.73
1974	5.96	7.48	1.52	8.92	1.44
1975	6.21	7.71	1.50	9.01	1.30
1976	6.31	8.00	1.69	8.99	0.99
1977	6.39	8.26	1.87	9.01	0.75
1978	6.56	8.50	1.94	9.54	1.04
1979	7.29	8.86	1.57	10.77	1.91
1980	8.78	9.34	0.56	12.46	3.12
1981	10.71	9.91	−0.80	14.39	4.48
1982	11.19	10.68	−0.51	14.73	4.05

SOURCES: U.S. League of Savings Associations, '78 *Fact Book* and '82 *Source Book*; Federal Home Loan Bank Board, *Savings and Home Financing Source Book*, 1982; Federal Home Loan Bank Board (1984, Table S5.1).

rate risk). This risk arose because interest rates payable on liabilities were deregulated (in order to avoid disintermediation) while asset earnings remained constrained.[4] As market interest rates rose, the industry faltered, as the data in Table 6.5 attest.

The reliance on long-term, fixed-rate assets, despite unexpectedly high liability costs, led to two results. The first was visible in the industry's declining and (ultimately in 1981 and 1982) substantially negative accounting profits. These are reported in Table 6.5. The second result was not so evident. The economic net worth of the industry (the market value of assets less that of liabilities) fell, as shown in Table 6.6, substantially below its accounting net worth and became negative (Kane, 1983a; Kopcke, 1981). Indeed, according to Kane (1983a), S&L net worth, when adjusted for the estimated value of unbooked losses on the mortgage portfolio, was continuously and increasingly negative from 1971 through 1981. By the early 1980s, it was clear that the industry's viability was at stake, regardless of whether economic or accounting valuations were used.

Consequently, increasing numbers of S&Ls faced insolvency. FSLIC policy has always been to avoid S&L failure by arranging mergers for problem institutions. As a result, statistics on the number of S&L failures are not as revealing as are those provided by the FDIC for insured commercial banks (Table 6.7). However, the comparisons provided in Table 6.7 do illustrate the industry's deterioration. The number of associations has declined monotonically since 1962, as shown in Table 6.8. Nevertheless, few of these industry consolidations have been closures by the FSLIC. The insurance agency, since its inception in the 1930s, has followed a policy of avoiding forced closure of associations, and only 21 associations have been closed by the FSLIC throughout its history. Seven of these closures occurred before 1960.[5] Five associations

TABLE 6.4
S&L PROBLEM LOANS

Year	Foreclosure Percentage[a]	Percentage Scheduled Items[b]
1970	0.19	n.a.
1971	0.19	n.a.
1972	0.20	0.78[c]
1973	0.21	0.74
1974	0.20	0.90
1975	0.20	1.25
1976	0.17	1.24
1977	0.14	0.99
1978	0.12	0.79
1979	0.11	1.69
1980	0.13	0.75
1981	0.18	0.97
1982	0.33	1.44
1983	0.39	n.a.

[a]The foreclosure percentage is the number of mortgages foreclosed as a percentage of the number of mortgages held.

[b]The percentage of scheduled items represents the value of slow and nonconforming loans and of real estate acquired as a result of foreclosure or repossession as a percentage of the value of total assets.

[c]Data available for July through December only, and not for the years 1970 and 1971.

SOURCES: Federal Home Loan Bank Board, *Savings and Home Financing Source Book*, 1975, 1978, 1982; MS League of Savings Institutions Sourcebook, 1984.

TABLE 6.5
PROFITABILITY OF INSURED S&Ls

	NET INCOME AS A PERCENTAGE OF	
Year	*Total Assets*	*Total Net Worth*
1965	0.64	9.41
1966	0.49	7.00
1967	0.45	6.61
1968	0.58	8.40
1969	0.66	9.29
1970	0.54	7.71
1971	0.66	9.84
1972	0.71	11.45
1973	0.72	11.61
1974	0.52	8.38
1975	0.44	7.58
1976	0.59	10.53
1977	0.71	12.90
1978	0.77	14.00
1979	0.64	11.63
1980	0.13	2.42
1981	− 0.71	− 16.64
1982	− 0.62	− 16.86

SOURCES: Federal Home Loan Bank Board, *Combined Financial Statements* (1975, 1982).

were closed in the 1960s. Only one closure was forced in the 1970s, but during the 1981–1983 crisis eight were closed (Table 6.7). The agency has, in fact, followed a policy of encouraging mergers for troubled associations. The Financial Institutions Regulatory and Interest Rate Control Act of 1978 gave the FSLIC limited powers to provide limited financial assistance to troubled merging associations. However, by the summer of 1982 a major crisis threatened. The Garn–St Germain Act was, therefore, enacted to significantly extend these emergency powers. More associations were closed in 1983 than in any earlier year, despite the number (149) of troubled associations that received assistance to merge during the years 1980–1983.

By contrast, the experience of the commercial banking industry has been somewhat different. Even after the FDIC was established, failures were common during the 1930s, when 402 banks failed; 116 banks failed in the 1940s, mostly during the first three years; 46 failed during the 1950s; and since that time 248 have failed, of which 110 failed in the years 1980–1983. In the first half of 1984 bank failures occurred at double the 1983 rate. However, the number of banks has risen over the same period (although not monotonically), reaching a peak in 1982.

INDUSTRY RESPONSES

Depository institutions responded to the various problems they faced in a variety of ways. The response to disintermediation is readily understood by industry outsiders. Commercial banks, for example, responded to disintermediation and to competition from thrifts by inventing new liability instruments that could attract funds by offering the higher market rates. As we discuss further in the next chapter, banks adopted large CDs, repurchase agreements, and Eurodollar borrowings in order to attract funds from their corporate customers. In the 1960s and 1970s S&Ls generally avoided these devices, fearing that they would raise interest costs beyond their ability to earn.

The S&L industry preferred to maintain and attract funds via the implicit payment of interest. After imposition of Regulation Q, gift promotions (toasters, barbeque grills, electric can openers, etc.) were offered; later they were

TABLE 6.6
NET WORTH OF INSURED S&Ls

Year	Book Value of Net Worth ($ billions)	Net Worth After Deducting Estimated Unrealized Mortgage Losses ($ billions)
1971	13.1	(20.7)
1972	14.7	(19.4)
1973	16.5	(18.5)
1974	17.9	(32.7)
1975	19.2	(38.6)
1976	21.4	(41.6)
1977	24.5	(44.4)
1978	28.3	(52.8)
1979	31.8	(79.3)
1980	32.4	(118.3)
1981	27.8	(150.7)
1982	25.3	n.a.

SOURCES: Kane (1983a); Federal Home Loan Bank Board, *Combined Financial Statements* (1975, 1982).

TABLE 6.7
S&L INDUSTRY OUTCOMES

Year	Number S&Ls Closed[a]	Number S&Ls Receiving Assistance When Merging[b]	Commercial Bank Failures
1960	0	0	2
1961	0	0	9
1962	0	0	3
1963	0	0	2
1964	0	0	8
1965	1	0	9
1966	2	0	8
1967	0	0	4
1968	2	0	3
1969	0	0	9
1970	0	0	8
1971	1	0	6
1972	0	0	3
1973	0	0	6
1974	0	0	4
1975	0	0	14
1976	0	0	17
1977	0	0	6
1978	0	0	7
1979	0	0	10
1980	0	11	10
1981	1	27	10
1982	1	65	42
1983	6	46	48

[a]The FSLIC has, in general, had a policy of avoiding closures. This policy differs from that of the FDIC.
[b]In some cases mergers were arranged among more than two associations. The numbers of mergers arranged are 11, 23, 44, and 27 for the years 1980–1983.
SOURCES: Federal Home Loan Bank Board, *Savings and Home Financing Source Book, 1982*; FDIC annual reports; FSLIC, FDIC Public Information Departments.

limited in value by the federal regulators. Free services (such as safety deposit boxes, traveler's checks, checking accounts at cooperating banks) were commonly offered in the early 1970s. In states permitting it, S&Ls increased the number of their branches. As Kane (1982) has pointed out, during the disintermediation period S&Ls increased the number of their branches much more quickly than did the commercial banking industry, whose large institutions were more committed to paying explicit interest on their managed liabilities. Table 6.8 shows that the number of S&L offices rose from 1.25 per S&L in 1960 to 5.16 in 1981.[6] It remains to be seen whether this trend will be reversed in a less regulated environment. Finally, associations offered "finder's fees" at the end of the 1970s in order to attract funds. In turn, finder's fees became subject to regulations imposed by the DIDC during 1981.

To increase the catchment area for funds and to expand the range of their profitable outlets for funds, commercial bank holding companies adopted techniques to operate interstate (Whitehead, 1983a and 1983b). S&Ls had less recourse to this device until the 1980 and 1982 acts freed them from many of their asset-side restrictions. Since the 1982 act, S&Ls and their holding companies have had substantial freedom to operate interstate and expand the range of their activities. Permissive laws in some states (such as California) have encouraged this process. As a consequence, the federal insurance agen-

TABLE 6.8
S&L IMPLICIT INTEREST: BRANCHING

Year	Number of Associations[a]	Number of Offices per Association[b]	Number of Commercial Banks	Number of Offices per Bank[b]
1960	6,320	1.25	13,484	1.79
1965	6,185	1.48	13,818	2.15
1970	5,669	1.76	13,705	2.60
1971	5,474	1.91	13,804	2.69
1972	5,298	2.10	13,733	2.81
1973	5,170	2.36	13,976	2.91
1974	5,023	2.75	14,230	3.01
1975	4,931	3.13	14,385	3.10
1976	4,821	3.47	14,697	3.14
1977	4,761	3.75	14,740	3.25
1978	4,725	4.02	14,741	3.36
1979	4,684	4.31	14,738	3.50
1980	4,613	4.62	14,870	3.61
1981	4,292	5.16	14,913	3.74
1982	3,833	n.a.	14,994	3.66

[a]Includes all S&Ls, state or federally chartered, insured and uninsured.
[b]Includes both head offices and branches.
SOURCES: Federal Home Loan Bank Board, *Savings and Home Financing Source Book, 1982*; U.S. League of Savings Associations, *'82 Savings and Loan Source Book*; FDIC annual reports.

cies have taken steps to limit their exposure by refusing insurance to associations deemed to be undertaking excessive risk through portfolio expansion.

COMPETITOR RESPONSES: RIPPLE EFFECTS

The restrictions and difficulties faced by S&Ls and other depository institutions provided opportunities to other financial agents. The rapid growth of money market mutual funds can be readily related to their ability to bypass the restriction applied to depository institutions. They offered market-competitive rates, often small denominations and minimum balances, ready availability, no minimum maturity, and some ability to serve as transactions vehicles.

The volume of credit card balances (both bank and nonbank) grew. Credit cards offer the opportunity to generate credit and may be used as transactions media (Garcia, 1980). Although their interest charges were typically high, as the 1970s progressed, their rates did not rise with market rates and became less usurious. For other users, credit cards offered the ability to make purchases without maintaining, as in depository institutions, large deposit balances that earned no interest. With judicious timing, the credit card monthly balance can be repaid from one's salary check without incurring interest charges. The average balance that would otherwise be retained in a checking account could then be used elsewhere (to earn interest in a money market mutual fund or to purchase consumer goods—items at a premium as inflation escalated).

Nonbanks came increasingly to offer deposit and lending services. Merrill Lynch pioneered its Cash Management and Ready Asset Accounts in the mid- and late-1970s. During the 1980s, it moved into consumer lending by offering its Equity Access Account to provide second mortgages to homeowners. Sears moved to increase its financial services beyond its traditional insurance (Allstate Insurance) and consumer lending, by providing a bank in Chicago, an S&L in California (Allstate S&L, which became Sears Savings Bank in January 1984), full service brokerage services (Dean Witter Reynolds), a real estate brokerage firm (Caldwell Banker), and by purchasing a bank—to become a nonbank bank—in Delaware. Rosenblum and Siegel (1983) provide careful documentation of the proliferation of nonbank banking.

Foreign competition in the banking area within the United States proliferated. Competition from Europe, Japan, and Hong Kong increased. Foreign competitors possessed an advantage prior to the passage of the International Banking Act of 1978 because they were subject to less regulation while operating within the United States than were domestic banks. Frequently, U.S. banks operating in foreign countries were not given the same advantage of diminished foreign regulation.

THE ECONOMIC AND
FINANCIAL EFFECTS OF REGULATION

The question arises whether credit crunches, as observed in 1966, 1969, 1974–1975, 1979–1980 and 1981–1982, were attributable to regulation. Would they not have occurred or would they have been less severe in the absence of regulation?

The answer is yes. Credit crunches might not have occurred in a deregulated environment. They would certainly have been less severe. It is clear that regulation made the S&L industry unstable in the environment of the late 1970s and early 1980s. Regulation also induced instability in the supply of mortgage credit. It is widely held that Regulation Q exacerbated the degree of credit rationing, particularly in the mortgage industry, during the cycles from 1966 through 1980. After that time, it seems more likely that mortgage and other lending dropped off at cyclical interest rate peaks, not because of a shortage of the supply of funds, but in response to a movement along the demand curve for funds as rates rose.

It has been argued that the Federal Reserve used disintermediation as a tool in economic policy in the 1960s and 1970s. Because of credit rationing during the 1960s and 1970s, Federal Reserve policy restraint could be transmitted readily to certain sectors of the economy with only a limited increase in interest rates. The housing and consumer durable goods industries, in particular, felt the brunt of such policies. In the 1980s, in the absence of these supply constraints, interest rates would need to rise to higher levels in order to restrain the demand for funds and the level of economic activity. This viewpoint is expounded clearly by Wojnilower (1980).

Others have argued that the threat of disintermediation acted as a constraint on Federal Reserve policy. Given the social contract with the housing industry, policymakers were prevented during the 1970s from pushing restrictive policies far enough to prevent escalating inflation. More restrictive policies would have increased interest rates further and would have exacerbated disintermediation and the ensuing decline in the housing industry.

Some analysts (Hendershott, 1983) have criticized the emphasis on the housing industry, arguing that the substantial subsidies the industry received caused a misallocation of investment funds away from more productive sectors. As a result, the housing industry grew at the expense of U.S. industry in general.

Further, the success of government-subsidized lending to housing, through the advantageous access to the capital markets available to quasi-government housing agencies (Fannie Mae, Freddie Mac, etc.), caused other industries to copy this approach. The use of government-sponsored or government-guaranteed loans escalated. The Student Loan Marketing Association (Sally Mae) was formed to provide guaranteed, and therefore subsidized, loans to students. The Farm Credit Administration (FCA), although established as a result of the experiences of the Great Depression, strongly increased its acquisition of funds for farmers during the 1970s. Only mainstream U.S. manufacturing industry appeared to lack subsidized access to the loan market (Fried, 1983). Some analysts have attributed this industry's loss of competitive position and productivity problems of the 1970s to inadequate investment resulting in part from the subsidization of other industries.

Above all, the structural weaknesses of depository institutions (particularly S&Ls) have been attributed to the regulatory environment that confined them within narrow bounds in the nation's flow of funds. Constraints that put them in a world of unexpectedly rising interest rates, which they were forced to match, first implicitly and then explicitly. These constraints not only threatened stability of S&Ls while they were binding, but they also made it more difficult for S&Ls to operate in the later, deregulated environment. In dedicating their physical assets to competing in the implicit rate environment, S&Ls prejudiced their ability to compete in the deregulated-rate world. In this world, the ownership of branches, for example, raises association costs above competitive levels.

At the same time that the liability barriers began to fall for S&Ls with the advent of the money market certificate in 1978, asset restrictions remained in place. While freedom to make nonmortgage loans was enhanced under the 1980 and 1982 acts, the S&L industry could not successfully move rapidly into new ventures, for it lacked expertise in these areas and tax considerations were not conducive to diversification. More useful to the industry would be the ability to avoid interest rate risk through the offering of variable rate mortgages (VRMs) in different forms. However, the 1980 act made no such provision, and it was left to the delayed responses of the federal regulators to authorize the VRM.

REGULATORY RESPONSES

The responses of regulators to these events have been both diverse and delayed. A long battle was waged between proponents of relaxing, and ultimately eliminating, Regulation Q as counterproductive and inequitable, and those favoring its retention in an effort to curtail depository institution costs. This battle is now drawing to a close with the anti–Regulation Q forces in command, as of early 1984 and for the foreseeable future.

Early recommendations by the Hunt and FINE Reports to liberalize S&L asset portfolios were not embodied in legislation until the 1980 and 1982 acts.

Now flexibility is at hand for these S&Ls that can handle the potential tax disadvantages in the way Baer (1983) recommends.

The letter of the geographic restrictions on assets and liabilities remain, but such restrictions are widely violated in practice. The restrictions on deposit flows (restrictions that geographically confine the ability to accept deposits) remain the most widely enforced regulations.

In the available three-year-period after the passage of DIDMCA, seventeen states partially or totally overrode the 1980 pre-emption of usury ceilings (Conference of State Bank Supervisors, 1984). Ten states took a more free-market stance than the act and removed the ceilings completely. Three states (Maine, Massachusetts, and North Carolina) reinstated their old ceilings, while four states (Kansas, Minnesota, New Jersey, and Washington) instituted new ones. In some cases, state usury ceilings have been bypassed by relocating (particularly in the case of credit card operations) the depository institution's head office to one of the permissive states. Several states (for example, Delaware, New York, Nevada, and South Dakota) have enacted permissive state legal frameworks in order to attract financial service corporations to their territory.

CONCLUSION

The S&L crisis of 1980–1983 appeared, at the time of initial writing in early 1984, to have been weathered. However, by mid-1984 several months of increasing market interest rates have poised the industry on the brink of another crisis. Repositioning the S&L asset portfolio will take time, even where it is feasible, given the current tax laws. In the meantime, Federal Reserve and administration policies are constrained by the threat of a recurrence of the 1980s thrift crisis. Further, Congress has yet to consistently evaluate its position on the social contract with the housing industry. In the meantime, that social contract, though modified, has not been terminated.

7 MONETARY CONTROL AND FINANCIAL INNOVATION

In the years following the Great Depression, monetary policy was in disrepute. It was held to have contributed importantly to the great debacle. It remained a little-used tool of economic policy. As such, it stayed in the background, largely undeveloped.

As the decades progressed, however, monetary policy re-emerged as a prime determinant of the economic climate and as an important tool of economic policy. In the process, economists and others gained greater insight into the transmission mechanism by which monetary policy exerts its influence over the economy. This insight led to suggestions of ways to make policy more effective. At the same time, an appreciation was emerging of the interrelationships between financial structure and financial policy.

Changes in the financial structure (that is, financial reform) and changes in monetary policy have mutual repercussions. This chapter examines these interrelationships. We first examine the evolving role that monetary policy has played in the economy. Second, we report developments in the economic environment and the shifting incidence of economic problems. Third, these developments altered the Federal Reserve's goals, or at least the relative emphasis shared among its several goals. At the same time, the financial system also evolved in response to economic problems and advancing technology. Fourth, we will briefly enumerate the series of financial innovations initiated by market participants.

The progression of financial innovations, together with the change in Federal Reserve goal priorities, led to revised methods employed by the monetary authority to implement its policies. These monetary reforms are summarized in the fifth section of the present chapter, which reports legislation, regulatory adjustments, and Federal Reserve initiatives. These last-mentioned initiatives included revisions in the money stock definitions and in its operating procedures.

The Federal Reserve employs a two-stage process for implementing its policies, a process called intermediate targeting. Under intermediate targeting, in the strategic phase of policy the Federal Reserve first chooses its final goals for the economy in terms of the growth of real GNP, employment, and the inflation rate. It also sets targets for some intermediate variable (such as the money stock or the level of interest rates) that it can influence and that determines, in some vital way, the achievement of the final goals. Since the central bank does not have direct control over the chosen midway variable, in the second tactical policy stage it chooses settings for its instruments. These are variables over which the Federal Reserve has more direct control (such as the level of nonborrowed reserves or the federal funds rate, the discount rate, and the level of reserve requirements) and which exert an important determining influence on the intermediate target variable (or variables). Schematically, the two-stage procedure may be represented as:

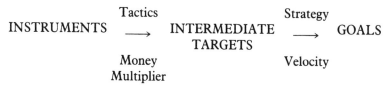

Consequently, in the sixth section of this chapter we will discuss the strategic stage in policy. Tactical or monetary control issues will be addressed in section seven. The chapter concludes with a summary and some comments on monetary policy's achievements.

MONETARY POLICY'S CHANGING ROLE

As a result of the experienced faults of central bank policy during the Great Depression of the 1930s, monetary policy was held in low esteem through the 1940s and 1950s. Stabilization policy was regarded principally as the preserve of fiscal policy. Monetary policy played a subsidiary role.

In general, policy at this time was easy to conduct because the economic environment was favorable. By the 1960s economies around the world had substantially recovered from the losses resulting from World War II. Optimism prevailed that the world economy faced a period of uninterrupted economic growth. The task of policymakers was to position any individual country to derive maximum advantage from participating in this growth and, at the same time, to solve whatever pressing social problems were given high priority. Monetary policy's contribution to this process lay in the background. It was envisaged as holding the economy on a steady course by gently leaning against the winds stirred by the business cycle.

As the 1960s progressed, however, the economics profession became more ready to listen to the early monetarists, who were arguing that monetary policy deserved greater recognition for playing an important part in economic stabilization. At this time, however, central bank behavior was constrained by fiscal policy, which was attempting simultaneously to solve social problems and to prosecute the Vietnam War.

During the 1970s, the world economy suffered a series of supply shocks that arrested the generalized advance. As a result, both industrialized and developing countries faced a number of problems: sharply rising oil prices, climatic disruptions, and demographic shifts. These problems would reduce the growth rate of world income and redistribute that income both among and within countries. Technological change also put strains on economic and social structures. Substantial changes in policy and in economic and sociopolitical institutions would be required to enable economies to adapt to the new environment. The age of optimism had ended.

As the 1970s progressed, professional opinion favored an increasing role for monetary policy; however, two factors cautioned against extravagant confidence in its efficacy. The first misgiving was the recognition that lags in the policy process could lead policy to be procyclical rather than stabilizing (Milton Friedman, 1968). Consequently, a fixed money growth rate was proposed to avoid procyclical stimuli. The second misgiving was the doubt cast by the rational expectations school on the stability of policy multipliers in the face of changes in policy regimes—a doubt about the usefulness of stabilization policy of any kind. Nevertheless, by the end of the 1970s, in the United States the major role in stabilization lay with the Federal Reserve.

U.S. MACROECONOMIC PROBLEMS

An important economic problem facing the world economy during the 1970s and early 1980s was a series of escalating inflation and recession cycles. The adverse supply shocks of the 1970s, following on the excessive demand policies of the Vietnam era, caused the severe downturn of 1973–1975 in the United States. In general, U.S. policymakers failed to recognize the structural implications of the mid-1970s crisis. Attempts to treat the situation as a typical excess/deficient demand cycle gave rise to policies that alternately attacked inflation, thereby causing recession, and then stimulated the economy to remedy unemployment. For example, by the late 1970s the structural problems were being masked under a fog of inflationary demand stimulation. The true nature of the problem was that adverse supply shocks simultaneously reduced GNP and accelerated price increases.

Figure 6.2 shows the progression of nominal interest rates, rising with inflation at each cyclical peak to new heights. Figure 7.1 shows the inflation recession escalation in the years following the Treasury Accord, which restored the Federal Reserve's ability to conduct policy independent of Treasury financing needs. As time passed, a consensus analysis was established about the nature of the problem. The dangers, both economic and sociopolitical, of inflation were emphasized, and resolutions were made to end the cyclical escalation.[1] Fiscal policy, despite the rhetoric, was regarded as unequal to the task. Table 7.1 shows that government expenditure continued to grow and that government receipts did not grow as quickly; as a result the budget deficit rose in total and as a percentage of GNP both during and following recessions. While the deficit's share in GNP is not unprecedented, it is remarkable for years in which the country was not at war. Such escalating budget deficits complicate the task assigned to the monetary authority of setting the scene for the structural adjustments that are necessary for the economy to adapt to the new era.

FIGURE 7.1
UNEMPLOYMENT AND INFLATION

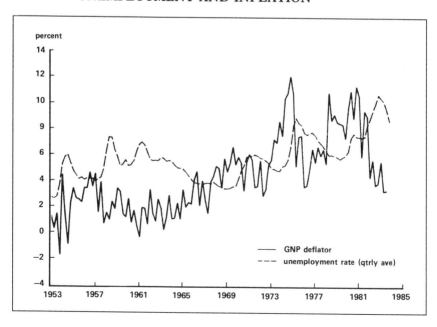

TABLE 7.1

FEDERAL GOVERNMENT RECEIPTS, EXPENDITURES, AND DEFICITS

| Year | $ Billion | | Deficit | Deficit as a Percentage of GNP |
	Receipts	Expenditures		
1948	43.2	34.9	− 8.3	− 3.2
1949	38.7	41.4	2.7	1.0
1950	50.0	40.8	− 9.2	− 3.1
1951	64.3	57.8	− 6.5	− 2.0
1952	67.4	71.1	3.7	1.1
1953	70.1	77.2	7.1	1.9
1954	63.8	69.9	6.1	1.7
1955	72.6	68.1	− 4.5	− 1.1
1956	77.9	72.0	− 6.0	− 1.4
1957	81.9	79.7	− 2.2	− 0.5
1958	78.6	89.0	10.4	2.3
1959	89.8	91.0	1.1	0.2
1960	96.1	93.1	− 3.0	0.6
1961	98.1	102.0	3.9	0.7
1962	106.2	110.4	4.2	0.7
1963	114.4	114.2	− 0.3	− 0.0
1964	114.9	118.2	3.3	0.5
1965	124.3	123.8	− 0.5	− 0.1
1966	141.8	143.6	1.8	0.2
1967	150.5	163.7	13.2	1.6
1968	174.4	180.5	6.1	0.7
1969	196.9	188.4	8.4	− 0.9
1970	191.9	204.3	12.4	1.2
1971	198.6	220.6	22.0	2.0
1972	227.5	244.3	16.8	1.4
1973	258.7	264.3	5.5	− 0.4
1974	287.8	299.3	11.5	0.8
1975	287.3	356.6	69.3	4.5
1976	331.7	384.8	53.1	3.1
1977	375.2	421.1	45.9	2.4
1978	431.6	461.1	29.5	1.3
1979	493.6	509.7	16.1	0.7
1980	540.8	602.1	61.3	2.3
1981	627.0	689.2	62.2	2.1
1982	617.4	764.4	147.0	4.8
1983 [a]	640.5	819.8	179.3	5.5

[a]Figures for 1983 are projected on the basis of data for the first three quarters.
SOURCE: U.S. Department of Commerce (1983).

CHANGING FEDERAL RESERVE GOALS

As the 1970s ended, the Federal Reserve (responding to the social consensus that the problem of inflation must be addressed) began to pay more attention to limiting the monetary growth rate and to restraining inflation. At the same time, major investments would be needed for the U.S. economy to adapt to the new distribution of world economic power and to take advantage of the technological revolution under way. To provide the investment funds, savings were to be encouraged by allowing savers to receive a market-determined rate on their funds, which Regulation Q had previously denied them. The market was also to become freer to allocate funds according to profitability rather than to politically determined priorities. The "reindustrialization" and computerization of America would reduce the emphasis on housing-related investments.[2]

LIABILITY MANAGEMENT
AND FINANCIAL INNOVATION

Monetary policy and financial reform are closely interwoven. Indeed, changes in the conduct of monetary policy constitute part of the financial reform process. Moreover, changes in the financial structure condition the ability of the central bank to implement its policies and to achieve its goals. The financial system evolves whenever the Federal Reserve changes its role, its goals, or the procedures it adopts to attain these goals. Such changes shift the set of constraints under which financial firms operate; when these constraints are binding, new positions of equilibrium are sought. Firms innovate either to take advantage of new opportunities or to avoid restrictions that curb their profitability. In turn, these innovations influence the ability of the Federal Reserve to achieve its goals and to readily implement its strategies. The Washington agencies may then "re-regulate."

This "regulatory dialectic" (Kane, 1981) is illustrated in the financial developments of the 1970s and 1980s. Several regulations, particularly Regulation Q, became increasingly burdensome as market interest rates rose with inflation. Rising market interest rates increased the extent and the frequency with which Regulation Q ceilings became binding (see Figure 6.2). This led to disintermediation, as discussed in the previous chapter. Institutions engaged in liability management, and they invented new financial instruments that allowed them to pay market rates and to combat disintermediation. Liability management also allowed institutions to better meet the economy's demands for credit, but, in doing so, they often reduced the Federal Reserve's direct constraints over the quantities of money and credit. Where reserve requirements are placed equally on all depository institution liabilities, reserve restraint will translate directly to control over the quantity of credit supplied by depository institutions. The constrained quantity of credit can be either allocated by price or rationed by quantity. Credit rationing can be used as a way to apply economic restraint to selected industries without raising interest rates substantially. That rationing will be the more severe if disintermediation occurs. However, the newly innovated assets typically carried low or no reserve requirements, so that a reserve squeeze and credit restraint arising from open market operations could be alleviated, if not entirely eliminated, by liability management and financial innovation. Where direct quantity constraints can be circumvented, restraint must be exercised through increases in interest rates, whose effect is to curtail the demand for loans more than they raise the supply.

Table 7.2 presents a summary of financial innovations initiated by the financial and retail sectors. It gives the date of each innovation's introduction and analyzes it by source and class of customer. Large certificates of deposit, repurchase agreements (RPs), NOW and ATS accounts, and Money Market Mutual Funds (MMMFs) were introduced by financial institutions to ease the pressure of the Federal Reserve's restrictions. These transactions media (or close substitutes) altered the relationship of traditional money to the final economy. Credit cards, which might be seen as principally a technological response to ease transactions and credit generation, also held the potential for similar effects (Garcia, 1980).

This situation presented two problems for the conduct of monetary policy. First, it was difficult for the Federal Reserve to judge the impact of any given money growth rate when newly innovated financial instruments allowed the public and financial institutions to accomplish their business, to an increasing extent, by bypassing measured money. The measured money stock underrepresented the stimulatory impact of monetary growth. The monetary aggregates would need to be revised to acknowledge the impact of RPs, NOW and ATS accounts, and MMMFs. Second, the impact of any reserve stringency was reduced by liability management's alleviation of generalized credit rationing on the supply side. Wojnilower (1980) stresses the important role of credit crunches in the execution of monetary stimuli. Increasingly, the burden of credit rationing would fall disproportionally on institutions not able to manage their liabilities: small banks and thrifts heavily reliant both on households for funds and on the industries that utilize these funds, such as housing, autos, and durable goods. These industries then lost some of the benefits or subsidies that they had received in the past. Further, the substantial removal of usury ceilings under the 1980 act eliminated a second restraint on the supply of funds that had earlier led to credit rationing in areas subject to the ceilings.

Technical advances in the collection, storage, and transmission of information facilitated the financial innovation process. Cash management became increasingly feasible. As interest rates rose, the economies from cash management increased, raising its benefits; as technology progressed, cash management's costs were reduced. These dual developments enabled the impact of cash management to spread from the largest corporations to the next largest, to businesses of all sizes, and finally by the 1980s, to households. Thus, these events hampered the Federal Reserve's ability to contain, via quantity constraints, money and credit growth and the stimulus they conveyed to the economy. In the future, central bank policy would rely more on the price mechanism to convey its policy to the financial system. Financial reforms would be needed to make this new *modus operandi* feasible.

MONETARY POLICY REFORMS

Congress and the financial regulators responded in several ways to the macroeconomic problems and the need for financial reform. Concurrent Resolution 133 required the Federal Reserve in 1975 to report quarterly its money and credit growth targets to Congress. This requirement did not serve to contain monetary growth, however, since the monetary authority each quarter systematically adjusted the base from which the reported growth was calculated each time that it missed its target. This "base-drift" led to the Humphrey-Hawkins Act of 1978, which mandated the Federal Reserve to publish and report semiannually to Congress its annual money and credit growth targets, calculated from the fourth quarter in one year to the fourth quarter next year. A serious step toward the deregulation of interest rates was taken with the authorization of six-month money market certificate accounts in June 1978. In October 1979, the Federal Reserve changed its operating procedures to controlling M1 growth through the management of nonborrowed reserves. The monetary aggregates were substantially redefined in February 1980 and were periodically readjusted thereafter.

The 1980 act significantly extended Federal Reserve quantity controls from member banks to all depository institutions by making all subject to reserve requirements. This ended the declining membership problem, which had been widely acknowledged as reducing the precision of Federal Reserve monetary control. Restrictions were relaxed on both the asset and liability sides of thrift balance sheets. Further steps were taken toward the deregulation of interest rates. State usury ceilings on mortgage securities were removed, and those on other loans were raised. In January 1981, as authorized in DIDMCA, NOW accounts were offered nationwide. The DIDC was mandated to remove Regulation Q ceilings on time and savings deposits by 1986.

TABLE 7.2
PRIVATE FINANCIAL MARKET INNOVATIONS

Issuer	Instrument	Year Originated	Holder
State-chartered banks	Demand deposits	Late 1800s	Households, businesses, and governments
Hotels	Credit cards	early 1900s	Households and businesses
Oil industry	Credit cards	1914	
Railroads, airlines	Credit cards	1947	
Diners Club	Travel and entertainment credit card	1949	Households and businesses
Banks:			
Franklin National Bank of Long Island, N.Y.	Bank credit card	1951	Households and businesses
Bank of America, Chase Manhattan Bank, and Marine Midland Bank	Bank credit card	1958	Households and businesses
Commercial banks in New York City	Federal funds	1921[a]	Other commercial banks
Federal Reserve	FR Open Market Operation Repurchase Agreement (RP)	c. 1924	Discount and acceptance houses
Securities dealers	Dealer RP	1948[b]	Banks and non-financial corporations

Commercial banks	Bank RP	1963[a,c]	Large corporations; state and local governments
First National City Bank of New York	Large negotiable CD[d]	1960	Foreign customers
	Large negotiable CD[d]	1961	Large corporations
Securities dealers	Secondary market in large negotiable CDs	1961	Foreign and domestic customers
Banks and thrifts in Massachusetts and New Hampshire	Negotiable Order of Withdrawal (NOW) Account	1972	Households
Securities industry	Money Market Mutual Funds	1972	Households, bank trust departments, corporations
Commercial banks	Automatic Transfer Account	1978	Households
Banks, thrifts	Household RP	late 1970s	Households

[a]The Boston Clearing House anticipated federal funds–type trading (sometimes subject to a repurchase agreement) between 1880 and 1910 (see Parker B. Willis, 1970, p. 2).

[b]Antecedents to dealer RPs go back to the national banking era (see Willis, 1972, p. 24).

[c]The Comptroller of the Currency gave impetus to the market when it freed RPs from the National Bank Act's lending and borrowing limits.

[d]Large regional commercial banks had issued large negotiable CDs to foreign customers and large domestic corporations for many years, but their origin is usually attributed to Citibank because its entrance into the market sparked the catalyst—the secondary market.

The Garn–St Germain Act of 1982, although having less obvious intended relevance to monetary policy, authorized the Money Market Deposit Account (MMDA) to compete with MMMFs. Because MMDAs have proved so popular, they rose with unprecedented speed, reaching $360 billion within six months. Questions were then raised concerning the sources of these funds and their implications for the growth rates of the monetary aggregates. MMDAs have limited transactions features; nevertheless, they enter the aggregates only at the M2 level.

In January 1983, SNOW accounts became available. These accounts pay market-determined rates on transaction accounts of $2,500 or more. The DIDC's authorization of the accounts took a step toward the removal of the zero-rate restriction on demand deposits. Together these new accounts made it difficult to choose appropriate growth rates for the M1 and M2 aggregates in particular (see Garcia and McMahon, 1984). The deregulation of interest rates progressed. The implications for monetary policy of each of these reforms will be discussed in the remainder of this chapter.

STRATEGY: WHICH INTERMEDIATE TARGET?

It is not clear when the intermediate targeting process became formalized, although the development of the Board's quarterly econometric model in the late 1960s and early 1970s contributed to the process. That model emphasized the role interest rates played in the transmission of central bank stimuli to the final economy. For much of this period, a nominal short-term interest rate held center stage as the intermediate target. However, during the period, emphasis shifted continuallly to emphasizing money (and credit to a lesser extent), a natural outcome from the increasing attention to controlling inflation as a principal central bank goal.

Several economists (Benjamin Friedman, 1977; and Robert J. Gordon, 1982) have questioned whether any two-stage process is an efficient way to conduct policy. Gordon, in particular, argues strongly that the Federal Reserve could better achieve its objectives by aiming its instruments directly at the final targets, as represented by the nominal value of GNP. Nevertheless, within the Federal Reserve System it seems to be largely taken for granted that the policy will continue to be conducted in this way. Officers concerned with policy implementation typically argue as follows: the Humphrey-Hawkins Act, by mandating that the Federal Reserve report targets for money and credit semiannually to Congress, ensures that the Federal Reserve will continue to operate in the two-stage way, at least until other legislation is passed to revise the process. In short, direct targeting on nominal GNP, for example, is regarded as of mainly academic (and disputable) appeal.

Within the Federal Reserve System, more interest is shown in the practical question of determining which intermediate target to adopt. In the years immediately before October 1979, the central bank used the federal funds rate as its instrument, and both the level of interest rates and the rate of money growth as its intermediate targets. But the rates used were nominal rates, whereas a real rate (making allowance for inflation) is the variable relevant to influencing spending decisions and GNP. Furthermore, the two targets set were frequently inconsistent, in which case the money growth objective was sacrificed. By fall 1979, a consensus was being reached that U.S. monetary policy procedures were contributing to world inflation. By attempting to stabilize the federal funds rate between upper and lower bounds chosen by the Federal Open Market Committee (FOMC) at rates set too low, the central bank was supplying reserves and stimulating money growth at an inflationary pace. It was felt that the FOMC would not in the future, as it had not in the past, raise the federal funds rate high enough to contain money growth. A more direct approach to monetary restraint would be needed.

At this time, the Federal Reserve, recognizing the changing national priorities, reflected that change in its own behavior. In order to better control inflation, it changed its intermediate target and its operating procedures. Using interest rates as an intermediate target had been appropriate in an era of Keynesian-type aggregate-demand management. For example, in the Board's large econometric model, interest rates provided the channels through which Federal Reserve policy stimuli were transmitted to the final economy. By the close of the 1970s received economic theory held that the long-run Phillips curve is vertical, but acknowledged a short-run trade-off between inflation and unemployment. Consequently, in October 1979 in the context of an international crisis caused by a continued inflationary depreciation of the dollar's value, the central bank switched to making money growth its overriding intermediate target in order to give greater emphasis to fighting inflation. In this way it would be less likely to be deflected from its anti-inflationary emphasis by the recession that would accompany the dampening of inflation. In turn, to better control the money growth rate, the monetary authority would also change its operating procedures from stabilizing the federal funds rate to monitoring the supply of member bank (and, after the passage of DIDMCA, also depository institution) reserves.

Much of the reform initiated and effected in the monetary area has been concerned with facilitating the two-stage, M1-intermediate-target-control process. In particular, most of the changes that have been made appear intended to improve the operation of a reserves-to-money control procedure. In the event, at the time of this writing in early 1984, these reforms fall short of their logical conclusion, and so they do not permit full control to be attained.

In the context of the two-stage process, we will discuss reforms intended to strengthen the ties of the intermediate target to the final economy before dealing with those that pertain to the instrument to achieve the intermediate-target relationship. In our terminology, we call the former the relevance issue and the latter the control question.

RELEVANCE

Many analysts within the Federal Reserve System concentrate attention on the control issues. It is logically clear that if the Federal Reserve decides that it seriously wishes to control some intermediate target, it can do so. What the central bank cannot determine, however, are the implications that the controlled variable has for the economy.[3]

Recent history provides a good example of this dilemma. If the Federal Reserve decides to control the quantity of traditional money (currency and demand deposits) through the limitation of depository institution reserves and through a system of legally enforced reserve requirements, it can hone the system to provide any degree of control it wants. But reserve requirements act like a tax on depository institutions, and the prohibition of the payment of interest on demand deposits (and, *de facto*, on currency) limits money-users' earnings. Consequently, both deposit-holders and deposit-suppliers have incentives to avoid the restrictions placed upon them. To circumvent these restrictions they will innovate and have, in fact, done so increasingly over the past quarter of a century.

Fama (1980) makes this point dramatically. He argues that the central bank in the United States controls the price level in two stages. First, it imposes bank reserve regulations that create an artificial demand for reserves. Second, it controls and limits the supply of reserves. Its success in achieving its price control goal depends on the efficiency of the demand creation and its supply restraint, which financial institutions and the public have incentives to bypass. This cautionary observation remains true whether the market operated on is that for depository institution reserves or any alternative "numeraire" market such as the licensing of spaceship trips to the planets—a twenty-first century control alternative mentioned by Fama (1980).

MONEY STOCK REDEFINITIONS

To maintain its influence over the economy in the face of extensive financial innovations, the Federal Reserve made successive redefinitions of the money aggregates to encompass the new financial assets. The principal redefinition occurred in February 1980, but since then definitional readjustments have been made from time to time. The principle on which the redefinitions have been conducted is that M1 should encompass the major media of exchange. Consequently, M1 currently includes currency in circulation, demand deposits, other checkable deposits, and traveler's checks, all of which are assets held by the public or by state and local governments. The principle underlying the broader money aggregates—M2, M3, and L—is that a financial asset should enter the hierarchy in a position reflecting its relative liquidity.[4]

However, in the execution, these principles are not carried to their logical conclusion. For example, MMMFs and MMDAs can be used for transacting, but they enter the aggregates at the M2 level; they are not included in M1. Credit cards and trade credit can be utilized to make purchases, and so may influence spending patterns: however, they are not included in any of the monetary aggregates.[5] Their omission can be justified, however, because their use incurs a debt by the public that will later be settled by the transfer of the appropriate amount of a medium of exchange. Hence credit card and trade credit data are excluded from all of the monetary aggregates (which represent assets in the public's balance sheets). However, trade credit and credit card data, as a matter of fact, are relevant to any appropriately defined credit aggregate. And they are both included in the credit data (total domestic nonfinancial debt) that the Federal Reserve has recently chosen to report to Congress and monitor in addition to the monetary data.

A second illogicality in the money aggregate definitions concerns the inclusion in M2 of small time deposits, whatever their maturity (from 7 days to eight years), whereas large CDs (whose maturity is typically 90 days) enter the aggregates at the M3 level. Yet large CDs are more liquid than long-term personal time deposits. Such illogicalities seem doomed to reduce the precision of Federal Reserve influence via the monetary aggregates to the final economy.

The recent process of innovation, begun with Citibank's adoption of the large CD at the beginning of the 1960s, accelerated during the 1970s as rising interest rates made interest rate ceilings increasingly burdensome. The monetary authorities began to feel that they were losing their regulatory hold over the financial system. As a result, the regulators (FHLBB, FDIC, Comptroller of the Currency, Federal Reserve, National Credit Union Administration, and the Treasury), first in the guise of the Inter-Agency Co-ordinating Committee (ICC) and later as the DIDC, began to create specific accounts which permitted a limited (if not very logical) deregulation of interest rate ceilings. From 1973 to 1983, there resulted, in succession, the wild card experiment, money market certificate, small saver's certificate, 7–31-day and 91-day accounts, MMDAs, and SNOW accounts. Table 7.3 reports regulatory innovations by sector and date.

TABLE 7.3
REGULATORY INNOVATIONS

Source	Instrument	Date	Ceiling Rate	Holder	Minimum Maturity
Congress	Keogh accounts	1962	Depending on maturity[a]	Self-employed individuals	Various[b]
Congress	IRA	January 1975	Depending on maturity[a]	Individual employees	Various[b]
Regulatory authorities	Large CD "Wild Card" Certificate	1973 July–November 1973	Removed None	Large corporations Households	7 days 4 years
ICC	Money Market Certificate	June 1978	Tied to 6-month T Bill rate[a]	Households	6 months
FRB	ATS accounts recognized	November 1978	Passbook rate	Households, businesses	None
ICC	Small Saver Certificate	1979	Tied to T Bill rate[a]	Households	30 months

Authority	Account	Date	Interest rate	Eligible holders	Minimum maturity
Congress (DIDMCA)	NOW accounts permitted nationwide	January 1981	5.25 (passbook savings rate)	Households[c]	None
Congress	All Savers Certificate	October 1981	70 percent of 52-week T Bill rate (tax free)	Households	1 year
DIDC	91-day Certificate	May 1982	Tied to 91-day T bill rate[a]		91 days
DIDC	7–31-day account	September 1982	Tied to 91-day T bill rate[a]		7 days
DIDC	Money Market Deposit Account	December 1982	None	Households, businesses	None
DIDC	Super NOW Account	January 1983	None	Households[c]	None

[a]Ceilings on MMCs, SSCs, IRAs, 7–31- and 91-day certificates and Keogh accounts were removed on October 1, 1983.

[b]Minimum maturities on IRA and Keogh accounts were removed on October 1, 1983.

[c]Governments are permitted to hold NOW and SNOW accounts as a result of the 1982 act.

INTEREST RATE DEREGULATION

On October 1, 1983, the system of interest rate restrictions had a more logical basis restored to it with the removal of ceilings on longer-term accounts. After this date, institutions became substantially free to set rates in order to attract the maturity mix of deposits appropriate to their lending practices. At the outset of 1984, only passbook savings, demand deposits, ATS, and NOW accounts retain ceilings, although there are still minimum balance requirements on MMDAs and Super-NOWs. Under the 1980 act ceilings on savings deposits are scheduled to be removed on or before March 31, 1986. Further legislation will be required, however, before the zero ceiling on demand deposits can be removed.[6]

The question that arises is: How will the deregulation of interest rates affect the conduct of monetary policy? Two subquestions are relevant here: How will deregulation affect stage-one monetary control, and How will it alter the relationship of the intermediate target to the final economy? The second issue will be addressed here; the first will be discussed in the later section devoted to the control question.

The profession's consensus view is that permission to pay market-determined rates on transaction accounts will reduce the opportunity cost of holding money. If money demand retains the same interest elasticity with respect to this opportunity cost, it will be less elastic with respect to changes in the level of interest rates paid on money substitutes. The traditional LM function will become less interest-elastic, and the economy will more closely approximate a monetarist world. In which case, M1 should become a more viable target.

However, this simple analysis addresses only the question of the expected value of the economy's response to a monetary stimulus, which is predicted to be stronger in a deregulated world. It does not consider the question of the variance of the economy's response to a monetary stimulus. This variance can be captured graphically by shifting the LM function. As Figure 7.2 shows, for an equal lateral shift in the LM function, the variability of GNP and the interest rate are greater, the lesser is the interest elasticity of the LM function (that is, the steeper is the LM function). Thus, where shocks to the system originate from shifts in the money demand function, monetary policy's effects on the final economy may become more difficult to predict as a result of interest rate deregulation.

However, if the shock originates in the real sector of the economy, from unexpected changes in either aggregate demand or supply (so that the IS function shifts), the variability of nominal GNP is reduced by interest deregulation's steepening of the LM function. The variability of the interest rate remains greater for the steeper LM function, concomitant with the smaller variability in GNP. These responses are illustrated in Figure 7.3

In another respect the deregulation of interest rates should unambiguously improve the Federal Reserve's influence over the final economy. The innovation of financial instruments has derived its strength from two sources. On the one hand, depository institutions and other financial sector participants have had incentives to avoid reserve requirements in order to increase their ability to hold profitable assets. On the other hand, the public has been induced to accept the new bank liabilities because they have been offered a chance to obtain higher interest earnings. As interest rates are deregulated, more and more regular deposit instruments can carry market rates. When the process is complete, the only way for the public to increase interest earnings may be to decrease liquidity or to increase risk. Then, one of the incentives to innovate will have been removed. Then, also, the Federal Reserve should have

FIGURE 7.2
INTEREST RATE DEREGULATION SHOCK TO
THE MONETARY SECTOR

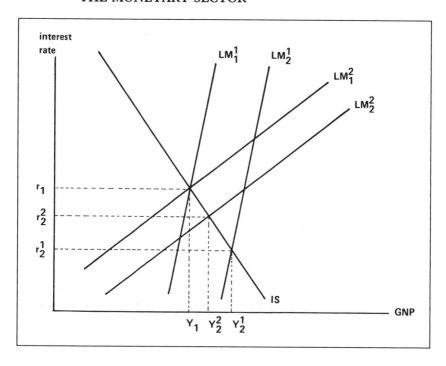

less need to periodically redefine the monetary aggregates and to concern itself with shifts in the relation between the measured aggregate and the ultimate economic goals.[7]

THE 1982–1983 VELOCITY SHIFT

The transmission of Federal Reserve policy stimuli to the final economy is made easier if the velocity of circulation (the ratio of the annual flow of GNP to the stock of money) is constant or accurately predictable. Then it is easier for the Federal Reserve to predict the outcome of any monetary growth rate that it chooses. Since the Second World War, the velocity of M1 has grown fairly regularly at approximately a 3 percent annual rate. As Figure 7.4 demon-

FIGURE 7.3
INTEREST RATE DEREGULATION SHOCK TO THE REAL SECTOR

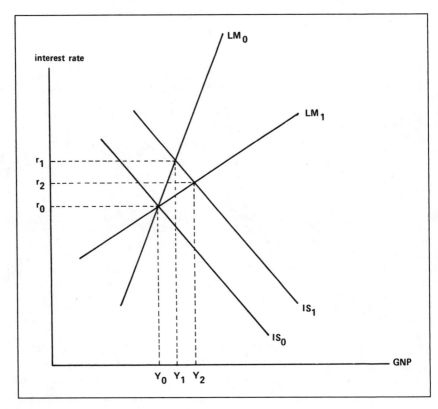

FIGURE 7.4
M1 VELOCITY VS. TREND

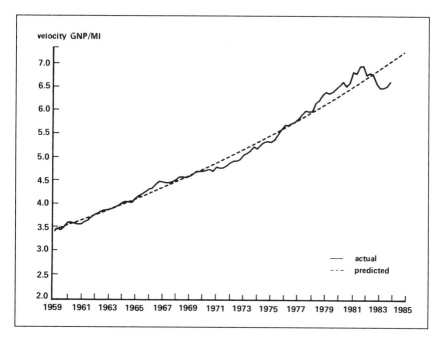

strates, this regularity ceased in 1982. Moreover, it is interesting to note that the relationships of GNP to M2, M3, and the central bank's credit measure (total domestic nonfinancial credit) were all substantially below trend during this period. Further, it was not restored during 1983, although the chart shows evidence of some return to normality.

At the time of writing in early 1984, an active debate has developed over the causes of the velocity shift. This issue is important because, if monetary and financial reform has altered the behavior of velocity in ways unknown and poorly understood, the attempts to control the final economy through a money stock target will fail. Some (Hamburger, 1983; Judd, 1983; Tatom, 1983) argue that the recent experience does not represent an end to the old relationship. They contend that the usual velocity increase has been delayed by the 1981–1982 recession and the volatility in money growth, but that it will ultimately recover its lost ground. Others (Gordon, 1983) argue that the change may be more permanent and therefore a more important consideration for policymakers.

Thus, Congress and the financial regulators instituted several financial reforms that were intended to facilitate the conduct of an anti-inflationary, money-growth-containing monetary policy. Nevertheless, the responsibility ultimately lies with the central bank itself to utilize these reforms to achieve its objectives. It was clear, for example, that Federal Reserve operating procedures would need to adapt in order to effect the new anti-inflationary goal and the new emphasis on the money stock as the principal intermediate target.

MONETARY CONTROL

At the outset of the 1950s the Federal Open Market Committee (FOMC) expressed its policy instructions to the open market desk in New York in general terms of ease, restraint, or neutrality (Wallich and Keir, 1979). With the renaissance of monetary policy, the FOMC felt the need to analyze the effects of its decisions and to more clearly guide its policy executors. During the 1950s and 1960s, it experimented with several key instrument variables and used short-term interest rates, the amount of member-bank borrowing, the value of excess reserves, and the difference between the latter, that is, net free reserves.

In time, as the Federal Reserve gave increasing attention to controlling the supplies of money and credit, the FOMC from 1966 to 1970 expressed policy in terms of two sets of variables, one conditional on the achievement of the other. For example, the manager of the system account might be told to maintain prevailing money market conditions until the next meeting of the FOMC, unless bank credit (or some other intermediate target) deviated from some specified behavior (Maisel, 1973).

Later, at the beginning of 1970, the emphasis on the use of proviso clauses changed. The principal instruction to the desk was issued in terms of one or more intermediate-target variables, which were to be pursued subject to the state of the money market. To achieve these intermediate target values, the manager of the system account was to conduct open market operations in order to maintain the federal funds rate within a narrow band, which was calculated to be consistent with the intermediate targets.

To better judge the chain of relationships from open market operations to the federal funds rate, to money growth, the Federal Reserve developed an elaborate econometric model during the early 1970s. This model, modified by subjective evaluation, provided the basis for the instructions given to the money market desk in New York. Nevertheless, despite the modeling and forecasting, the outcomes achieved for the money and credit aggregates often deviated significantly from the targeted values (Poole, 1982).

In response to its inability to hit the targets, in 1972 the FOMC shifted to using a bank reserve measure instead of the federal funds rate. In turn, the committee experimented with total reserves and reserves against private deposits before it reverted to using money market conditions, because of variability in the reserves-to-money (multiplier) relationship and the difficulty of using a reserve instrument under lagged reserve accounting.

By the late 1970s, the Federal Reserve had re-established its intermediate-growth target for money. However, it was frequently prevented from achieving these objectives by a strong proviso clause, which constrained the federal funds rate within a narrow (50 to 100 basis point) range. In an attempt to achieve better monetary control, operating procedures were changed in October 1979. In fact, the Federal Reserve (Board of Governors, 1981, p. 1) itself characterized its October 1979 action as a change in "open market operating procedures to place more emphasis on controlling reserves directly so as to provide more assurance of attaining basic money supply objectives."

The interaction between the policymaking arm of the Federal Reserve (the Federal Open Market Committee) and the day-to-day policy execution of open market operations by the system account manager at the Federal Reserve Bank of New York has always been arcane (Maisel, 1973). But it has become more complex and obscure since October 1979. Prior to that date, outsiders could infer that the FOMC set bounds for the federal funds rates and that the desk in New York bought or sold Treasury securities to keep the actual rate within these bounds.

As mentiond, since October 1979 the process has been more difficult to divine. Outsiders rely principally on the articles by Robert L. Hetzel (1982), George Kaufman (1982), Peter Keir (1981), Fred J. Levin and Paul Meek (1981), William Poole (1982), and David E. Lindsey (1983), which describe the procedures adopted in 1979. It is perhaps less widely known, however, that these procedures were again changed in late 1982.

OCTOBER 1979–LATE 1982

The central bank bases its money control operations on the money multiplier relationship (m) between the money stock (M) and the supply of total reserve (TR), as formulated in equation 7.1:

$$M = mTR \tag{7.1}$$

If m remains relatively constant over time, or if it is accurately predictable, this equation can be used to control the money stock. Then, the Federal Reserve would implement its policy by supplying the level of total reserves (TR_{obj}) likely to produce the desired money stock (M_{obj}). Unfortunately m is not stable, and it is not clear that it is precisely predictable. Moreover, under a system of lagged reserve accounting (LRA), the Federal Reserve is unable to control the level of total reserves. Under lagged reserve accounting (the system in operation from September 1968 through January 1984), reserve obligations today are related to deposit levels held two weeks earlier. If institutions are to be allowed to meet their legal obligations, the Federal Reserve must supply the necessary level of reserves, either in borrowed (BR) or non borrowed (NBR) reserves for:

$$TR = BR + NBR \qquad (7.2)$$

Consequently, under LRA, the central bank's attempts to influence the financial system's behavior are complex. For example, for three years, the Federal Reserve described itself as setting a nonborrowed reserve operating target (NBR_{obj}). It initiated this tactical stage of policy by estimating the level of borrowed reserves that would be issued to depository institutions each week in the period between FOMC meetings.

Immediately after October 6, 1979, the Federal Reserve staff estimated the level of borrowed reserves by extrapolating recent experience at the borrowing window. Later, when this estimation procedure was found wanting, the staff turned to econometric estimates of borrowings, which were derived from a structural equation relating borrowings to the spread between the discount rate and the federal funds rate (Kaufman, 1982).

The staff then subtracted the estimate of BR (called the borrowing assumption) from the desired level of TR in the initial week of the intermeeting period. This produced an estimate of NBR in the initial week that was projected to provide the desired money stock. That is,

$$NBR_{obj} = TR_{obj} - BR_{est} \qquad (7.2')$$

Instructions were then transmitted to the open market desk in New York to provide this level of NBR_{obj} in the first week of the new intermeeting period. In later weeks NBR was to grow (after seasonal adjustment) at the rate calculated to produce the desired rate of money growth.

The question then arises whether NBR_{obj} is consistent with another, definitional relationship which divides total reserves into required reserve (RR) and excess reserve (ER) components. Thus, as stated in equation 7.3

$$BR = RR + ER - NBR \qquad (7.3)$$

Banks, typically under LRA, keep ER as near zero as possible. Moreover, under LRA, in any week, RR is already determined. In these circumstances, the borrowing assumption may not be met, for NBR has been set by policy.

As the intermeeting period progressed and more information became available, the FOMC could possibly revise its borrowing assumption. But would this lead the committee to revise its NBR_{obj} to compensate in order to obtain the desired money stock? The variability in money growth rates during this period suggests that it did not, or did not quickly, respond. Beyond adjusting the provision of reserves during any week to obtain the money growth planned for that week, the desk could compensate in any one week for deviations from target that occurred in earlier weeks. And likewise the FOMC would compensate for the errors made in earlier intermeeting periods of the FOMC. The speed with which the Federal Reserve should react to indications that its original longer-term plans were not being met is a subject of continuing debate. Ann-Marie Meulendyke (1983) suggests that, prior to 1983, a partial adjustment was made, but that during 1983 past misses were forgiven and reserves were targeted week by week. It is expected that these procedures are again being revised following the February 2, 1984, introduction of two-day lag accounting (semi-contemporaneous accounting).

Even after the 1979 change, however, for the next two years inflation continued at a historically high rate. Interest rates rose and became more volatile. At the same time, the variance of the money growth rate also increased, an event that the majority of economists had not expected. This significant increase in monetary volatility is shown in Figure 7.5, which reveals, month by month, the growth occurring over the previous twelve months. And the economy experienced two recessions within a short interval (January 1980–July 1980 and July 1981–November 1982). Many observers argue that the change in goals, as well as in intermediate target and in operating procedures, exacerbated the economy's ills.[8] Accordingly, a lively debate has developed both within and outside the Federal Reserve on the relative merits of several potential intermediate targets (Garcia, 1984) and on appropriate operating procedures (Board of Governors of the Federal Reserve, 1981).

By fall 1982, at the nadir of the worst recession since the Great Depression, the experience with money stock targeting was generally held to have been unsuccessful. These sentiments were shared by both monetarists and non-monetarists alike. Monetarists (Milton Friedman, 1982) argued that monetarism had not, in fact, been tried, because money growth was volatile; non-monetarists contended that it had failed (Gordon, 1982, 1983; Kaldor, 1982) and had exacerbated the recession caused by the second oil price shock. Several bills were being considered by Congress to compel the Federal Reserve to switch to targeting some other variable, such as credit or real or nominal interest rates. At this time, the Federal Reserve was increasingly concerned about the severity of the recession, the potential for crisis in the S&L industry, and the international economy, where substantial foreign debt problems threatened defaults by several developing countries, defaults that could lead to the failure of several of the world's largest banks. As a result, it announced another change in intermediate target and in operating procedures.

FIGURE 7.5
ANNUALIZED GROWTH RATE OF M1

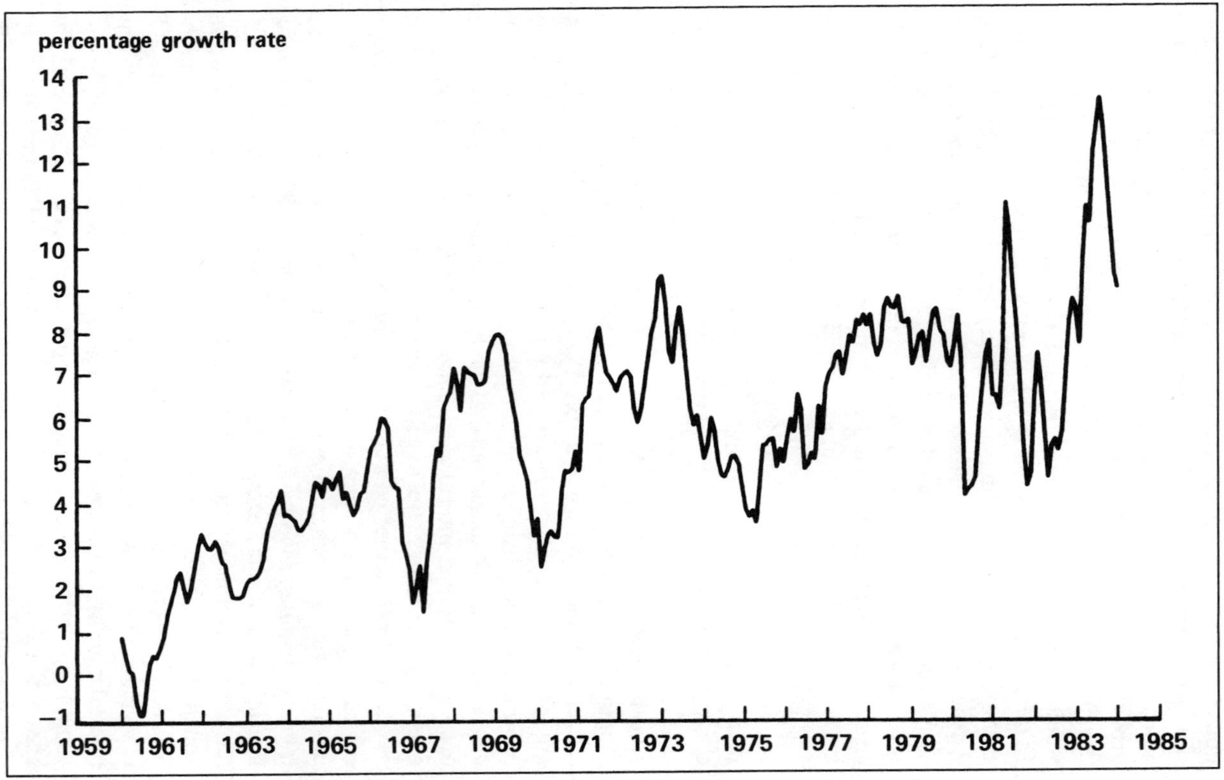

The Federal Reserve pointed out that movements in M1 were likely to be obscured by the phase-out of the All-Savers Certificate and the introduction of the MMDAs and SNOW accounts.[9] Portfolio shifts resulting from these instrument changes would most likely be effected by M1, the medium of exchange. Consequently, observed changes in M1 growth might reflect temporary (or even permanent) portfolio shifts rather than foretell future movements in nominal GNP. This possibility was regarded as the more likely since velocity was decreasing more strongly than usual during the 1981–1982 recession.

THE FALL 1982 CHANGE

Consequently, the Federal Reserve changed its intermediate target in fall 1982 to give major emphasis to M2 and M3 instead of M1, and it also changed operating procedures again to coincide with the introduction of the MMDAs and SNOW accounts in December 1982 and January 1983.

The success of the nonborrowed reserve objective, as adopted in 1979, depended on the accuracy of the forecasts of borrowed reserves and on the Federal Reserve's willingness to adjust its nonborrowed reserve objective in light of new information. The staff had previously had difficulty in forecasting the borrowing variable, and these difficulties did not decrease as borrowing became a more important reserve management tool for banks and grew under the post-1979 procedures.

In any week, RR has been predetermined under LRA, NBR has been set by policy, and ER is likely to be negligible. Consequently, BR falls out from equation 7.3. At this point in time, it should be readily estimable by Federal Reserve staff. But BR, at this stage, may be very different from the forecasts made earlier at the time when the FOMC set NBR_{obj}. In fact, neither the extrapolative nor the econometric forecasts of borrowing proved accurate (Kaufman, 1982). Indeed, John Judd and Adrian Throop (1981) show that errors in the borrowing assumption proved to be the major factor contributing to money target misses in the period immediately following October 1979.

Misforecasting BR had consequences for the behavior of the federal funds rate. Under concurrent reserve accounting, a shortage of reserves would drive up the federal funds rate and induce banks to reduce assets, deposits, and required reserves. But under LRA, depository institutions cannot ease the shortage by reducing their current need for reserves. That need must be met, first, in the federal funds market and, next, as the federal funds rate rises above the discount rate, at the borrowing window. Thus, under LRA, the demand for reserves is interest-inelastic in the short run. Yet, it is the rise in the federal funds rate and the anticipation of future increases that must curb assets and deposits. The increase is likely to be substantial. Conversely, under LRA when reserves are plentiful, the federal funds rate may have to fall precipitously to induce banks to hold excess reserves. Consequently, under the October 1979–fall 1982 procedures, the federal funds rate was highly volatile—unacceptably so.

As a result, as Meulendyke (1983) reveals, the Federal Reserve again changed its procedures—this time to a borrowed reserve objective. That is, the FOMC in its deliberations establishes a targeted level for borrowed reserves.[10] Indeed, the intention was to keep the level of borrowed reserves stable during FOMC intervals and to revise it between periods only on rare occasions when changes in market conditions were clearly evident.[11] Stability in borrowing levels was intended to reduce unnecessary variability in the federal funds rate. In the event, both the level of borrowed reserves and the federal funds rate became less volatile during the period between fall 1982 and February 1984.

Thus, the NBR objective for any reserve maintenance period is derived from the staff's best estimates of required and excess reserves. That is, the new procedures result in a relationship in which a level of NBR is set to keep borrowed reserves close to a fixed level $\overline{BR}_{obj}$:

$$NBR = RR + ER_{est} - \overline{BR}_{obj} \tag{7.4}$$

The level of NBR is revised during the reserve maintenance period when RR or ER estimates are updated. Meulendyke observes that these revisions occurred most often on Tuesdays and Wednesdays as the LRA reserve maintenance period neared completion.

Some economists (Kaufman, 1982; Laurent, 1982) doubt that the monetary authority can conduct a reserve targeting procedure under lagged reserves. Laurent argues that the Federal Reserve continued to directly determine the federal funds rate, although it did not peg it even after the 1979 change. Certainly by 1983 many market analysts had reverted to using the funds rate to judge the tenor of policy. Further, the Federal Reserve Bank of San Francisco's money market model (Judd and Scadding, 1982b) draws inferences from the federal funds rate to the level of borrowed reserves to money stock growth, rather than directly from reserves to money.

Poole (1982) also dissents from the Federal Reserve's view of its operating procedures. He argues that the Federal Reserve in fact used a borrowed reserve instrument during the immediate post–October 1979 period. In its derivation of the appropriate nonborrowed reserve supply from equation 7.2, the FOMC estimated the average level of borrowing for each week of the intermeeting period. It then set the nonborrowed reserve supply to effect this average borrowed reserve level during the period. That is, Poole claims, the

Federal Reserve was, in effect, targeting borrowed reserves, not nonborrowed reserves.

These different interpretations of the Federal Reserve's operating procedures can be synthesized in Figure 7.6 (which is an adaptation of a diagram from Avery and Kwast, 1983), which shows the transmission of open market operations on the reserve supply, interacting with reserve demand to determine the federal funds rate.

In the diagram, the federal funds rate (r_f) and the discount rate (r_d) are measured on the vertical axis, and reserves and money on the horizontal axes. Initially, in the left-hand half of the diagram, the Federal Reserve supplies the level of nonborrowed reserves NBR_1 and sets the discount rate at r_d. The supply of total reserves is then given by the upward-sloping line TR_1^s. That supply equals NBR_1 for federal funds rates equal to or below r_d. But at federal funds rate levels above r_d, banks find it profitable to borrow reserves from the Federal Reserve. So the level of borrowed reserves $(TR_1^s - NBR_1)$ rises with the level of market interest rates. Administrative restrictions and institutional reluctance restrain the elasticity of the borrowing function. The demand for total reserves is given by the function TR^d. Under lagged reserve accounting, RR is predetermined and insensitive to current interest rates. Total demand for reserves is shown having some (likely very small) interest sensitivity on the part of excess reserves. The intersection of TR^d and TR^s determines the equilibrium federal funds rate, which, in turn, determines the money stock from the money demand function in the right-hand half of the diagram.

Figure 7.6 illustrates the interrelationships among the Laurent, Meulendyke, and Poole interpretations of Federal Reserve operating procedures. Given these relationships, under the Laurent interpretation the federal funds rate cannot be influenced by changes in the demand for reserves arising from changes in deposit levels, so that as a result the monetary authority determines (by the level of nonborrowed reserves it supplies) the federal funds rate, and thereby the money stock. Under Meulendyke's view of the first post–October 1979 episode, the Federal Reserve first sets NBR, and then the federal funds rate and the level of BR follow from market behavior. Poole, on the other hand, sees the central bank as setting BR, which implies a level of NBR or an equilibrium federal funds rate, given the predetermined level of required reserves.

REFORMS TO IMPROVE MONETARY CONTROL

The Federal Reserve has several options available to it in setting its operating procedures to control money. The primary distinction is between control via a price (the federal funds rate) or via a quantity. The choices among

FIGURE 7.6
MONETARY CONTROL

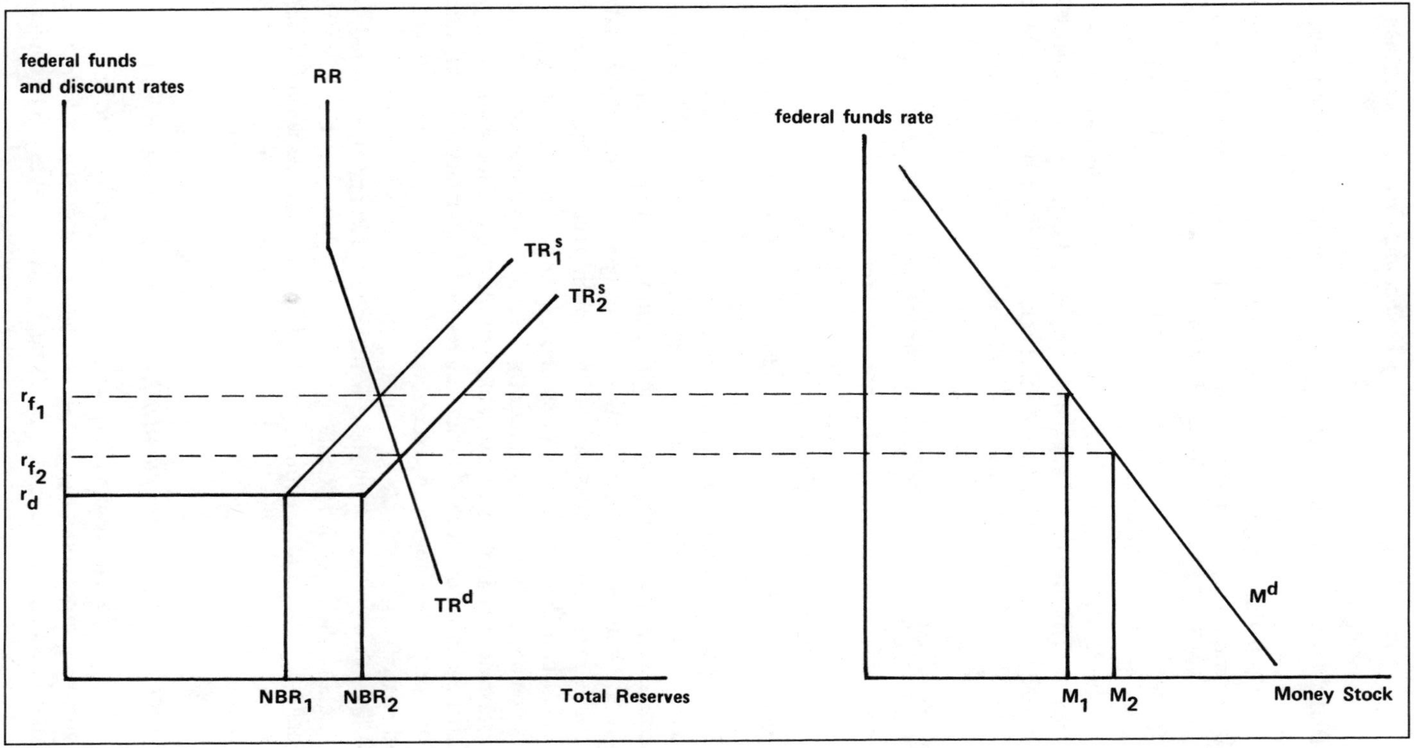

quantities are illustrated in the Federal Reserve balance sheet, presented in simplified form in Table 7.4, which shows the sources and uses of reserves, regulated by one of the Federal Reserve's principal operational activities — open market operations.

Ralph C. Bryant (1983) discusses the advantages and disadvantages of five instrument possibilities for the Federal Reserve: (1) the federal funds rate, (2) the Federal Reserve's security portfolio, (3) the monetary base, (4) the supply of reserves in total, or (5) nonborrowed reserves. Bryant concludes that no instrument unambiguously dominates all others. The strengths and weaknesses of the alternatives derive from the different sources of uncertainty and shocks to the financial system.

The 1979 change in the Federal Reserve's operating procedures involved the adoption of a reserve-aggregate instrument. The system of lagged reserve accounting prevented the use of a total reserve instrument because the level of required reserves had been predetermined. In recognition of this problem, as described above, a nonborrowed reserve procedure was initially implemented. Although the use of *NBR* recognized the problem, also, as described above, it did not solve it. Many other changes were needed.

Many of the revisions in laws and regulations accomplished by the Federal Reserve in recent years were undertaken to improve its control over the money stock when it is using a reserve-aggregate instrument. In this context, an article by William Poole and Charles Lieberman (1972) appears to have had an important bearing on monetary reform. That paper established a laundry list of necessary revisions needed to improve central bank control.

The argument in the previous section showed that it is unlikely under LRA that depository institutions will alter their demand for reserves quickly in response to Federal Reserve policy stimuli. Nevertheless, the demand for reserves does vary, sometimes unpredictably. Moreover, the supply of reserves may vary unintentionally. Such variability makes the conduct of policy more difficult.

With respect to the side of the Federal Reserve's balance sheet showing the uses of reserves, Poole and Lieberman recommend stabilizing reserve demand and making it more predictable by: (1) limiting the effects on reserves of fluctuations in the level of Treasury deposits; (2) bypassing the membership problem by extending the Federal Reserve's reserve requirements to nonmember banks; (3) eliminating reserve requirements on non-M1 components of the aggregates; and (4) ending the system of lagged reserve accounting.

On the supply-of-reserves side of the balance sheet, Poole and Lieberman recommend: (5) reducing the level of Federal Reserve float, (6) controlling bank borrowing of reserves through the adoption of a penalty discount rate, and (7) improving the seasonal adjustment factors (whose inadequacies often cause substantial later revision of the monetary data). Implementing items

TABLE 7.4
FEDERAL RESERVE SIMPLIFIED BALANCE SHEET

Assets	Liabilities
Security portfolios of the monetary authorities	Currency in circulation
Federal reserve float	Total reserves Required reserves Excess reserves
Borrowed reserves	Government deposits at Federal Reserve
Other assets (including tangible assets)	Surplus and capital accounts (net worth)

(1)–(7) would enhance Federal Reserve control of the money supply process. Most of these recommendations have now been implemented, although not always in the form that Poole and Lieberman specified. Once again, the reforms made to date fall short of achieving their full logical implementation.

THE DEMAND FOR RESERVES

It has been shown that the imposition of formal, legally enforced reserve requirements is not essential for monetary control (Kaminow, 1977; Kanatas and Greenbaum, 1982). In fact, the Bank of England executes (if not with sterling precision) its monetary control without such formal requirements. It operates on the basis of voluntarily held and minuscule reserve requirements (Meek, 1982). Nevertheless, in the United States, reserve requirements have legal force. The percentage requirements are set by the Federal Reserve within bounds established by, and on instruments determined by, the 1980 act.

Monetary control is enhanced if the Federal Reserve knows with considerable accuracy the multiplier relationship between reserves and the money stock. This knowledge may be based on constancy in the relationship or on ready predictability. Constancy of the multiplier is enhanced if all the components of the aggregate that are to be controlled carry equal reserve requirements. Equality prevents movements among different types of accounts or among different kinds of institutions from muddying the relationship. Stability is also improved if accounts excluded from the aggregate do not carry reserve requirements (Garcia, 1983).

This ideal situation was far from being met during the 1970s. Reserves at the Federal Reserve Banks were required to be held by banks that were members of the Federal Reserve System. Nonmember banks were not obliged to hold such reserve balances, although they did face other obligations

(Gambs, 1980; Conference of State Bank Supervisors, 1979). State-chartered banks were governed by different state laws, which typically required that they hold reserve balances, but usually at a lower rate than member banks. Moreover, these balances usually could be held as government securities or as deposits at other commercial banks, not at the Federal Reserve Banks. As interest rates rose, the reserve tax on Federal Reserve members became more burdensome (because reserves held at Federal Reserve Banks do not pay interest). In contrast, nonmembers typically received some form of implicit compensation for their balances. In consequence, member banks increasingly left the Federal Reserve System, and the proportion of demand deposits covered by Federal Reserve regulations declined, as shown in Figure 7.7.

The value of the multiplier became more uncertain as the reserved proportion of the money stock declined. Adding to the uncertainty, the Federal Reserve regulations that were imposed on member banks themselves varied according to the size and location of the bank. The complexity of reserve

FIGURE 7.7
RATIO OF DEMAND DEPOSITS AT MEMBER BANKS
TO TOTAL DEMAND DEPOSITS

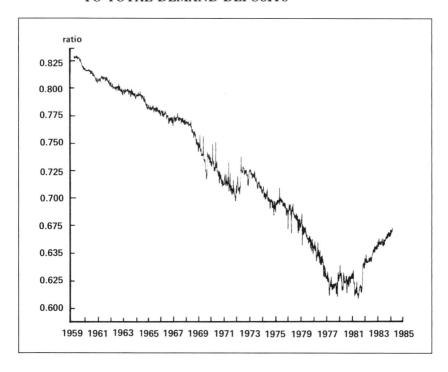

requirements (ranging from 7 percent to 16.25 percent on demand deposits, and from 1 percent to 6 percent on savings and time deposits) that were in effect before the passage of the 1980 act is illustrated in Table 7.5. Moreover, Treasury deposits held at designated commercial banks were treated anomalously, in that they were reserved but were not included in the money supply. Consequently, shifts into and out of Treasury accounts at commercial banks caused the multiplier to vary. Again, Federal Reserve reserve regulations were not extended to nonbanks, although some were beginning to offer transaction accounts, and most offered accounts included in the broader aggregates.

The variability of the incidence of reserve requirements was tackled in four stages. First, the Treasury deposit anomaly was largely ended in 1977. Beginning with that year, commercial banks were allowed to put Treasury deposits into special tax and loan accounts that pay interest. This reduced the incentive for the Treasury to shift its balances, which had previously been held as demand deposits at zero interest, to the Federal Reserve Banks. There they were invested to the benefit of the Banks' and ultimately (as central bank

TABLE 7.5
RESERVE REQUIREMENTS BEFORE DIDMCA

Regulator	Institution	Percentage Rate
State legislatures	Nonmember banks	various
Federal Reserve	Members banks[a]	
	Net demand deposits	
	<$ 2 million	7.00
	$ 2–10	9.50
	$ 10–100	11.75
	$100–400	12.75
	over $400	16.25
	Savings Deposits	3.00
	Time Deposits	
	$ 0–5 million:	
	30–179 days	3.00
	180 days–4 years	2.50
	4 years or more	1.00
	over $5 million:	
	30–179 days	6.00
	180 days–4 years	2.50
	4 years or more	1.00
FHLBB	S&Ls: federal-chartered	various
States	S&Ls: state-chartered	various

[a]Source for these data is the *Federal Reserve Bulletin*, October 1983, Table A8.

profits are paid to the government) the Treasury's advantage. Henceforth, Treasury demand deposits were reduced in value, so that their variability became a less important determinant in the demand for reserves (Lang, 1979). Second, the Federal Reserve itself revised Regulation D in 1978 to remove the distinction between country member banks and reserve city member banks, along with the difference in their reserve requirements. Third, the membership issue was solved by the 1980 act. Fourth, reserve requirements are ultimately, after a phase-in period ending in 1984 for member banks and in 1988 for other institutions, to be determined according to the type of account, not the size, location, or type of institution offering it. Banks and thrifts alike after 1987 will be required to maintain equal reserves against their transaction accounts included in M1. The simplification and regularization of reserve requirements after 1987 is illustrated in Table 7.6.

Nevertheless, again the principle is not carried to its logical conclusion. The first tranche or stratum of deposits at any bank or thrift carries a lower reserve requirement than do subsequent deposits. Moreover, the 1982 act relieves small institutions of the legal requirement to maintain reserves. The effect of these relaxations of principle may not be too important in contributing to the observed variability in the money supply because they cannot be systematically manipulated by the attempts of depository institutions to maximize profits.

More important are other slips between the cup and the lip—slips that individual households and firms can manipulate to their advantage. Money

TABLE 7.6
RESERVE REQUIREMENTS AFTER FULL
IMPLEMENTATION OF DIDMCA IN 1988

Institution	Regulator	Account[a]	Percentage Rate
Member banks	Federal Reserve	*Net transaction accounts*	
Nonmember banks	Board	$0–26.3 million[b]	3.0
Thrifts		Over $26.3 million	12.0
		Nonpersonal time deposits	
		Less than 3.5 years	3.0
		3.5 years or more	0
		Eurocurrency liabilities	
		All types	3.0

[a] The first $2 million of reservable liabilities are exempt from reserve requirements at all institutions.

[b] This upper bound is amended (raised) each year.

market mutual funds and MMDAs can be used for transacting. Yet MMMFs and personal MMDAs carry no reserve requirement. Moreover, reserve requirements are currently enforced on some accounts that are excluded from M1. For example, nonpersonal time deposits and business MMDAs carry reserve requirements, although at a 3 percent rate rather than the 12 percent rate imposed on transaction accounts. Thus, at times when the demand for credit is strong, commercial banks and others engaging in liability management may increase their offerings of large CDs, RPs, or Eurodollar borrowings. This may use up reserves and deplete the volume available for transaction accounts. Then non-M1 components of M2 may rise relative to M1. It could happen then that M2 rises, and with it the supply of depository institution credit, while M1 falls (Thornton, 1983).

In short, the logical implication of using reserves to control M1—equal and exclusive reserves on M1 deposits—is not attained. This may have occurred because the central bank has compromised between this principle for setting reserve requirements and one or another of two alternative principles: either concern with aggregates broader than M1 or concern for credit.

If we assume that the central bank focuses on aggregates broader than M1, then a logical way to structure reserve requirements would be to impose a hierarchy of requirements according to the "moneyness" of the deposits. Deposits with the largest set of monetary attributes would deserve the highest rate, and successively poorer substitutes would have successively lower requirements. As liquidity determines the proximity to transaction ability, M2's components would rationally include the closest money substitutes. Application of this principle would suggest that M2's non-M1 components would carry a second tranche or stratum of requirements at a lower rate than M1 components. That this principle is not applied at the time of writing (early 1984) can clearly be seen by contrasting the treatment of RPs with that of large CDs. Overnight RPs are included in M2 but carry no reserve requirements. They are highly liquid assets. Large CDs are included in M3, not M2, because they have 90-day maturity and so are less liquid. But they carry a 3 percent reserve requirement.

The reason for this anomaly appears to be a relic from the pre-1979 era, before the emphasis on money and reserves. The Federal Reserve has long been ambiguous as to whether it should control money or credit. One way to control credit would be to place reserve requirements equally on all depository institution liabilities. If not applied to all liabilities, the requirements might be placed on those used importantly in liability management strategies. Large CDs are recognized as belonging to this category. This would constitute a second alternative reserve requirement principle. However, this principle is not comprehensively applied, because RPs are also used for liability management. The extension of emergency and supplementary credit control reserve requirements to RPs, large CDs, and Eurodollar borrowings in 1979 and 1980, recognized this argument. Nevertheless, in the normal course of events RPs are not reserved, whereas large CDs are.

Moreover, recent empirical work by Benjamin Friedman (1982) has shown that depository institution credit is too limited a concept to be a viable intermediate target. Since credit is fungible, Friedman advocates a broader intermediate target, total domestic nonfinancial credit, and this indeed is the variable that the System uses in its report to Congress. The Federal Reserve currently does not have the legal authority to impose reserve requirements on all components of this credit measure, even should it want to do so. So it cannot fully implement precise credit control. Nevertheless, the imposition of reserve requirements on large CDs seems best rationalized as an attempt to control credit.

In short, there remain vestiges of illogicality and compromise in the composition of reserve requirements, and these, no doubt, contribute to the variability in monetary control. For example, R.W. Hafer and Scott E. Hein (1983) argue that it is variability in the money multiplier, rather than instability in the supply of reserves, that has been responsible for the much-criticized variance in money growth rates during 1982.

THE SUPPLY OF RESERVES

In order to control the money supply, the Federal Reserve also needs to control the supply of reserves. That is, it needs to control the components of its balance sheet that supply reserves, or to be in a position to know about and offset any changes in those components that it does not directly control. Balance sheet items supplying reserves are shown on the asset side of the Federal Reserve's balance sheet in Table 7.4.

Lack of control over several components has posed problems for the Federal Reserve in using a reserve aggregate to control a monetary aggregate. Poole and Lieberman point out that float and the system of lagged reserve accounting contribute to these difficulties. For example, when utilizing open market operations to implement a nonborrowed reserves procedure, the actual level of nonborrowed reserves is not unambiguously under desk control. It is, for example, affected by aberrations in the behavior of currency in circulation, Treasury deposits held at Reserve Banks, and the Federal Reserve float. Currency in circulation has always been amenable to prediction (Garcia and Pak, 1979), and this is especially true when seasonal factors are taken into account. The behavior of Treasury balances also, since the 1977 introduction of a market-interest-paying tax and loan account, follows a largely predictable pattern; money market analysts and professional Fed-watchers regularly anticipate such events as the Treasury's payment of social security allowances and its receipt of tax installments. The Federal Reserve float has presented a more difficult problem, however. At the beginning of the 1979–1982 experiment, errors in the nonborrowed reserve supply arising from Federal Reserve float equalled all other errors combined (Meulendyke, 1983).

FLOAT

Float was only a minor inconvenience to policy execution under federal-funds-rate targeting. Float did not prevent or even particularly complicate the keeping of the federal funds rate within FOMC-specified bounds. In fact, after an initial decline in float due to technological advances in speeding check clearing in the early 1970s, the volume of float grew rapidly during the later 1970s. Several factors contributed to this advance. High and rising interest rates made float an interest-free way for member banks to acquire reserves. Cash management techniques, such as remote disbursement, deliberately set out to utilize float (Federal Reserve float, bank and mail float). Table 7.7 and Figure 7.8 show the yearly progress in daily average Federal Reserve float levels.

As greater attention was paid toward the end of the 1970s to the money growth rate, the central bank became concerned about this uncontrolled source of reserves. The problem was not only that the level of float was growing, for this could be compensated by slowing the growth of open-market-supplied nonborrowed reserves, but also that the float level for any week was difficult to predict.

Table 7.7 is derived from weekly data on the daily average level of float. It shows for different years, beginning in 1965, the average value of float and two measures of the variability in float data. The first variability measure is the coefficient of variation during each year of the weekly float data, and the second is the range over the year in weekly float data.[12]

At the same time that the Federal Reserve became concerned with the money growth implications of the surge in float, Congress noted that its growth involved a loss of revenue to the Treasury. When the Federal Reserve creates reserves through open market operations, it does so by buying Treasury securities. On these it earns interest. Float involves no such interest earnings. Thus, replacing open-market-created reserves by float-created reserves lowers Federal Reserve interest earnings, which are passed (less expenses) annually to the Treasury. Although Benjamin Wolkowitz and Peter R. Lloyd-Davies (1979) argue that this is not a true cost to society, Congress in the 1980 act, nevertheless, instructed the Federal Reserve to charge the banking system for float and it began to do so during 1983. Since DIDMCA's enactment, the level of float has declined, as shown in Figure 7.8, and so also has the range of its volatility (see Table 7.7).

TABLE 7.7
LEVEL AND VARIABILITY OF
FEDERAL RESERVE FLOAT
($ MILLION)

Year	Mean[a]	Range[a]	Coefficient of Variation
1965	1,830.8	1,500	18.6
1966	2,087.9	1,588	16.3
1967	1,633.9	1,343	18.6
1968	1,888.0	2,441	24.1
1969	2,589.2	1,929	16.1
1970	2,930.7	2,358	15.6
1971	3,033.2	2,211	16.5
1972	3,333.8	2,239	15.6
1973	2,744.9	3,033	25.0
1974	2,311.4	2,633	23.8
1975	2,145.9	3,214	25.5
1976	2,646.5	2,567	19.6
1977	3,656.1	3,958	24.4
1978	5,428.9	6,731	26.5
1979	6,615.8	7,895	26.8
1980	4,712.1	6,011	27.1
1981	3,322.7	3,551	20.6
1982	2,544.1	5,242	34.9
1983[b]	1,785.1	2,200	30.4

[a] The basic data are weekly averages of daily data, not seasonally adjusted. The means, range, and coefficient of variation are calculated from the weekly data.
[b] Data for 1983 end on November 16.
SOURCE: Board of Governors of the Federal Reserve.

LAGGED AND CONTEMPORANEOUS RESERVE ACCOUNTING

In the pre–October 1979 world where interest rates were used both as instrument and as intermediate target, the system of lagged reserve accounting did not present insurmountable problems for monetary policy. That situation changed after 1979, however, when the monetary authority began to control reserves. Although the Federal Reserve retains control of the supply of non-borrowed reserves, the value of required reserves (the major component of total reserves) is determined, in effect, two weeks earlier by the banking system. What would be the response if institutions knew that the Federal Reserve would not readily supply the level of required reserves determined earlier, but would force deficient institutions to borrow reserves at a penalty rate? They would be reluctant to supply deposits beyond that consistent with the total nonborrowed reserve base that they expected the Federal Reserve to willingly (that is, profitably) supply. But the central bank has refused to impose a punitive discount rate, and so, on occasions, it has lost control over the supply of total reserves.[13] Consequently, policy analysts and economists, although not industry participants, have almost universally argued that the monetary authority should revert to contemporaneous reserve accounting (CRA).

On February 2, 1984, the Federal Reserve moved toward a system of semi-contemporaneous reserve accounting. For transaction accounts the new system involves a two-day lag in reserve accounting. That is, the period over which an institution incurs its reserve obligation (called the reserve computation period) is a two-week span ending on alternate Mondays. The period (called the reserve maintenance period) over which reserves must be held to

FIGURE 7.8
MONTHLY AVERAGE OF DAILY FLOAT

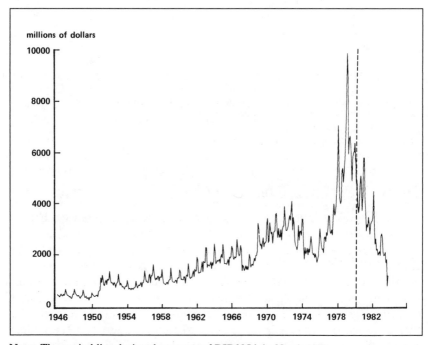

NOTE: The vertical line depicts the passage of DIDMCA in March 1980.

match the average daily deposit levels held in the computation period, is a two-week period ending every other Wednesday. That is,

Reserve Computation Period

M T W T F S S M T W T F S S M T W T

Reserve Maintenance Period

Thus, for 12 days of every 14-day period, the maintenance and computation period overlap. For nontransaction accounts the system of lagged reserve accounting continues, but the length of the lag has increased. Required reserves on nontransaction accounts are based on a two-week computation period ending 30 days before the end of the maintenance period.

These changes are significant and will involve major alterations in the way depository institutions, Federal Reserve Banks, and the FOMC act. The changes also involve a good deal of uncertainty about the way in which the new system will operate. It remains to be seen whether this last item to be implemented on the Poole and Lieberman list will improve monetary control. Robert B. Avery and Myron L. Kwast (1983) forecast that it will make a small, but not substantial, difference. Laurent (1984) argues that it will likely be no improvement, and, at best, a minor improvement.

SEASONAL ADJUSTMENT

As the Federal Reserve observes deviations of the actual growth of money from its targeted path, it must consider whether to take corrective action or not. This process is complicated by the possibilities that the observation may be due to temporary factors that will naturally be reversed later, or that it may represent merely an error in the data. Inappropriate seasonal adjustment factors have contributed to data errors and sometimes have required substantial revision of the initial estimates.[14] Difficulties the Federal Reserve has experienced with its seasonal adjustment process have complicated short-term fine-tuning. A substantial research effort is under way at the Board to improve the seasonal adjustment process (Pierce, Grupe, and Cleveland, 1983).

THE MONEY MULTIPLIER

Accurate control of the money supply requires that the monetary authority must accurately predict the demand for reserves, and also that it must anticipate and counteract any changes in the value of the money multiplier by adjusting the supply of reserves to compensate.

This task is made easier if the money multiplier is relatively constant or if it grows at a regular rate. Bryant (1983) stresses the variability observed in the multiplier within recent years. Garcia (1984) argues that this variability, illustrated in Figure 7.9, which plots the ratio of transaction deposits to total reserves, is influenced by the configuration of reserve requirements and by the incomplete process of interest rate deregulation. In the past LRA has also contributed to the multiplier's variability. Multiplier variability is likely to be greater in the following circumstances: where reserve requirements are positioned unequally on components of the aggregate to be controlled and where rates are regulated on the components carrying high reserve ratios but are unregulated elsewhere. Such is the case, for this situation encourages financial innovation. As Figure 7.9 illustrates, the multiplier was more stable in the pre–financial innovation days of the 1960s, but more unstable in the financial innovation heydays of the 1970s and in the interest rate deregulation era that commenced in 1978.

FIGURE 7.9
TOTAL RESERVES MULTIPLIER

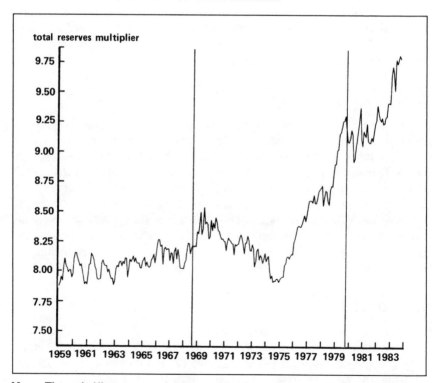

NOTE: The vertical lines represent the change to lagged reserve accounting in September 1968 and the October 1979 change in operating procedures.

It is clear that the multiplier has not been stable in the recent past, nor is it likely to become so at least until the completion of the transition phase for the 1980 act's revision of reserve requirements. Variability, however, does not necessarily mean that the multiplier is unpredictable. Economists at the Federal Reserve Bank of St. Louis have devoted a substantial research effort to forecasting the relationship of M1 to the monetary base (Johannes and Rasche, 1979). But forecasting this ratio is made easier by the relatively steady behavior of currency, which is included in both the numerator and denominator of the St. Louis multiplier. A demonstration of the ability to predict the ratio of transaction deposits to total or nonborrowed reserves would encourage greater confidence in the Federal Reserve's ability to successfully manage the money supply.

Nevertheless, after 1987, when the reserve-requirement transition phase is ended and interest rates are fully deregulated, monetary control should become more feasible. This would be more true if the Federal Reserve Board exercised the option available to it under the Monetary Control Act to reduce the reserve ratio on large CDs to 0 percent.

ACHIEVEMENTS, SUMMARY, AND CONCLUSIONS

Recent changes in Federal Reserve policy reflect a studied reaction to the public's and the economics profession's analysis of macroeconomic policy requirements. In setting its goals, the Federal Reserve plays a senior statesman role, reflecting professional analysis and political reality.[15] It readjusts its goals with the times and changes its policy techniques to better achieve the new goals. In this context, the central bank changed its goals in order to emphasize combating inflation at the close of the 1970s. At that time, it altered its intermediate-target and operating procedures accordingly.

At the time of this writing, in early 1984, it is clear that the inflation rate has been reduced. Analysts differ in their assessment of whether the reduction is permanent or temporary. Further, it is disputed to what extent the Federal Reserve can claim credit for the reduction that has occurred. Apologists for the Federal Reserve claim that it has succeeded in reducing the average growth of M1, which, in turn, has been translated into lower inflation. Others (Gordon, 1982) argue that the reduction in inflation was caused principally by a lowering of energy prices (just as the two inflation escalations in the 1970s were due to adverse supply shocks). The central bank's contribution to the economy, Gordon posits, was to unnecessarily exacerbate the two early 1980s recessions. R. W. Hafer (1983) attributes some importance to the rule of energy prices in reducing inflation, but finds that the reduction in the growth of money has been the major factor. On the basis of a St. Louis equation relating inflation to current and lagged money growth and decreases in the relative price of energy, Hafer estimates that three factors contributed to the decrease in the actual GNP deflator from 10.01 percent in 1981 (first quarter) to 3.65 percent in 1982 (fourth quarter). Decelerating money growth reduced the inflation rate to 6.26 percent; energy prices contributed a smaller 1.41 percent (reduction); a 1.20 percent reduction remains unexplained by the model.

It is clear that structural problems in the financial sector prevented the Federal Reserve from pursuing an anti-inflationary monetary policy as vigorously as it initially wished. For example, in 1982, the difficulties facing depository institutions restrained the central bank from raising interest rates to the high levels demanded under lagged reserve accounting in order to contain money growth in the way it wished. Fears of widespread failures among S&Ls and banks generated the marked change in the direction of policy in the summer of 1982.

The structural problems had arisen because unanticipated increases in deposit interest rates that rose faster than rates charged on assets caused solvency problems for S&Ls in the early 1980s. At the same time, many commercial banks faced potentially large loan losses on their international and energy-related loans. Even as the recovery accelerated in 1983, the financial system still showed serious signs of strain. Both S&Ls and commercial banks experienced substantially higher failure rates, as discussed in Chapter 6. Interest rate levels were reduced (see Figure 6.2), but real rates remain high. There was repeated concern that they would prematurely stall the cyclical recovery that began in November 1982, and, once the recovery was complete, that high real rates would curtail the ensuing cyclical advance. However, no one has yet invented a way to finance structurally high budget deficits without either raising interest rates or creating money. And the creation of money is being avoided in order not to rekindle inflation.

The signs of strain in the financial system restrain Federal Reserve action. In the domestic arena the recovery of S&Ls was reversed in mid-1984, as interest rates rose significantly once more. Large commercial banks are exposed by their international lending, while banks of all sizes in some regions of the country have experienced losses from defaults on energy and agricultural loans.

In short, the Federal Reserve can claim (disputed) successes in policy, and it still faces significant problems. It is not clear, at the time of writing in early 1984, what intermediate-target and operating procedures will be used in 1985 and thereafter. Will the adoption of partially contemporaneous reserve accounting finally allow the Federal Reserve to restrain and stabilize monetary growth or will the Federal Reserve again adopt some other set of operating procedures and priorities?

8 ISSUES BEYOND 1984

It is clear that considerable progress has been made toward reforming the financial system and making it and monetary policy conformable to the economic environment of the 1980s. But several important issues remain unresolved.

HOW FAR DEREGULATION?

The movement toward the deregulation of U.S. industries, including the financial services industry, reached a crescendo as President Reagan took office. As the president's term progressed, however, a reassessment was made concerning further deregulation of the financial system. Questions were raised, and still remain to be satisfactorily answered, about what, if any, minimum level of financial regulation should be preserved and how it should be imposed.

The first cautionary question arises from the reflection that the laws and regulations that so visibly overburdened the financial system at the close of the 1970s had originally been put there for some purpose. Some had come in response to financial crises; others had been initiated to foster congressional goals. So, should the offending regulations now be removed? Should all or most regulations be eliminated? Or should an alternative way be found to achieve any still-desired objectives?

DEREGULATORY RATIONALES

Four valid types of arguments for the removal of specific regulations can be listed. The first would be that the particular instigating financial crisis was past and believed unlikely to recur. This is the case, for example, with respect to bank exposure to domestic liquidity crises. The established system of cash and reserves held at the Federal Reserve Banks, plus the Federal Reserve System's well-understood readiness to act as lender of last resort, has served to calm fears of the effects of liquidity crises. Even the run on Continental Illinois Bank in May 1984 was contained by cooperative responses between the federal regulators and the private banking community. Similarly, it could be that the desired congressional goals had been achieved and were now no longer a consideration. In short, the regulations may have become superfluous.

Second, the laws and regulations could have been found ineffective in forestalling crises or achieving goals. Quite possibly, they had never worked, or they had given rise to serious unwanted side effects. On the one hand, these unwanted consequences may not have been foreseen at the time the law or regulation was introduced. Regulation Q comes to mind here. On the other hand, the economic, social, political, or technological environment may have changed so as to render counterproductive laws and regulations that were originally appropriate. Technical advances that have produced scope and scale economies that are breaking down the segmentation of the financial series industry are relevant here (Panzar and Willig, 1981).

One important factor is that the pattern of laws and regulations was not consistently designed when they were initiated. Laws and regulations accrued piecemeal over a fifty-year period in response to different events and problems. Consistency among the numerous motivating goals has rarely been a consideration. Indeed, consistency has long been recognized to be a casualty of the political process (Arrow, 1951). Further, the interactions of the different laws and regulations and their combined impact have not been systematically assessed in more recent times, as new layers of regulation were superimposed on the old.[1] In short, the existing system of constraints could have become— and, indeed, did become—counterproductive. By the close of the 1970s, the resulting inefficiencies and misallocation of resources had become unacceptable.

Third, society's goals may have changed. New priorities may require the replacement of old regulations by a new, less regulated environment or by a financial system re-regulated to achieve other goals. Here Patric Hendershott's (1983) discussion questioning the system of the implicit subsidization of housing in the United States is relevant.

The fourth type of deregulatory rationale is particularly relevant to many of the financial reforms still pending during the second half of the 1980s. Although some of the objectives of regulations may remain valid, a better way of achieving them is now available. The resulting process of re-regulation is, therefore, legitimate. In particular, the current trend is toward promoting society's goals through price incentives rather than quantity restrictions. This is the situation with respect to both deposit insurance and the conduct of monetary policy.

REGULATORY ANOMALIES

In short, by the end of the 1970s, it was clear that financial reform was imperative. But the processes of deregulation and re-regulation suffer from the same problems as those affecting the initial accumulation of regulation. The mutual consistency of the new goals—to improve the efficiency, viability, and functional performance of the financial system—has not been determined. Moreover, deregulation is also proceeding piecemeal. The theory of the second best warns that the results of such an *ad hoc* process may not produce an optimal allocation of resources. It may even worsen that allocation.[2] Moreover, the dynamic process of re-regulation has not been thought through.

A more detailed discussion of the examples is in order. One will be provided to relate to the problems of partial deregulation of the financial structure; a second illustrates the difficulties attendant on deregulation and re-regulation for monetary policy.

S&L PORTFOLIOS

The first example concerns the regulation, the partial deregulation, and the re-regulation of S&L portfolios, along with their impacts on the financial structure and performance of the industry.

Restrictions on the asset portfolios of thrifts were imposed initially to foreclose opportunities to acquire unduly risky assets and to provide funds for mortgage financing. In the period before interest rate risk became an important factor, the resulting portfolio composition proved viable and profitable for thrifts. However, during the 1960s, when market rates began to rise, portfolio constraints were recognized as detrimental to the profitability of S&Ls. Consequently, Regulation Q was extended to thrifts to provide them with a stable, low-cost supply of funds. Henceforth, Regulation Q was administered restrictively; it no longer rose *pari passu* with market rates. As inflation progressed,

Regulation Q became unworkable. Consequently, it has been largely eliminated at the time of this writing in early 1984. Nevertheless, the costly process of overcoming disintermediation through bypassing Regulation Q, along with the unsuccessful handling of interest rate risk, jeopardized the viability of S&Ls. Moreover, the inability to handle interest rate risk was at least partly attributable to regulation.

By the 1980s, recognition could no longer be postponed of the problems arising from those regulations that may have been initially appropriate, but had become destructively restrictive. Consequently, the 1980 act sounded *de jure* the death knell for Regulation Q. The act also began the asset-portfolio deregulation necessary to ensure the viability of thrift institutions in the new environment. The 1982 act accelerated progress toward deregulation. Yet, this process is hampered by the tax laws, which continue to encourage mortgage specialization by S&Ls and savings banks.

Asset Diversification.   Thus, the piecemeal removal of regulations contributed to the thrift crises of 1980–1982. Although this solvency crisis was successfully contained, questions have been raised concerning the possibility of a recurrence. S&L portfolios still rely heavily on mortgage loans, even where thrifts have the legal opportunity to diversify. John Crockett and A. Thomas King (1982) have shown that state-chartered S&Ls in Texas diversified cautiously after they received broader powers during the 1970s. Most remained heavily specialized in mortgages and mortgage-backed securities. By the end of 1981, state-chartered stock associations had 77.2 percent of their assets in mortgage loans and securities. This compares with 80.6 percent held at federal mutual associations and 80.3 percent at state mutual associations.[3] Thus, despite several years of opportunity to diversify, only a modest restructuring has occurred in Texas.

Data in Table 8.1 show the nationwide portfolio composition of S&Ls and savings banks two and three years after the 1980 deregulation.[4] The percentage of total assets held as mortgages declined five percentage points during 1983. The proportions held as mortgage-backed securities and liquid assets increased. Small increases were evident in the proportions of consumer loans (which still measured less than 3 percent of assets at the end of 1983) and of other loans. In comparison, state-chartered stock associations in Texas held 5 percent of their assets as consumer loans. Consequently, some modest additional growth of consumer lending may be forthcoming nationwide as S&Ls have time to develop this area of expertise.

Diversification is likely to be a slow process. Expertise in other than real-estate lending can be hired or learned. If done quickly, the diversification may be costly or unsuccessful. If done slowly, portfolios remain exposed to interest rate risk (Dunham and Guerin-Calvert, 1983).

TABLE 8.1
PORTFOLIO COMPOSITION OF S&Ls AND SAVINGS BANKS

	Total Assets ($ billion)	Mortgage Loans (percentage)	Mortgage-Backed Securities (percentage)	Consumer Loans (percentage)	Liquidity[a] (percentage)	Other Loans (percentage)
December 1982[b]	692.6	68.4	8.9	2.3	11.9	8.4
June 1983	756.8	64.7	10.4	2.5	13.9	8.4
November 1983	807.8	63.9	11.2	2.7	13.3	8.8

[a] Liquidity includes required and nonrequired cash and nonmortgage securities.

[b] Data for December 1982 are for S&Ls only. At that date S&L assets constituted 99.0 percent of combined S&L and savings bank assets.

SOURCE: Federal Home Loan Bank Board, *News*, February 1, 1984.

Variable Rate Mortgages.   There has, however, been greater success in immunizing S&L portfolios against interest rate risk via the adoption of variable-rate mortgage instruments. The Federal Home Loan Bank Board's research staff compiles data on the use of variable-rate mortgage instruments by the major mortgage lenders. In this regard, S&Ls have undergone greater transformation than have other lenders. At the end of 1981, S&Ls made less than 2 percent of their mortgage loans in the form of variable-rate loans. By January 1984, over 60 percent of their new single-family conventional mortgages were variable-rate loans. In comparison the percentages of similar mortgage loans at commercial banks, savings banks, and mortgage companies were 23.3, 39.1, and 49.7 percent, respectively.

The S&L adoption of variable-rate instruments has not been monotonic. The data in Figure 8.1 show that the public's acceptance of variable-rate instruments has increased, in general, over time, but also that it has suffered setbacks at times. Actual interest rates, expectations of future interest rate movements, and the promotional activities of thrifts, and, in particular, the relative prices of fixed and variable-rate instruments have influenced the relative acceptance rates of fixed- and variable-rate mortgage instruments.

Thus, it would seem that S&Ls are considerably less exposed to interest rate risk in 1984 than they were even two years ago. Fears of a recurrence of a nationwide thrift crisis are correspondingly reduced. However, the data discussed refer only to new loans, so that there is now a new S&L mortgage backlog problem—that of fixed rate mortgages still held in thrift portfolios. Moreover, promotional interest rate discounts to buyers of new homes, caps on rate increases, and the aggravation of credit risk—if the homeowner cannot afford the increased monthly mortgage payments when interest rates rise— insure that VRMs are not a panacea. Consequently, if interest rates were to rise significantly again, as they have during the first several months of 1984, those thrifts that have remained reliant on fixed-rate instruments would suffer losses once again. The specter of a second thrift crisis looms ahead. Fears of this outcome constrain monetary policy from allowing interest rates to rise significantly again in the near future.

Moreover, S&Ls and savings banks remain heavily invested in mortgage securities. Housing is still given priority as a social goal as a result of this encouraged reliance. Moreover, single-family homeownership is encouraged by a second feature of the tax laws, which allows the deduction of mortgage interest from taxable income. The social contract favoring housing is still intact. If Congress were to decide that this priority should be reduced, the tax laws that give thrifts incentives to invest in mortgage instruments must be changed. Moreover the tax advantages of homeownership would need to be

FIGURE 8.1
SAVINGS AND LOAN ASSOCIATIONS' VARIABLE RATE MORTGAGES

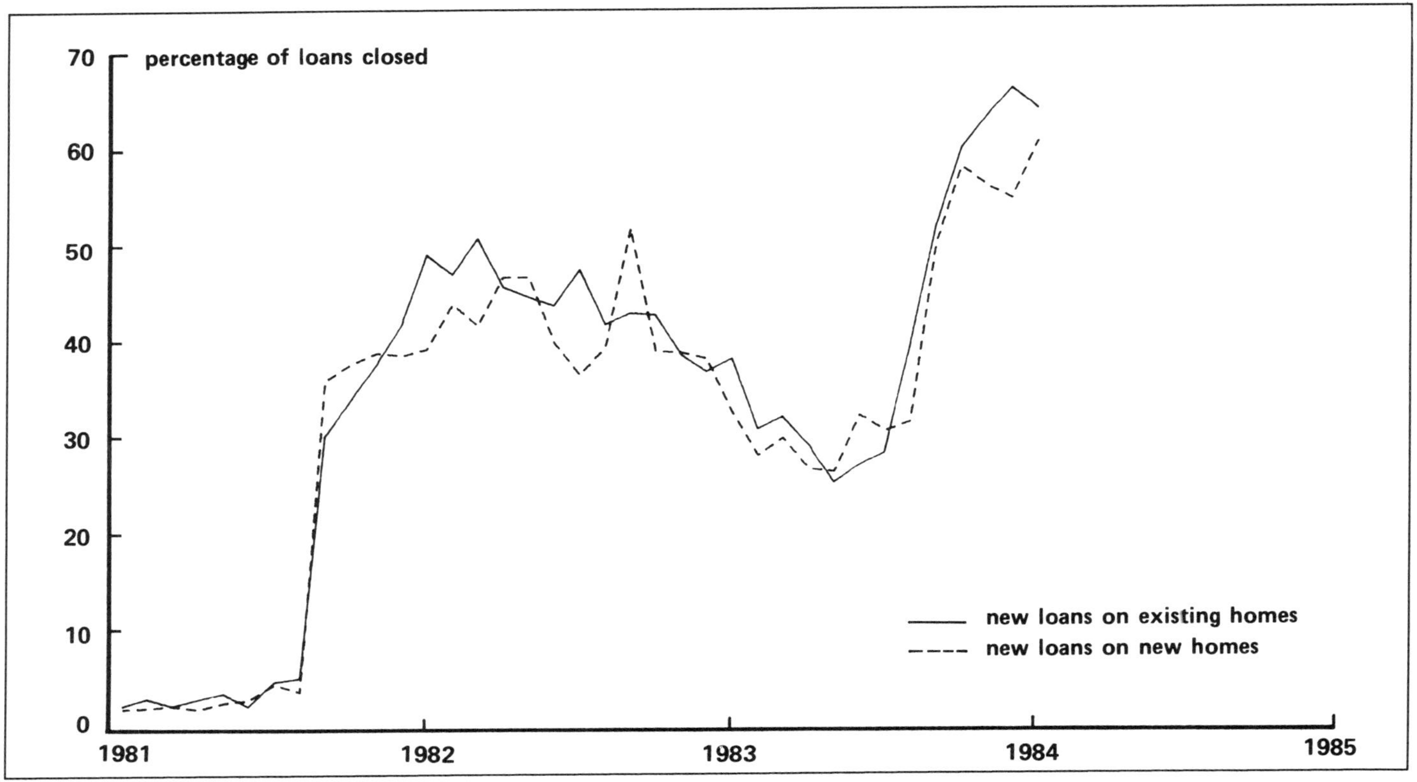

percentage of loans closed

——— new loans on existing homes
----- new loans on new homes

reduced. Herbert Baer's analysis of thrift tax concessions has shown that the tax incentives can be adapted by jointly diversifying out of mortgage securities and into "nonqualifying" state and local government securities. Nevertheless, this strategy gives a preference to state and local government borrowing that Congress did not intend and may not desire. Does society wish to further subsidize non–federal government borrowing by artificially stimulating the demand for its debt instruments? Social financing priorities need to be discussed and clearly established in this regard. This stricture is particularly appropriate as the present and projected federal budget deficits strain the nation's supply of loanable funds.

MONETARY DEREGULATION

The process of piecemeal deregulation has adverse implications for monetary policy, at least in the short run. Research has shown that the money multiplier will be relatively stable in an environment where the interest rates of all deposit components of the chosen aggregate are controlled or where all are unregulated (Garcia, 1983). Control is potentially more difficult where some components have regulated rates and some do not. But this is the world as it exists at the beginning of 1984.

Partial deregulation applies regardless of whether M1, M2, or M3 is the chosen aggregate. Within M1, explicit rates payable on demand deposits are regulated at 0 percent; NOW accounts pay 5.25 percent, whereas SNOW rates are unregulated. A similar admixture describes the components of M2 and M3: some rates are regulated and some are not. In short, partial deregulation is hampering monetary control during the mid-1980s.

In the meantime, the appropriate configuration and the timing of the steps to take toward further deregulation remain to be analyzed by the policymakers. This consideration is the more relevant because Fama's analysis (1980) emphasizes that control of the price level, being a legitimate central bank function, has to be exercised through regulation in one form or another. The present process of monetary reform can be characterized as a switch in the mechanisms by which that control is exercised. Quantity restraints and outright prohibitions are being replaced by influences conveyed via the price mechanism. This process is far from complete, however.

REGULATORY OBJECTIVES

An historical examination of financial regulations suggests that different motives have led to successive waves of regulation, one superimposed on the other. Initially, the objective was the safety and soundness of the post-depression financial system. Later, during the 1950s and 1960s anti-monopoly considerations came to the forefront of regulatory attention. In the 1970s, consumer protection was in vogue (Benston, 1983). Over the years, many of the predictions of the regulatory capture theory that regulators would become the guardian of the property rights of existing financial institutions—were fulfilled. The legal concept of "competitive equity" among competitors is a reflection of this last approach.

SAFETY AND SOUNDNESS

Banks became the object of particularly stringent regulation because of their special characteristics. They were, and still importantly are, the guardians of the nation's payments mechanism, a vitally important responsibility. At the same time, the liability composition of banks is heavily reliant on fixed-price, immediately callable deposits of shorter duration than their assets. As such, banks, like S&Ls, are subject to interest rate and liquidity risks. Moreover, a large number of banks were believed to have failed during the Great Depression because of defaults on the loans they had made. Some of these defaults arose because the central bank failed to immunize the financial system from the contagion of failure. Other defaults resulted from management's inappropriate lending practices.

Consequently, many bank regulations were imposed to pre-empt the making of risky loans. At that time, risk was interpreted as credit risk. To this end, banking was separated from commerce under the Glass-Steagall Act. Loans to insiders were limited, exposure from excessive lending to individual borrowers was restricted, borrowing by parent holding companies and their affiliates was controlled, and regulations were established concerning acceptable collateral. All of these measures aimed to contain exposure to default risk.

In the past these regulations may be judged to have been largely successful. Bank lending practices changed. The failure rate among commercial banks was drastically reduced after the Great Depression. It is fashionable to attribute this success to the establishment of nationwide deposit insurance, but the new regulations all played a part: risky activities were prohibited or restricted. The restrictions were successful until the 1980s. In recent years questionable lending decisions with respect to energy, agricultural, and international loans have again raised the issue of credit risk as a threat to the stability of the banking system.

By the 1970s, banks could claim three decades of successful handling of credit risk. Consequently, relaxations were made under the Garn–St Germain Act to the regulations concerning lending to single borrowers and to insiders.

Although there has been no legislative change permitting it, the walls separating banking and commerce are being breached to a significant degree. Nonbanks, such as Merrill Lynch, Sears, and American Express, are progressively encroaching on the banking domain, especially in the areas of consumer lending and deposit taking (Rosenblum and Siegel, 1983).

Conversely, banks are advancing into nonbank territory. Citicorp of New York is using the 1982 act's opportunities to purchase failing S&Ls across state lines. Citicorp has acquired thrifts in California, Florida, and Illinois—states with strong or growing markets. Several banks have moved into the discount brokerage business. The Bank of America is planning to allow an insurance company to sell auto, homeowner, and life insurance from a select number of its branches. South Dakota allows its state-chartered banks to underwrite insurance and permits out-of-state banks to buy in-state banks, thus offering an avenue into the insurance business for those banks wishing to take that route. New York State, at the beginning of 1984, is proposing to allow its state-chartered banks, together with thrifts and their holding companies, not only to sell and underwrite all kinds of insurance but also to own insurance companies. Delaware is also courting financial institutions by providing a favorable regulatory environment. California allows state-chartered thrifts so wide a discretion over their activities that the deposit insurance agencies have taken steps to limit their risk exposure by restricting the range of activity that they are willing to insure. Others argue that diversification into nonbanking businesses could reduce bank risk, if earnings from the new activities are negatively correlated with normal bank earnings.

Although scope economies exist and are motivating the breaching of the interindustry walls (Kane, 1983c, 1984), doubt exists about how advisable it is to allow banks to enter industries subject to high risk, and vice versa. For example, Lowell R. Beck (1984) argues that property and casualty insurance is a volatile business inappropriate for banks.

Is it reasonably certain that banks will continue to handle credit risk successfully in the absence of discouragement from undertaking highly risky projects? Past problems with real estate investment trusts in the mid-1970s, with agricultural and energy loans in the early 1980s, and with international lending up to the time of this writing (early 1984), suggest that banks are not immune from management error or fad. Failure rates for banks (and thrifts) in the early 1980s are the highest rates since the 1930s (see Table 6.7), and failure rates for the first seven months of 1984 were double those of 1983. Stephen Buser, Andrew Chen, and Edward Kane (1981) show that the deposit insurance system, as it is currently priced, encourages bank risk-taking and heavy leverage.

In these circumstances, until a risk-reflecting pricing system is instituted, other, quantity constraints on risk-taking remain necessary. As such, the safety and soundness of quantity restrictions on depository institutions, and their careful enforcement by the supervisory agencies, have shared in the success of deposit insurance systems in promoting the safety and soundness of the financial system in the decades following the Great Depression. However, technical progress is markedly enhancing scope economies. To prevent depository institutions from taking advantage of them is to make the financial system unnecessarily inefficient. As technical progress proceeds, the regulatory barriers will inevitably be breached. Some other method of handling depository-institution risk exposure becomes imperative.

Risk-Adjusted Deposit Insurance Premia.[5]   The advances in the technology of collecting, storing, processing, and transmitting data now make it feasible and necessary to change the way in which restraint on depository-institution risk-taking is exercised. In the past, two aspects of the availability of information have presented problems. First, information is more readily available to managers than to regulators, raising the potential for fraud and the exposure of the insurance funds to moral hazard. Second, information necessary for management to appropriately exercise its functions has not been available to all but the largest depository institutions.

The magnitude of these problems is potentially reduced in the computer age. As a consequence, a system of risk-adjusted deposit insurance premia becomes feasible. This system could achieve the legitimate dual purposes of governmental persuasion: first, to guarantee deposits in order to forestall the risk of runs on banks; second, to influence the degree of risk aversion maintained by bank managements. It would also improve the equity of the insurance guarantee system. At present, risk-averse institutions subsidize risk-prone banks and thrifts.

Deposit insurance is unlike insurance on property, accident, or life, all of which typically insure against losses that are not under the control of either the insuree or the insurer. While the deposit guarantor cannot fully control the probability of failure, it can reduce it by enforcing higher capital-adequacy requirements. Moreover, the FDIC and the FSLIC can, and currently do, influence the extent of the losses that result from failure. They exert that influence through regulation, supervision, and examination. If the institution is closed as, or before, its net worth becomes zero, the insurance agency will suffer no loss beyond its transaction costs. Higher ratios of capital to assets reduce insurance agency risk. Higher capital ratios could be encouraged by scaling premiums to charge less to depository institutions having higher capital ratios. This approach to variable interest rate premia appears more practicable than some others because capital ratios are readily measurable. Some other schemes are likely to lead to contention between industry participants and the regulators over the measurement and the pricing of risk.

Closure. The right to declare the institution closed is important to the question of future financial reform.[6] In general, private insurers, if they had the power to close institutions, would tend to close them early in order to conserve the insurance-fund resources. On the other hand, if the right of closure remains under public control via the regulators, as at present, there will remain a tendency to delay closure until net worth is negative. This is particularly likely to be the case where financial troubles are widespread, because there are serious externalities or consequences to innocent parties from financial failure. This tendency manifested itself strongly during the S&L crisis of 1982, when large numbers of thrifts were permitted to continue in operation despite negative book-networths (Carron, 1982, 1983). The net worth certificate program specified in the Garn–St Germain Act exacerbates the risk of loss to the insurance funds by helping thrifts and real estate banks to operate with negative net worths as measured under generally accepted accounting practices. Of course, the intention is to reduce the actual, realized loss by buying time for the industry to overcome its problems.

The closure issue is one of the important aspects of future financial reform that remain to be considered. In this regard, it should be noted that private insurance, which some advocate, is unlikely to be made available in the absence of the private, or completely impartial, exercise of the right to close a troubled institution. The former may be socially unacceptable and the latter realistically unlikely. The government must retain the ultimate responsibility for guaranteeing the financial system's integrity, although private insurance could no doubt relieve the government of some of the present burden.

FAILURE: PUBLIC OR PRIVATE RESPONSIBILITY?

The reason why impartial exercise of the right to closure by a public agency is unlikely is that the demarcation of public and private responsibility for risk-taking has not been formally or informally agreed upon. Although a social consensus has been reached on some aspects of risk exposure, it remains undecided on other aspects. Where insolvency occurs as a result of fraud, management is held responsible. Mishandling credit risk is also regarded as management's responsibility. In these circumstances, it is generally agreed that regulators should allow the institution to fail. Depositors should be protected to prevent a liquidity crisis, which can accelerate otherwise preventable default and may spread into runs on other banks. But management and company owners should be allowed to suffer losses. Until recently, large depositors were also protected, *de facto*, by the insurance regulator's preference for merging rather than closing troubled institutions. But in 1982, when Penn Square National Bank failed, a change in policy was made. Henceforth, large depositors were to be expected to exert a risk-restraining influence on institution activities.

As merger partners become more difficult to find during the early 1980s, the insurance agencies changed their practice. Large depositors (over $100,000) did not receive a full and timely replenishment of their funds. For example, the costs of the Penn Square failure were allowed to pass to its creditors. Continental Illinois of Chicago and Seafirst of Seattle are well-known bank casualties of the Penn Square failure. The idea behind this change in policy is that large depositors, having better access to relevant information, are in a position to exert market pressure on depository- institution activities. When they perceive risk, they demand a risk premium. This premium causes the borrowing institution to evaluate risk as a determinant of its lending activity—a discipline otherwise reduced by the existence of deposit insurance that allows banks and thrifts to borrow funds at a risk-free rate.

Recent developments have pointed in the opposite direction, however. These developments are challenging the principle of management responsibility for credit risk. For example, to this time of writing, banks have been insulated from formally recognizing the market value of the losses on their international loan portfolios. Further, a proposal has been made in the Congress to extend the net worth certificate program to agricultural banks. Thus, it appears that credit risk, on an individual bank basis, remains management's responsibility—unless the bank is very large. However, if the problem is widespread, the onus for its handling is increasingly passing to the government.

Market Discipline: Continental Illinois Bank and Trust Company.   This policy of imposing discipline through the surveillance of large depositors was formally enunciated by the FDIC in March 1984. The announcement of the new policy was followed two months later by an extensive run on Continental Illinois Bank and Trust Company. Uninsured depositors, particularly those in the Eurodollar market, did more than demand a risk premium for lending to Continental—they simply withdrew their funds at any price in response to new information on the poor condition of Continental's loan portfolio and the FDIC's (in the event, unsuccessful) attempt to avoid underwriting the loan portfolio.

The FDIC's attempt to use the private market to exercise risk-restraining discipline on banks was unsuccessful. Deposit insurance was established in 1934 to prevent bank runs, yet a system-threatening run occurred in May 1984. Evidently, the system of deposit insurance must be reformed. It was established originally to insure small deposits. If small depositors were the ones most likely to make a run in the first half of this century, large depositors are now the ones most likely to withdraw their funds irreplaceably. That the threat to the U.S. payments system and to the integrity of the financial system was judged to be substantial is evidenced by the size of the federal aid package announced initially on May 17, 1984, and by the ultimate nationalization of the bank, announced in July 1984.

The regulator response evidences an asymmetry in the treatment of large and small banks that the Congress may perceive to be inequitable. Small banks are to be allowed to fail because they do not threaten the system. But large banks will be supported at substantial cost because their loss would violate the integrity of the system.

Market Response: Brokered Deposits.   However, in the continuing dialectic between the regulators and the regulated, the attempt to impose market disciplines produced another response—a market response. Merrill Lynch innovated the now-common brokering of deposits. The broker accumulates large volumes of funds for an individual bank or thrift—a volume comprised of many contributions, each less than $100,000 and fully issued. Market discipline to risk restraint is thus avoided. A proposal to eliminate this practice is available for public comment at the time of writing (early 1984). It is an issue remaining to be resolved.

Regulatory responsibility in the case of interest rate risk is more contentious. When occurring in isolated instances, it is regarded as the responsibility of management, so that failure would be permissible. But in recent years, exposure to interest rate risk has been pervasive. Moreover, in the case of S&Ls such exposure was largely unavoidable not only because of the restrictions on asset and liability portfolios that resulted from social policy but also because the high levels of interest rates experienced in the early 1980s were unforeseen and, possibly, unforeseeable. Research by Brewer and Garcia (1984) shows that behavior associated with profitability for S&Ls in 1976 detracted from profitability in 1981. Thrift management requires more than finding a golden rule and adhering to it.

Thus, while there has been a tendency for the administration to deny responsibility for the plight of the thrift industry, Congress' actions have been otherwise. Throughout its history, Federal Home Loan Bank Board (FHLBB) regulators have avoided declaring insolvency as an act of policy. They have promoted merger wherever feasible. When the supply of suitable merger partners for failing thrifts was exhausted during 1981 and 1982, other recourses were exercised. Minimum net worth requirements were successively lowered, accounting changes artificially raised measured net worth, and FHLBB assistance was offered. Ultimately, the regulatory assistance program was formalized under the emergency provisions of the Garn–St Germain Act.

In short, the social consensus currently places the responsibility for incidences of default risk that are not system threatening on management, that for liquidity risk on the central bank, whereas no consensus has been reached concerning interest rate risk or on the handling of waves of defaults. Wider discussion and the attribution of this responsibility will be needed before the issue of the right and responsibility for closure can be resolved.

Other risks, beyond default and interest-rate risk exposure, face depository institutions. Fraud remains a problem both for the insured and insurer. It is best discouraged by a surveillance system under government, or impartial, control. The present fragmented system of supervision needs to be consolidated (Federal Reserve Bank of New York, 1984). The Bush Commission on the Regulation of Financial Services (1984) is finding how difficult this objective is to achieve, but the commission does offer an opportunity to study the theoretical issues as well as the practical problems attendant on such financial reform.

Regulatory Overlap.   Banks and thrifts are currently regulated by the Federal Reserve Board, the FDIC, the Comptroller of the Currency, the Federal Home Loan Bank Board (including the FSLIC), the DIDC, and the Securities and Exchange Commission. The National Credit Union Administration is also involved with the regulation of credit unions. The interweaving, often overlapping, scatter of regulatory responsibilities is shown in Table 8.2. This fragmentation of responsibility is a deterrent to consistent application of current law.[7]

Deposit institutions are also exposed to other risks: liquidity and political (called country-risk in the current terminology of international banking). Guaranteeing against liquidity risk has long been the responsibility of the central bank. But, liquidity risk interrelates with default and interest rate risk. The deposit insurance agencies cope primarily with these latter two risks. Consequently, both the central bank and the deposit insurance agencies become involved in guaranteeing the integrity of banks and thrifts. The resulting involvement of the central bank with the other regulatory and guaranteeing agencies is a subject of major disagreement in the Bush Commission, which is trying to rationalize the currently confusing overlapping of responsibilities. It is also the subject of ongoing research (Kanatas, 1984).

The Central Bank's Role in Promoting Safety.   At the outset of the discussion of bank safety and soundness, it was emphasized that their portfolio composition, heavily leveraged with immediately putable debt (meaning that demand depositors can demand their deposits immediately), exposed banks to liquidity risk as well as credit and interest rate risks. Kenneth Cone (1982) emphasizes and explores the implications of this peculiarity of depository institutions.

TABLE 8.2
DEPOSITORY INSTITUTIONS AND THEIR REGULATORS

	National Banks	State Member Banks	Insured Nonmember Banks (FDIC)	Uninsured Banks (Non-FDIC)
Chartering and Licensing	Comptroller	State Banking Dept.	State Banking Dept.	State Banking Dept.
Branching				
Intrastate	Comptroller	Federal Reserve State Banking Dept.	FDIC State Banking Dept.	State Banking Dept.
Interstate	[a]	[a]		
Mergers and Acquisitions				
Intrastate	Comptroller	Federal Reserve State Banking Dept.	FDIC State Banking Dept.	State Banking Dept.
Interstate	[b]	[b]	[b]	
Reserve Requirements [c]	Federal Reserve	Federal Reserve	Federal Reserve State Banking Dept.	Federal Reserve State Banking Dept.
Access to the Discount Window [d]	Federal Reserve	Federal Reserve	Federal Reserve	Federal Reserve
Interest Rate Ceilings on Deposits				
Rulemaking [e]	DIDC	DIDC	DIDC	State Banking Dept.
Enforcement	Comptroller	Federal Reserve	FDIC	State Banking Dept.
Deposit Insurance	FDIC	FDIC	FDIC[f]	None State Insurance Funds[g]
Supervision and Examination	Comptroller	Federal Reserve State Banking Dept.	FDIC State Banking Dept.	State Banking Dept.
Prudential Limits, Safety, and Soundness	Comptroller	Federal Reserve State Banking Dept.	FDIC State Banking Dept.	State Banking Dept.

Consumer Protection				
Rulemaking	Federal Reserve	Federal Reserve State Banking Dept.	Federal Reserve State Banking Dept.	Federal Reserve State Banking Dept.
Enforcement	Comptroller	Federal Reserve State Banking Dept.	FDIC State Banking Dept.	State Banking Dept. State Banking Dept.

[a] The McFadden Act, as amended in 1933, has prevented interstate branching by national banks and state member banks, but banks can offer various services on an interstate basis.

[b] Presently, the Garn–St Germain Act provides the statutory framework in which the FDIC and the FSLIC may arrange interstate and interindustry acquisition or mergers of closed or failing federally insured depository institutions. Details differ across type of institution. Furthermore, the legislation specified priorities, including the following, which the agencies must consider in arranging the mergers and acquisitions: "First, between depository institutions of the same type within the same state; Second, between depository institutions of the same type in different states; Third, between depository institutions of different types in the same state; and Fourth, between depository institutions of different types in different states." The authority to arrange interstate and interindustry mergers and acquisitions expires in 1985. Similar authority was also granted to the National Credit Union Administration with regard to credit unions.

[c] Under the Monetary Control Act of 1980, the Federal Reserve Board sets reserve requirements and promulgates reserve requirement regulations for nearly all depository institutions. The nearly uniform system of reserve requirements dictated by the Monetary Control Act will replace the reserve requirements, which varied; for example, the reserve requirement of state nonmembers varied across states and from the reserve requirements of member institutions. The new system of reserve requirements is being phased in. Until the phase-in is complete, the reserve requirement of many depository institutions will reflect the reserve requirements imposed by their State Banking Department as of March 1980. State Banking Departments set the reserve requirements for those depository institutions not subject to Federal Reserve reserve requirements.

[d] Nearly all depository institutions in the United States, including branches and agencies of foreign banks, have access to the discount window. These depository institutions are expected to make reasonable use of their usual sources of funds before turning to the Federal Reserve. These usual sources of funds include special industry lenders such as the Federal Home Loan Bank Board and the Central Liquidity Fund of the National Credit Union Administration.

[e] The Depository Institutions Deregulation Committee has the authority to establish classes of deposits and applicable interest rate ceilings at all federally insured depository institutions, except credit unions. DIDC is required to phase out interest rate ceilings by March 31, 1986.

[f] Deposits of up to $100,000 in federally chartered mutual savings banks are insured by the FSLIC. Deposits in state-chartered mutual savings banks are insured by the FDIC. However, under the Garn–St Germain Act, state-chartered savings banks that convert to federal charters may continue to have their deposits insured by the FDIC.

[g] Some deposits that are not insured by the FDIC are insured by state insurance funds.

TABLE 8.2 (*continued*)

	Savings Banks (Federal/State)	S&Ls (Federal/State)	Credit Unions (Federal/State)	Bank Holding Companies
Chartering and Licensing	FHLBB State Banking Dept.	FHLBB State Banking Dept.	NCUA State Banking Dept.	Federal Reserve
Branching				
Intrastate	FHLBB/FDIC State Banking Dept.	FHLBB/FDIC State Banking Dept.	[a]	
Interstate	[b]	[b]	[c]	
Mergers and Acquisitions				
Intrastate	FHLBB/FDIC State Banking Dept.	FHLBB/ FSLIC[d]	NCUA/ State Banking Dept.	Federal Reserve State Banking Dept.
Interstate	[d]	FHLBB/ State Banking Dept.	NCUA State Banking Dept.[d]	Federal Reserve State Banking Dept.[e]
Reserve Requirements	Federal Reserve State Banking Dept.[f]	Federal Reserve State Banking Dept.[f]	Federal Reserve State Banking Dept.[f]	[g]
Access to the Discount Window	Federal Reserve[h]	FHLBB Federal Reserve[h]	NCUA Federal Reserve[h]	[i]
Interest Rate Ceilings on Deposits				
Rulemaking	DIDC State Banking Dept.[j]	DIDC State Banking Dept.[j]	NCUA State Banking Dept.[k]	
Enforcement	FSLIC/FDIC State Banking Dept.	FSLIC State Banking Dept.	NCUA State Banking Dept.	
Deposit Insurance	FSLIC/FDIC State Insurance Funds[l]	FSLIC State Insurance Funds[m]	Credit Union Share Insurance Fund[n]	

Supervision and Examination	FHLBB/FDIC	State Banking Dept.°	FHLBB	State Banking Dept.	NCUA	State Banking Dept.	Federal Reserve
Prudential Limits, Safety, and Soundness	FHLBB/FDIC	State Banking Dept.	FHLBB	State Banking Dept.	NCUA	State Banking Dept.	Federal Reserve
Consumer Protection Rulemaking	Federal Reserve	State Banking Dept.	Federal Reserve	State Banking Dept.	Federal Reserve	State Banking Dept.	
Enforcement	FSLIC/FDIC	State Banking Dept.	FSLIC	State Banking Dept.	NCUA	State Banking Dept.	

[a] Federal credit unions are not required to receive approval from the National Credit Union Administration before opening a branch.

[b] As a matter of policy the Federal Home Loan Bank Board has prohibited interstate branching by federally chartered thrifts. Limited exceptions have been made in cases of failing institutions.

[c] Federal credit unions are not required to receive approval from the National Credit Union Administration before opening a branch.

[d] Presently, the Garn–St Germain Act provides the statutory framework in which the FDIC and the FSLIC may arrange interstate and interindustry acquisition or mergers of closed or failing federally insured depository institutions. Details differ across type of institution. Furthermore, the legislation specified priorities, including the following, which the agencies must consider in arranging the mergers and acquisitions: "First, between depository institutions of the same type within the same state; Second, between depository institutions of the same type in different states; Third, between depository institutions of different types in the same state; and Fourth, between depository institutions of different types in different states." The authority to arrange interstate and interindustry mergers and acquisitions expires in 1985. Similar authority was also granted to the National Credit Union Administration with regard to credit unions.

[e] The Douglass Amendment to the Bank Holding Act allows bank holding companies to acquire "banks" in other states if the state in which the bank to be acquired is situated has passed legislation that specially allows out-of-state holding companies to acquire in-state banks.

[f] Under the Monetary Control Act of 1980, the Federal Reserve Board sets reserve requirements and promulgates reserve requirement regulations for nearly all depository institutions. The nearly uniform system of reserve requirements dictated by the Monetary Control Act will replace the reserve requirements, which varied; for example, the reserve requirement of state nonmembers varied across states and from the reserve requirements of member institutions. The new system of reserve requirements is being phased in. Until the phase-in is complete, the reserve requirement of many depository institutions will reflect the reserve requirements imposed by their State Banking Department as of March 1980. State Banking Departments set the reserve requirements for those depository institutions not subject to Federal Reserve reserve requirements.

[g] Certain obligations of depository institution affiliates are regarded as reservable deposits of the depository institution.

[h] Nearly all depository institutions in the United States, including branches and agencies of foreign banks, have access to the discount window. These depository institutions are expected to make reasonable use of their usual sources of funds before turning to the Federal Reserve. These usual sources of funds include special industry lenders such as the Federal Home Loan Bank Board and the Central Liquidity Fund of the National Credit Union Administration.

TABLE 8.2 (continued)

[i] Bank subsidiaries of bank holding companies have access to the discount window.

[j] The Depository Institutions Deregulation Committee has the authority to establish classes of deposits and applicable interest rate ceilings at all federally insured depository institutions, except credit unions. DIDC is required to phase out interest rate ceilings by March 31, 1986.

[k] The National Credit Union Administration is authorized to set interest rate ceilings on deposits at federally insured credit unions through March of 1986. NCUA, however, has chosen not to exercise this authority. Interest rates at uninsured state-chartered credit unions, should they exist, are set by the State Banking Department.

[l] Deposits (up to $100,000) in federally chartered savings banks as well as in many state-chartered savings banks are insured by either the FDIC or the FSLIC. Some deposits in savings banks that are not insured by these federal agencies are insured by state insurance funds.

[m] Deposits (up to $100,000) in many state-chartered S&Ls as well as in all federally chartered S&Ls are insured by the FSLIC. Deposits in non–federally insured institutions may be insured by a state insurance fund.

[n] Shares (up to $100,000) in all federal credit unions are insured by the National Credit Union Share Insurance Fund, which is administered by the National Credit Union Administration. Shares in some state-chartered credit unions may be insured by a state insurance fund.

[o] The FDIC has the right to examine state-chartered savings banks that have converted to federal charter but whose deposits continue to be insured by the FDIC.

	Foreign Branches of U.S. Banks (Federal/State)	Edge Act (and Agreement) Corporations	International Banking Facilities	U.S. Branches and Agencies of Foreign Banks (Federal/State)
Chartering and Licensing	Federal Reserve, FDIC State Banking Dept.	Federal Reserve		Comptroller/ State Banking Dept.
Branching				
Intrastate		Federal Reserve		Comptroller/ State Banking Dept.[a]
Interstate		Federal Reserve		Comptroller/ State Banking Dept.[b]
Mergers and Acquisitions				
Intrastate		Federal Reserve		Comptroller/ Federal Reserve FDIC, State Banking Dept.[c]
Interstate		Federal Reserve		

Reserve Requirements	[d]	Federal Reserve[e]	[f]	Federal Reserve[e]
Access to the Discount Window				Federal Reserve[g]
Interest Rate Ceilings on Deposits				
Rulemaking	[h]	DIDC[i]	[j]	DIDC[i]
Enforcement		Federal Reserve	[k]	Comptroller/Federal Reserve; FDIC, State Banking Dept.
Deposit Insurance				FDIC[l]
Supervision and Examination	Comptroller, Federal Reserve; State Banking Dept.	Federal Reserve	Federal Reserve	Comptroller/Federal Reserve; FDIC, State Banking Dept.
Prudential Limits, Safety, and Soundness	Federal Reserve	Federal Reserve	Federal Reserve	Comptroller/Federal Reserve; FDIC, State Banking Dept.
Consumer Protection				
Rulemaking				Federal Reserve; State Banking Dept.
Enforcement				Federal Reserve; Comptroller/Federal Reserve; FDIC, State Banking Dept.

[a] Foreign banks with federal branches and agencies are subject to the within-state branching restrictions of the McFadden Act. The establishment of additional within-state branches or agencies by a foreign bank with state-license branches or agencies is regulated by state banking law.

TABLE 8.2 (*continued*)

[b] Foreign banks with state or federally licensed branches or agencies are not permitted to establish a federal or state branch or agency outside their home state unless (1) it is permitted by law in the state in which it will operate; and (2) in the case of a branch, it is agreed with the Federal Reserve that the non–home state branch will limit deposits to those permitted to Edge Corporations.

[c] The International Banking Act of 1978 specifies conditions under which foreign banks that have U.S. branches or agencies may merge in the United States.

[d] Deposits at foreign branches of U.S. banks that are payable only outside the United States are not subject to reserve requirements.

[e] Under the Monetary Control Act of 1980, the Federal Reserve Board sets reserve requirements and promulgates reserve requirement regulations for nearly all depository institutions. The nearly uniform system of reserve requirements dictated by the Monetary Control Act will replace the reserve requirements, which varied; for example, the reserve requirement of state nonmembers varied across states and from the reserve requirements of member institutions. The new system of reserve requirements is being phased in. Until the phase-in is complete, the reserve requirement of many depository institutions will reflect the reserve requirements imposed by their State Banking Department as of March 1980. State Banking Departments set the reserve requirements for those depository institutions not subject to Federal Reserve reserve requirements.

[f] By amendments to Regulation D (Reserve Requirements of Depository Institutions) deposits at international banking facilities satisfying the requirements of the regulation are exempted from reserve requirements.

[g] Nearly all depository institutions in the United States, including branches and agencies of foreign banks, have access to the discount window. These depository institutions are expected to make reasonable use of their usual sources of funds before turning to the Federal Reserve. These usual sources of funds include special industry lenders such as the Federal Home Loan Bank Board and the Central Liquidity Fund of the National Credit Union Administration.

[h] Interest rate ceilings do not apply to deposits of U.S. depository institutions payable outside the United States.

[i] The Depository Institutions Deregulation Committee has the authority to establish classes of deposits and applicable interest rate ceilings at all federally insured depository institutions, except credit unions. DIDC is required to phase out interest rate ceilings by March 31, 1986.

[j] Depository institutions have been exempted from interest rate ceilings on their IBF deposits.

[k] IBF deposits are exempt from interest rate ceilings.

[l] U.S. branches of foreign banks that accept retail deposits must subscribe to FDIC insurance.

SOURCE: Federal Reserve Bank of New York, 1984.

LEGEND
DIDC	Depository Institutions Deregulation Committee
FDIC	Federal Deposit Insurance Corporation
FHLBB	Federal Home Loan Bank Board
FSLIC	Federal Savings and Loan Insurance Corporation
IBF	International Banking Facilities
NCUA	National Credit Union Administration

The discussion, as originally written in early 1984 (before the writing of our section on "Market Discipline: Continental Illinois Bank and Trust Company"), largely ignored liquidity risk. The reason was that such domestic risk was considered to be under control. Nevertheless, the problems of Continental Illinois emphasize the fact that some important issues remain to be resolved in this context.

During the nineteenth century, it was judged that banks needed to be educated by regulation into correctly handling their exposure to liquidity risk. Reserve requirements were originally imposed to this end. Yet today, reserves are regarded principally as an instrument of monetary policy. No one doubts that depository institutions—when allowed to pay market rates on their liabilities—can handle their liquidity requirements in normal circumstances. In abnormal times, the central bank is trusted to act to avert runs on the banking system. It acts as the lender of last resort to any viable institution experiencing a liquidity crisis. Moreover, deposit insurance removes the prime incentive for a panic. In short, before the problems of Continental Illinois, it was felt that there was no longer any fear from this phenomenon; it had been conquered and no longer needed preventive regulation. But that complacency no longer exists. Uninsured deposits constitute an important source of funding for many, especially the large, banks, and they may be withdrawn rapidly. Consequently, it is becoming increasingly recognized that liquidity risk still remains relevant to the pricing of deposit guarantees, although it has not been included in most of the proposals for reform of the deposit insurance system. Research by George Kanatas (1984) is exceptional here. This work explicitly considers the appropriate pricing of liquidity risk together with default and interest rate risk.

The domestic liquidity responsibilities of central banks are internationally recognized. Nevertheless, concern still exists over the international responsibilities of central banks. Where loans are made and deposits are accepted across national boundaries, the question of which central bank should carry the lender-of-last-resort burden arises. This issue remains to be resolved during the second half of the decade.

INTERNATIONAL LOAN PROBLEMS

In the early 1980s, a new financial problem of major proportions emerged to occupy the attention of the policymakers. The growing difficulty that non-OPEC developing (particularly, Latin American) countries have experienced in servicing, let alone repaying, their large external debt has serious implications for the reform process in the United States for two reasons. First, the international debt problem has been acknowledged as extremely serious for the United States. Much of the borrowing by non-OPEC developing countries was from large banks, many of which are located in the United States. Table 8.3 illustrates the degree of risk exposure for U.S. banks. The concentration of risk exposure to Latin American countries is especially noticeable. The seriousness of the issue was stressed in early 1984 by Paul Volcker, chair of the Board of Governors of the Federal Reserve:

> The situation that emerged last year was unique in its scope and potential effects. It involved several major debtors at the same time, and threatened to spread to others, weak and strong alike. It is this potential for cascading liquidity pressures, undermining the stability of the financial system, that has demanded prompt and forceful action . . . to protect the economy . . . The international financial system is not separable from our domestic banking and credit system. The same institutions are involved in both markets . . . We are talking about dealing with a threat to the recovery, the jobs, and the prosperity of our own country, a threat essentially without parallel in the postwar period.[8]

This statement suggests that the international debt problem is perceived in the same light as the Great Depression in terms of its potential impact. There is considerable feeling that the international debt problem and the extreme risk exposure of U.S. banks has been partly the result of too much

TABLE 8.3
CLAIMS OF NINE LARGEST U.S. BANKS ON
NON-OPEC DEVELOPING COUNTRIES

	On All Countries			On Argentina, Brazil, and Mexico		
		As percentage of			As percentage of	
End of Period	$ Billions	Total Bank Assets	Total Bank Capital	$ Billions	Total Bank Assets	Total Bank Capital
1977	30.0	8.1	163	15.6	4.2	85
1978	33.4	7.9	176	16.4	3.9	82
1979	39.9	8.2	182	18.2	3.7	83
1980	47.9	9.0	199	22.7	4.3	95
1981	57.6	10.2	220	27.4	4.9	105
1982	64.1	10.9	221	31.3	5.3	108
1983	65.8	11.3	209	32.8	5.6	104

SOURCES: Board of Governors of the Federal Reserve (1983, 1984); Norman S. Fieleke (1983).
NOTE: Data are for domestic and foreign offices of the nine banking organizations and cover only cross-border and nonlocal currency lending.

emphasis on competition and that we should rethink the goals of deregulation and how they can be achieved while maintaining a safe and sound system. Others argue that unique forces produced the international debt problem and that the failure to clearly think through the reform process is at fault. Specifically, the lack of risk premiums in the present structure of deposit insurance encourages risk taking. If a risk-sensitive deposit insurance framework had been in place, many of the large U.S. banks would have been less willing to lend to the non-OPEC developing countries.

Whatever the outcome of this debate, one thing is clear. Policymakers have become more cautious in pursuing a more competitive environment. The international debt problem has made them more sensitive to the potential conflicts between efficiency and soundness, and, at the same time, the 1980 and 1982 acts have significantly reduced the most serious structural problems in the financial system.

The second implication for the reform process derives from the crisis orientation of reform in the United States. The international debt problem is certainly perceived as a world crisis that goes beyond adversely impacting only a few domestic economies. In fact, the *Wall Street Journal* of June 22, 1984, published a special five-page report entitled "World Debt in Crisis." This much attention devoted to one issue at one time is unusual for the *Journal*. As the crisis impacts the U.S. financial system, policymakers will react. It is reasonable to expect that policymakers and legislators will reduce their enthusiasm for removing more competitive constraints on the financial system. It is more likely that the concern with soundness will induce re-regulation to limit the risk exposure of depository institutions, especially banks, to all types of lending. Deposit insurance will be the focus of much of this effort as well as other types of portfolio constraints. The specifics of future financial reforms are uncertain; however, the remainder of this decade will continue to witness significant change in the financial system and the conduct of monetary policy.

In short, this promotion of the safety and soundness of the financial system remains an issue of continuing importance. It required government promotion following the Great Depression, and it continues to require encouragement today. The severe externalities arising from a breakdown of the financial system make its avoidance imperative. However, the acceptable ways of promoting safety and soundness differ in this decade from those established five decades earlier. Changing the methods to achieve these long-term ends demands continuing financial reform.

PREVENTING MONOPOLY

Other goals have prompted other regulations. By and large, these other goals are subsidiary to the goal of safety and soundness, as discussed at length above. These other laws and regulations established earlier in this century resulted from desires to restrain monopoly and to protect the consumer.

During the 1950s and the 1960s laws were passed and regulations were established that limited the aggrandizement of banking powers.[9] It is possible that the prohibition of interstate banking, which originated in an earlier period and was formalized in the McFadden Act of 1927, is also a manifestation of the fear of conglomerate bank power. However, the U.S. tradition of preserving state's rights and separate identities is also a factor that has inhibited explicit permission for interstate banking.

These considerations led to stringent regulations concerning the entry, exit, branching, merger, and the formation of a holding company by commercial banks. Typically, until the 1980s, regulatory permission was needed, and was often difficult to obtain, in order to establish a new bank or thrift. The restrictions on entry have more recently been criticized as manifestations of the regulatory-capture theory. New entrants were excluded by the regulators in order to preserve the property rights of existing institutions. However, as the new decade began, the regulators, particularly the Comptroller of the Currency (which charters national banks), relaxed the regulations on entry. Entry is now relatively easy, once requirements to insure viability are met. Safety, rather than turf protection, is now recognized to be the primary objective.

Nevertheless, further relaxations of the antimonopoly regulations can be made. Restrictions, even prohibitions, on bank branching are still common, particularly in the Midwest. Federal Reserve Banks, which are involved in evaluating merger applications by holding companies, still consider the proposed merger's potential effects on competition. Market shares are currently used as the principal evidence of concentration. Practice among Federal Reserve Banks differs as to what determines a market. Some consider only the competition among, and the market shares of, banks in a given market area. Geographical market area may also be defined narrowly or broadly. Narrow interpretations make it more likely that an application will be denied. Other Reserve Banks define the market region more broadly and include thrifts in the calculation of market shares. These practices make merger approval more likely. Indeed, in very recent months the practice has been to approve merger applications. Only one application was denied on competitive grounds during 1983. But this represents a significant change in approach. Moreover, the procedures used still tend to discourage merger applications, even when mergers may be rational.[10]

The need for change in policy with regard to preserving competition is particularly urgent when we consider the lessons of the recent theoretical developments in the area of contestable markets (Bailey and Panzar, 1980; Bailey, 1981). This work emphasizes that the potential for competition, equally with the current existence of competition, restrains anticompetitive behavior. Entry into the banking and thrift industries is now more readily available now that bank and thrift charters are being more readily granted. The potential competition from incipient depository institutions, together with the relaxation of barriers that previously segmented depository institutions, make the theory of contestable markets as applicable to the financial services industry as it is to transport, communications, and other industries.

These considerations should serve, in future legislation, to break down the barriers that exist on interstate deposit-taking and other activities. That these are now broadly breached in practice (Whitehead, 1983a, 1983b; Federal Reserve Bank of Atlanta, 1983) is not really the issue. Laws that are widely broken bring disrepute to other more justifiable laws. And the disregarded laws give rise to inefficiencies, if only in the efforts involved to circumvent them.

CONSUMER PROTECTION

Several laws were passed during the late 1960s and the 1970s that aimed to protect the consumer from overpaying for services or from being denied services supplied in a discriminating fashion. Truth-in-lending, anti-redlining, and other laws, described Carter H. Golembe and David S. Holland (1984), were enacted. It is not clear at the time of this writing in early 1984, what is the trend regarding consumer protection laws. Some consumer advocates are recommending further enactments. For example, at the beginning of 1984, several congressmen are pressing for restrictions on bank service charges. At the same time, the regulators, particularly the Comptroller of the Currency, have been taking a more permissive stance on such issues. The Comptroller, for example, initially claimed federal preemption of state-imposed restrictions on bank service charges. In mid-1984, however, he moderated his stand. In the meantime, some congressmen are pressing for inexpensive, "lifeline" banking services.

Moreover, it should be recognized that there are rational, economic reasons why service charges have been increasing in recent years. When interest rate ceilings suppressed depositors' earnings, banks and thrifts rewarded their depositors with implicit interest, often conveyed as free or low-cost services. Now that interest rates are substantially deregulated, depository institutions do not need to pay implicit interest and must "unbundle" their pricing in order to remain efficiently profitable.

Congress and the consumer lobby are also currently pressing banks and thrifts to accelerate their processes of clearing consumer checks. Some put arbitrarily long "holds" on deposited checks, at a time when technology and revised Federal Reserve practice has significantly accelerated the process of check clearing. In this instance, some depository institutions are placing implicit charges on depositors. This runs counter to the trend toward explicit, unbundled, pricing. Whether competition or legislation is the best remedy for this ill, however, is debatable.

In short, at the time of this writing in early 1984, it is not clear which force—that toward deregulation or that toward greater regulation—will prevail during the remainder of the 1980s in the area of consumer protection.

ISSUES REMAINING IN MONETARY POLICY

In regard to monetary policy, issues remain to be resolved at all levels: conceptual, theoretical, empirical, and practical. The role of monetary policy is still being debated. The goals of monetary policy are contested. The best intermediate target for use in the conduct of monetary policy is not indisputably recognized. Federal Reserve operating procedures are in transition.

THE CENTRAL BANK'S ROLE IN MONETARY POLICY

Classical monetary theorists have long contended that money is neutral. In this case, the sole legitimate responsibility for monetary policy is control of the price level. Even though the Federal Reserve has lately given prime emphasis to combating inflation, it typically acts as if it has wider responsibilities and the power to influence the real economy. Such actions also run counter to the more extreme manifestations of rational expectations theory, which imply that deliberate, anticipated policy is ineffective. These implications are largely ignored by the U.S. central bank and are disputed by some academic economists (Mishkin, 1982).

INTERMEDIATE TARGETS

The Federal Reserve typically describes itself as pursuing an intermediate targeting approach. Nevertheless, during 1983, the FOMC appeared to be gearing its actions directly to the behavior of the final economy. In fall 1982, Federal Reserve Chairman Volcker stated that M1, the previous target, was at least temporarily a potentially misleading indicator because of inflows into money market deposit and SNOW accounts and outflows from expiring All-Savers certificates. Congress considered legislating an alternative target.

M1. None of the potential intermediate targets is ideal. M1 typically excludes financial innovations that originate in the private sector. Market-sector financial innovations are usually close money substitutes—quasi-money—rather than true money. Consequently, they are excluded from M1, although they may alter the relationship of M1 to the final economy. The question whether the relationship of money to the final economy has been disrupted by financial innovations has been discussed at length most recently by John P. Judd and John L. Scadding (1982a). RPs and MMMFs have been found responsible for the well-researched downward shift in the money demand function in 1974–1975.

More recently, the sharp decline in velocity during 1982 has again caused concern about the relevance of M1 for GNP. Some have argued that the decline results from the severity of the recession. However, it seems more likely that, once again, financial innovation may be responsible for the disruption in the relationship between money and nominal GNP.

Two regulatory innovations—NOW and SNOW accounts—have grown rapidly since NOWs first became available nationwide in January 1981 as a result of DIDMCA. Consequently, the data series (other checkable deposits) has grown rapidly. Other checkables were valued at $20.9 billion at the end of December 1980; three years later they had reached $128.8 billion. During the same period, demand deposits had fallen in value from $266.8 billion to $239.8 billion. The growth of other checkable accounts has disrupted the regular upward trend in velocity because their rate of turnover is much lower than that of demand deposits.

Table 8.4 shows that the turnover of other checkable deposits was only one-twenty-seventh that of demand deposits at the end of 1983. The turnover of demand deposits has been rising concomitantly with the growth of other checkable deposits. This is an expected result of the public's portfolio readjustment among its transactions accounts. Those components that pay zero interest—demand deposits—are used for the most mobile of funds, while those that are less mobile are allowed to earn 5.25 percent as NOWs or market-determined rates as SNOWs.

TABLE 8.4
TURNOVER RATES
(NOT SEASONALLY ADJUSTED)

	December 1980	December 1981	December 1982	November 1983
Demand Deposits	202.8	286.1	325.0	381.7
ATS–NOW Accounts	9.7	14.0	14.3	14.0
MMDAs	0	0	0	2.8
Savings Deposits	3.6	4.1	4.5	4.8

SOURCE: Board of Governors of the *Federal Reserve Bulletin*, January 1984, Table A14.

These considerations have led to the suggestion that the money aggregates be measured as an index number, which reflects their differences in turnover rates. Paul Spindt (1983) has constructed such an index. His work aims to be an empirical implementation of the M in the income version of the quantity theory of money:

$$MV = PY. \tag{8.1}$$

Here M is the money stock, V is velocity, P is the price level, and Y is real GNP. All of these variables need to be estimated in index-numbers form for consistency. The behavior of M_Q—the turnover weighted monetary index— shows that its velocity slowed during 1982, as is common during recessions. Its velocity did not fall sharply, as did that for the unweighted M1 measure of money.

Thus, using M1 as the basis of monetary policy has potentially severe problems that result from financial innovations, both market and regulatory. Nevertheless, these problems can be alleviated by monitoring the behavior of Spindt's M_Q series. This series illuminates those occasions when M1 velocity is aberrant. Then, knowing this, the Federal Reserve can react accordingly.

The Broader Aggregates. If M1's behavior is disrupted by financial in-novation, it might be thought that using a broader money aggregate, M2 or M3 (which include the innovations), would compensate for M1's problems. In-deed, the Federal Reserve said in fall 1982 that it would pay more attention to the broader aggregate in the following months. However, there are also problems in using M2. One problem is a practical one. The FOMC monitors short-term movements in money growth, despite its admonition to the mar-kets to disregard short-term variability. Data on several M2 series are available only monthly, not weekly, as is the case for M1.

The second problem is more fundamental. M2 is not conceptually clear in its composition. It includes both money and money substitutes. That is, it consists of numerous nonhomogeneous components. Ross Starr (1982) has shown that M2 behaves procyclically. Because some important components, such as MMMFs and RPs (and now also MMDAs), pay market rates, their volumes grow when market interest rates rise. Increases in these series, during the late 1970s and early 1980s, were large enough to cause the growth of M2 to accelerate when market interest rates rose.

This put policy in the Alice-in-Wonderland world where the FOMC tightened policy by restricting the supply of nonborrowed reserves only to have M2 rise. As Figure 7.6 shows, constraining reserves raises the federal funds rate and other market interest rates. In the figure, this reduces the stock of money as the public moves down its demand curve. But for M2 this relationship does not hold. Instead there is a bizarre result: tightening policy to raise market interest rates increases the stock of M2. Conversely, when market rates fall, so will the growth rate of M2.

Moreover, the growth rate of M2 has been shown to have been raised by the unprecedented popularity of MMDAs (Garcia and McMahon, 1984). Consequently, its use as an intermediate target was subject to severe problems even during 1983, when interest rates were relatively stable in comparison with those observed in the late 1970s and early 1980s.

There are also potential problems with the use of M3 as an intermediate target. M3 is even more of a conceptual mishmash than M2. Moreover, it is subject to the same aberrant behavior as is M2 when rates rise. On the other hand, it was only marginally affected by the new accounts during 1983. The new accounts drew money from consumer savings and time deposits, from MMMFs, and, importantly, reduced bank (but not thrift) reliance on large CDs. These substitutions largely canceled out in their net effects on M3.

A Credit Aggregate.   Benjamin Friedman (1982) strongly advocated the use of total domestic nonfinancial debt as an intermediate target. This advocacy is subject to several criticisms, however. First, although Franco Modigliani and Lucas D. Papademos (1980) have presented a model of transmission mechanism for bank credit, credit is fungible. Consequently, bank credit is too restrictive a concept. This has been recognized in the extension of Federal Reserve authority via reserve requirements to all depository institutions under the 1980 act. But no theoretical model is available that describes the transmission mechanism for the broader credit variable that Friedman advocates. In order to exercise precise control over a credit aggregate, instead of a money variable, reserve requirements would need to be reconstituted to directly determine credit, rather than money. The Federal Reserve does not currently have the authority to undertake this revision. The Monetary Control Act gives the central bank power to require reserves for transaction accounts and a limited set of managed liabilities. Finally, Edward K. Offenbacher and Richard D. Porter (1983) have shown that the vector autoregression analysis, used by Friedman to demonstrate the empirical superiority of the credit variable, does not produce robust results. The M1 monetary aggregate is shown to be equally good, if not better than a credit aggregate.

Interest Rates.   Interest rates are frequently advocated as appropriate intermediate targets. It is frequently claimed, with more than a little justification, that the monetary authority in the United States still *de facto* uses nominal interest rates as its principal policy instrument and target. However, nominal rates were rejected in 1979 because policy based on interest rates is particularly subject to political pressure—pressure against increasing rates in order to reduce inflation.

Moreover, it is real rates that influence private spending on consumption and investment goods, aggregate demand, and real GNP. Consequently, some have advised Congress that the central bank be required to monitor real rates. However, there are several potential real rates available. Different estimates use different deflators, different time horizons, and different methods of representing expectations (for it is anticipated, not historical rates, that influence behavior). Christine Cumming and Cathy Miners (1982) have shown that several different measures of the real rate are not closely correlated, giving rise to markedly different policy prescriptions. Moreover, Owen F. Irvine, Jr. (1983), has shown that markedly different real rates are appropriate to production decisions made in different industries. Consequently, it is not clear what is the real rate nor which of numerous operationalizations should be used in monetary policy.

In any event, to this time of writing, the Congress has not passed legislation to change the intermediate target. Since the summer of 1982, the Federal Reserve has set its policy stance in the light of developments in both the real and the financial sectors. However, the passing of two problems—the disruptive effects of the recent financial innovations on the path of M1 and the puzzling steepness of the decline in velocity during 1982 and 1983—suggests that the case for reverting to M1 as the pre-eminent target is strengthening. Even so, a reinstatement would be cautious because interest rate deregulation is spreading to transactions accounts and the implications for the growth path of M1 are not well understood.

OPERATING PROCEDURES

At the time of this writing (early 1984), the conversion to almost contemporaneous reserve accounting has recently been made. The change introduces an extra element of uncertainty into monetary policy operations. Is the Federal Reserve being lenient during February and March 1984 in its willingness to accommodate the demand for reserves in order to facilitate the change? Will the FOMC later tighten to redress any earlier accommodation? How will the banking system react to the change?

Early evidence suggests that financial institutions are indeed, as expected, increasing their demand for excess reserves. The financial system began the adjustment to CRA by moving from a position of net borrowed to positive net free reserves. If this response is more than transitional, then the relationship of nonborrowed and borrowed reserves to interest rates and to the money stock will change. The Federal Reserve will need time to assess the extent of these changes. Substantial new adaptations of operating procedures may then transpire.

THE TRANSMISSION MECHANISM IN
A DEREGULATED ENVIRONMENT

Much of the 1960s–1970s modeling of the transmission of monetary policy is based on a quantity-constrained approach to monetary policy. The elasticity of the supply of funds with respect to interest rates was reduced by Regulation Q. In that world, a large budget deficit, such as that shown in Figure 8.2, could conflict with private capital market demands. Then, it would lead either to credit rationing or to high interest rates. High rates would be needed to allocate an inflexible supply of funds. However, where savers can earn market rates, the supply of loanable funds is not fixed; the supply can respond to increases in interest rates brought about by the government's demand for funds. Pressure on rates will cause consumers to forgo consumption and to increase savings. Interest rates will not need to rise so far to achieve equilibrium in this deregulated environment. Moreover, the importation of foreign capital will serve to keep interest rates below those in a closed economy.

This is just one example of the differences in the behavior of a deregulated and of a regulated macroeconomy. Much further research is needed in order to understand the operation of the interest-rate-deregulated world of the 1980s. Many old preconceptions, including those concerning the problems of budget deficits, need to be reconsidered.

Further elimination of quantity restrictions and their replacement by price stimuli will demand yet further analysis. For example, the historical configuration of reserve requirements may be changed later in this decade.

Reserve Requirement Reform. Reserve requirements act like a tax. High reserve requirements increase the accuracy of monetary control, but they also provide greater incentives for financial innovations. Financial innovation reduces the relevance of money for the control of GNP. That is, there is a trade-off between precision in the two phases of monetary policy inherent in the intermediate targeting approach. The trade-off results from the tax implications of reserve requirements. Consequently, three kinds of proposals have been made to reduce the taxation element of reserve requirements.

One suggestion, the least extreme of the proposals, is that the Federal Reserve should pay some rate of return (influenced by, but below, market rates) on required reserves. This would increase Federal Reserve costs and reduce its net earnings so that the value of Federal Reserve profits that are transmitted to the Treasury Department would decline. Despite its political

FIGURE 8.2
FEDERAL EXPENDITURES AND RECEIPTS

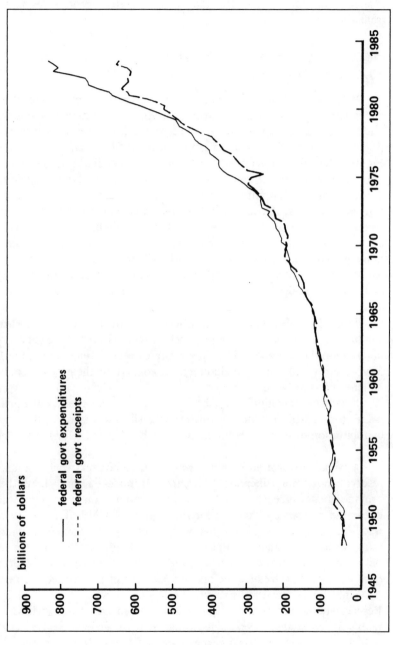

billions of dollars

——— federal govt expenditures
- - - federal govt receipts

disadvantage, this suggestion is likely to receive active consideration once the transitional period for contemporaneous reserve accounting is over.

A more innovative proposal is that of George Kanatas and Stuart I. Greenbaum (1982). Currently, the Federal Reserve executes policy by creating a demand for reserves via legally enforced reserve requirements. Then, it determines the price of reserves—the federal funds rate—through adjusting the reserve supply. Kanatas and Greenbaum examine an alternative world where the Federal Reserve would continue to control the supply of reserves, but would influence the demand for reserves via an alternative mechanism. The Federal Reserve would pay interest on whatever reserves depository institutions choose to hold voluntarily. By varying the rates payable on reserves, the central bank can influence the level of reserves held. The relative pressures from the demand for, and supply of, reserves determines the federal funds rate. In turn, the federal funds rate influences the demand for money and the supply of loans. The effects of these two variables transmit to the real economy. The authors argue that such an approach would reduce incentives to invent new financial instruments. This reduction would decrease the variability in the broader (innovation-including) money aggregates. However, it would not necessarily reduce variability in interest rates.

Robert Laurent (1981) has a third innovative proposal. He also remarks on the reserve-tax incentives to financial innovation. He points out that deposit insurance contributions are made voluntarily and suggests that risk-graduated reserve requirements be substituted for insurance premia. The combined system would provide money control, guarantee deposits, and remove the element of taxation from reserve-holding. Monetary control would be enhanced by simultaneously moving to a system of reverse-lag reserve accounting. That is, depository institutions would be allowed to supply deposits and make loans based on the level of reserves held two weeks earlier.

CONCLUSION

The financial system is currently (early 1984) undergoing a fundamental reconfiguration. Many old regulations have been removed and the finance system is adapting to the new environment. The removal of Regulation Q has wide implications, and not all of them have been recognized. Further theoretical and empirical work is needed.

Other financial reforms are in progress. Many quantity restrictions, imposed on portfolios in the 1930s, are being removed from depository institutions. Their removal should increase the efficiency and profitability of the financial system. But their removal can also expose institutions to greater variability in profits, that is, to greater risk. This factor must to be taken into consideration in the future reform of the deposit insurance system. Old barriers to the geographic expansion of bank and thrift activities are crumbling. Congress should recognize the reality of the present situation by enacting new laws. The McFadden Act restrictions need to be repealed; they are an anachronism.

Greater consideration needs to be given before the long-standing separation of banking and commerce is removed. Safety and soundness still need to be guaranteed. Yet scope economies are putting irresistible pressures on the old barriers between industries. It may be that safety can be assured by a reformed system of deposit guarantee — one that allows further mutual incursions between banking and commerce. But the path to reach that goal is not yet clearly illuminated.

On the other hand, it appears that many restrictions in banking that were imposed to thwart monopoly may now be relaxed. Now that entry into the banking and thrift industry is open, the new theory of contestable markets shows that potential, not just actual, competition can produce benefits of competition. Moreover, reduced compartmentalization among depository institutions brings greater competition. Finally, competition, together with the greater access to information that new technology is bringing, may prove to be better guardians of the consumer interests than are present laws and regulations.

In short, great strides toward financial reform have already been made in this decade. But many more steps remain to be taken. The form that future legislation will take is not clear. The chairman of the Senate Banking Committee, Senator Jake Garn, favors further deregulation, whereas the chairman of the House Committee, Congressman Fernand St Germain, is considering reversing the recent deregulatory tide. Nevertheless, further legislation is expected. As is typical of financial reform in the United States, it will probably occur in response to one or other of the impending crises. Both the banking and thrift industries are exposed to greater risks in the 1980s than at any other time during the past fifty years. Congress will need to address these problems wisely if the financial system is to function optimally during the remainder of this century.

Moreover, the Federal Reserve will need to continue the judicious policy it has pursued during the 1980s because the evolving structure of the financial system will also continue to raise new and serious problems for the achievement of prosperous but noninflationary money and credit growth.

NOTES

CHAPTER 1

1. The use of regulator or regulatory reform is meant to describe a broad range of legislative and nonlegislative actions by government or government agencies, primarily at the federal level, to change the structure of the financial system or monetary authority.

2. The most important financial instruments were NOW (negotiable order of withdrawal) accounts, repurchase agreements, bank holding company–related commercial paper, Eurodollar deposits, and MMMFs (Money Market Mutual Funds). See Glossary for clarification of these and other important terms and concepts in this study.

3. The term *thrift* currently refers collectively to savings and loan associations (S&Ls) and mutual savings banks because, at one time, they relied on savings deposits as their major source of funds and they allocate a major portion of their uses of funds to mortgages. Credit unions have on occasion also been referred to as thrifts, although they contribute little to the flow of mortgage credit. In any event, the term is not entirely accurate since S&Ls, (mutual) savings banks, and credit unions rely as much on transaction deposits in the current environment as they used to rely on savings deposits.

CHAPTER 2

1. Although less recognized for his work on the relationship between changes in the money supply and economic activity, Warburton's contributions are important (Warburton, 1966; and Cargill, 1979 and 1981) and, in several important respects, parallel those of Friedman and Schwartz.

2. The following brief summary of regulatory approaches has been drawn from Mackay and Reid (1979).

3. David Stockman, director of the Office of Management and Budget under the Reagan administration, described on a practical level in 1981 the influence of special interest groups in formulating the budget (Greider, 1981).

CHAPTER 3

1. In 1811, there were 88 state-chartered banks; however, by 1816, the number had increased to 246 (U.S. Department of Commerce, 1975, p. 1018).

2. The most notable were the Deposit Act of 1836, the Specie Circular of 1836, and the establishment of the Independent Treasury in 1840. The Deposit Act required federal deposits in state banks to be less than three-fourths of the bank's capital; the Specie Circular was an executive order that required payment in only specie or Virginia land scrip for public land; and the Independent Treasury was an attempt to reduce the federal government's reliance on state banks as fiscal agents. The Independent Treasury never achieved the objective of separating the federal government's fiscal activities from private banks. It was not very significant in the financial system and officially ceased to exist in 1920.

3. The political debate over the McFadden Act is briefly but well summarized by Verle B. Johnston (1983). Carter H. Golembe and David S. Holland (1983) provide a comprehensive discussion of federal banking regulation.

CHAPTER 4

1. Thomas Mayer (1968) provides a useful summary of these antimonetary policy views. In addition, Thomas F. Cargill (1983, Chapter 18) provides a technical discussion of these views.

2. The Fisherian mechanism refers to the relationship between market interest rates and anticipated inflation expressed by Irving Fisher at the turn of the century. The relationship is based on the notion that the market rate of interest is equal to a real interest rate (unobservable) and anticipated inflation. Since market participants are interested in real rates of return, market interest rates are adjusted to incorporate anticipated price changes. For more discussion of this relationship, see James C. Van Horne (1984) and for a recent empirical study of the relationship, see Thomas F. Cargill and Robert A. Meyer (1980).

CHAPTER 5

1. The most notable efforts at financial reform include those in Australia, Canada, France, Germany, Italy, Japan, Sweden, Switzerland, and the United Kingdom.

Hang-Sheng Cheng (1983) has summarized the reforms in Australia and New Zealand; Charles Pigott (1983) and Dorothy Cristelow (1981) have provided analyses of the reforms in Japan: and David H. Howard and Karen H. Johnson (1982) have provided an overview of financial reform in a number of countries, with special attention directed toward the experiences of Canada and the United Kingdom. Charles Freedman (1982) discusses recent reforms in Canada. The financial system in Italy is discussed by Mario Monti, Francesco Cesarini, and Carlo Scognamiglio (1983).

2. The summary of the 1982 act is drawn partly from material in Cargill and Garcia (1983), Garcia et al., (1983), and the Federal Reserve Bank of Chicago (1983).

CHAPTER 6

1. However, the advent and spread nationwide of credit lines (derived from second mortgages offered by brokerage houses) could lead to the creation of such data bases. The establishment of these services demands not only the assessment of the potential borrowers' creditworthiness, but also the valuation of the properties to be mortgaged.

2. S&L deposit levels, seasonally adjusted, have experienced declines from one month to another on eight occasions since the imposition of Regulation Q in September 1966. Deposit levels declined in April and July 1966, before the extension of Regulation Q, and in July 1969, January 1970, June, July, and August 1981, October 1982, and May and September 1983. These last two occurrences followed the introduction of the money market deposit account, which substantially increased S&L deposit levels. These recent events illustrate one of the serious shortcomings of using monthly declines to measure disintermediation.

3. Average liability costs decline from $t = 0$ to $t = 1$, and then rise again to new higher levels. If S&L management can successfully predict interest rate movements, and if the demand for mortgages at time $t = 0$ is sufficiently strong, the S&L can set the mortgage rate high enough to ensure that the area of the vertically shaded area in Figure 6.5 exceeds that of the sum of the areas of the two horizontally shaded areas. The vertically shaded area needs to exceed the area above the unprofitable periods by a margin sufficient to cover other costs of operation and to allow a measure of profit. Then the S&L will be profitable over this cycle.

4. Passbook savings deposits constituted 88.3 percent of total S&L deposits in October 1966 (the month after Regulation Q was imposed). By September 1982 this percentage had fallen to 16.8 percent.

5. The FSLIC closed three associations in 1940 and four in 1941. In contrast, the FDIC reports that 564 commercial banks failed prior to 1960.

6. In contrast, the number of banks has increased over the period, and so has the number of branches, which rose monotonically through 1981. It declined, however, in 1982, as did the number of offices per bank, which rose from 1.79 in 1960 to 3.74 in 1981. The decline observed in 1982 came, no doubt, in response to interest rate deregulation.

CHAPTER 7

1. Some macroeconomists (Gordon, 1982) point out that those policies to eliminate inflation that is caused by supply shocks will exacerbate the GNP downturn that is
caused by the supply shocks. Moreover, Gordon denies that inflation (measured by the
GNP deflator) was "out of hand" during the 1970s.

2. Thygerson (1983) discusses the weakening in the 1980s of the social contract
with the housing industry.

3. Charles Goodhart (1984) of the Bank of England has coined a law to describe
this process. Goodhart's law says that as the central bank acts to control an intermediate
target, its relationship to the final economy may, at worst, break down and, at best,
will change.

4. M2 consists of M1 plus most MMMFs (general purpose and broker-dealer
funds), MMDAs, savings and small denomination time deposits at all depository
institutions, overnight and continuing contract repurchase agreements at commercial
banks, and overnight Eurodollars issued to U.S. residents by foreign branches of U.S.
banks worldwide. For M3 and other monetary measures, see Glossary.

5. Robert Clower distinguishes between transactions media, which include credit
card lines of credit for households as well as trade credit lines for business, and
"settlement balances." M1 provides settlement balances for the public, whereas reserves are so used by banks.

6. The minimum balance requirements on MMDAs and SNOWs were set by the
DIDC and are being phased-out by the committee.

7. The incentive to innovate will not cease entirely, however. Technological
advances seem to suggest that instrument innovation will continue, but possibly at a
slower rate.

8. Angelo Mascaro and Allan H. Meltzer (1983) argue that monetary volatility
increased both short-term and long-term interest rates. As such it depressed economic
activity.

9. Paul Volcker (1983) provides the rationale for the change in operating procedures in the fall of 1982.

10. It should be noted that Poole (1982) argues that the Federal Reserve has, in fact,
been using a borrowed reserve target ever since October 1979. Poole argues that the
FOMC uses in equation 7.2 an average weekly interperiod forecast level of borrowing
and then adjusts the nonborrowed reserve supply to effect this average level for
borrowed reserves.

11. The FOMC meets 8 times a year. Typically, meetings are held monthly, but
some intermeeting periods are longer.

12. Weekly averages of daily float data are used because, until February 1984, the
week was the period over which reserve levels were calculated and maintained.

13. One argument expressed against the use of a penalty discount rate is that it
would increase the volatility (especially on the up-side) of the federal funds rate.

14. Jacob Grossman (1981, p. 415, footnote 9) has shown that the correlation coefficient between initial and final revisions of the monetary data is insignificantly different from zero. The authors thank Vance Roley for this citation.

15. Other authors have stressed the Federal Reserve's insulation from political pressure and have objected to that insulation. Keith Acheson and John F. Chant (1973), for example, criticize the Federal Reserve for operating as a bureaucracy pursuing its own aggrandizement. Milton Friedman (1962) has suggested that the Federal Reserve be made a subdivision of the Treasury Department. James Pierce (1978) and Robert Weintraub (1978) have argued for increasing the Federal Reserve's political accountability through greater congressional supervision.

CHAPTER 8

1. Empirical research on the inefficiencies of regulation has concentrated on regulatory problems one by one. This is particularly relevant in the research on the ill effects of Regulation Q.

2. Imagine two financial instruments: loans to housing and loans to manufacturing industry. Begin from an initially unregulated, perfectly competitive, optimal world. Then, suppose loans to manufacturing are taxed at a given rate. The tax proceeds are costlessly distributed as supplements to income. The tax will cause a suboptimal reallocation of resources. Suppose, next, that an equivalent tax is imposed on housing loans and the tax proceeds are costlessly distributed as negative income taxes. The misallocation is corrected and the optimal allocation of funds is re-established. A partial deregulation from this position will then prove detrimental to the optimal allocation of credit. However, a complete deregulation will be optimal.

3. As might be anticipated, stock associations are shown here to be more aggressive in seeking profit-generating diversification than are mutual associations. This is true regardless of whether the mutual associations have state or federal charters.

4. The Garn–St Germain Act gave depository institutions wide powers to change their charters. Consequently, during 1983 numerous S&Ls switched to savings bank designation. In October 1982, when the Garn–St Germain Act was passed, there were 3,387 S&Ls. This figure had fallen to 3,047 by December 1983. On the other hand, there were only 6 FSLIC-insured savings banks in December 1982. This figure had risen to 137 by December 1983. Thus, the thrift data for 1983 cover the experience of both S&Ls and savings banks.

5. Papers by Gerald D. Bierwag and George G. Kaufman (1983), Paul M. Horovitz (1983), Edward J. Kane (1983b), and Tim S. Campbell and David Glenn (1984) offer valuable discussions of, and viewpoints on, the reform of the deposit insurance system.

6. In this context "closure" need not imply the physical closing of the failed institution. The guaranteeing agency can sell the assets of the failing institutions and change its management without closing its doors.

7. Some have argued that the differences of implementation of the law among

regulators—regulatory competition—provides a healthy outlet for frustrations among the regulated and an avenue to financial reform (Kane, 1983c).

8. This statement is from Paul Volcker's testimony before the Committee on Banking, Finance and Urban Affairs, U.S. House of Representatives, February 2, 1984; quoted in Fieleke (1983).

9. Some relevant acts are the Bank Holding Company Acts of 1956, 1966, and 1970, and the Bank Merger Act of 1966 and their amendments.

10. For recent evidence on the economies of scale among depository institutions, see George J. Benston, Allen N. Berger, Gerald A. Hanweck, and David B. Humphrey (1983).

GLOSSARY

Adjustable Rate Mortgages (ARMs). Mortgages whose interest rates change in line with market interest rates. Also called variable rate mortgages (VRMs).

Automatic Transfer Service (ATS) Account. A savings account that provides transfers of funds into checking-type accounts under certain prearranged conditions.

Bank holding company. A separate company that holds a minimum number of shares in one or several banks. Bank holding companies also hold shares in nonbank businesses that are "closely related" to banking.

Bank Holding Company Act of 1956 and 1970 amendments. Legislation that established federal regulation through the Board of Governors of the Federal Reserve System over bank holding company activities.

Banking collapse during the 1930s. The period from late 1930 until March 1933 when almost 10,000 banks failed because of attempts of depositors to convert deposits into currency.

Bank Merger Act of 1960 and 1966 amendments. Requires federal regulators to consider the competitive implications of bank mergers and other acquisition activities in the banking system.

Bank notes. The major form of currency and bank lending prior to the 1880s. Bank notes were debt obligations of the issuing bank and circulated as the nation's medium of exchange.

Bank of the United States, First (1791–1811).   A quasi-public commercial bank that provided fiscal agent services to the federal government as well as some central banking services to the private financial system.

Bank of the United States, Second (1816–1832).   Functioned much like the First U.S. Bank and was notable for the famous "bank war" between Nicolas Biddle, the Bank president, and Andrew Jackson, president of the United States.

Board of Governors of the Federal Reserve System (the Board).   A seven-member group that (together with five of the presidents of the Reserve Banks) for all practical purposes is responsible for the formulation and execution of monetary policy in the United States.

Borrowed reserves.   Legislation and the Federal Reserve require banks and thrifts to hold reserves in the form of cash or deposits at Federal Reserve Banks. When a bank has insufficient reserves, it can purchase them in the inter-bank federal funds market or borrow them, in appropriate circumstances, from the Federal Reserve System.

Certificates of Deposit (large CD).   Large ($100,000 or more) negotiable certificate sold by commercial banks in the money market with maturities ranging from one week to several years. They have an active secondary market.

Charter.   Depository institutions require a legal charter issued by either the federal or state government in order to conduct business. The existence of both state and federal chartering agencies produces a "dual" system in the United States for banks, S&Ls, mutual savings banks, and credit unions.

Checkable deposit.   Any type of deposit subject to transfer by a check or written order, currently defined to include demand deposits, NOW and SNOW accounts, and credit union share drafts. Also called transaction deposits.

Commercial bank.   A business organized for the purposes of making commercial loans and offering demand deposits. Commercial banks can be either national or state-chartered.

Comptroller of the Currency.   Part of the U.S. Treasury Department established in 1863 to charter, regulate, and supervise national banks.

Consumer Bank.   A nonbank bank that escapes the definition of a commercial bank by not making commercial loans.

Contemporaneous reserve accounting (CRA).   A system that computes current required reserves for a depository institution based on current deposit levels.

Contestable market. Market that behaves competitively because of potential, rather than actual, competition.

Credit union. Small financial institution that specializes in short-term consumer lending and is organized as a cooperative.

Credit union share draft. A savings-type deposit offered by credit unions subject to transfer by check or draft. Similar to SNOW accounts.

Debt. Debt (or credit) measure used by the Federal Reserve System. It consists of the total domestic nonfinancial debt of federal, state, and local government sectors, together with that of private nonfinancial sectors, which includes corporate bonds, mortgages, consumer credit, bank loans, commercial paper, banker's acceptances, and other debt instruments.

Default risk. The risk that the issuer of an obligation will fail to meet interest or principal payments.

Deficit unit. Any economic unit (government, business, or household) whose total expenditures exceed their total nonfinancial receipts. Deficit units are net demanders of funds in the financial system since their borrowering exceeds their lending activities.

Demand deposit account. A deposit account subject to immediate transfer by check. By regulation, commercial banks have a virtual monopoly over demand deposit accounts. S&Ls and mutual savings banks, however, have limited authority to offer demand deposit accounts. Demand deposit accounts are subject to a zero-interest rate ceiling.

Depository financial institution. Financial institution that accepts deposits as the major source of funds, currently defined to include banks, S&Ls, mutual savings banks, and credit unions.

Depository Institutions Deregulation Committee (DIDC). Established by the Depository Institutions Deregulation and Monetary Control Act (DIDMCA) of 1980 to oversee the phase-out of Regulation Q and scheduled to be disbanded in March 1986.

Direct finance. The segment of the financial system in which funds and obligations are transferred directly between surplus and deficit units. In this segment of the financial system, the surplus unit directly assumes the default risk of the deficit unit.

Disintermediation. The transfer of funds from the indirect or intermediary sector of the financial system to the direct sector when deposit interest rate ceilings became binding on the intermediary sector during periods of high interest rates.

Diversification.   A strategy to reduce risk by holding a variety of assets or investments in such a manner so that the default (or other risk/exposure) of one or a group of assets does not threaten the entire portfolio.

Dual banking system.   The coexistence of both national and state-chartered banks in the United States.

Due-on-sale clause.   A clause in a mortgage agreement that permits the lender to call the loan "due-on-sale" if the title of the mortgaged property is transferred.

Duration.   The average life of a security, taking into account the time pattern of payments of interest and principal.

Efficiency.   An allocation of resources such that no reallocation can increase the output of any one product without lowering the output of other products.

Efficient market.   A financial market for debt or equity obligations whose current prices incorporate all available information affecting their valuation.

Eurodollar deposit.   A dollar-denominated deposit, almost always a time deposit, in a bank located outside the United States.

Explicit interest payment.   Monetary return in the form of interest payments to the deposit holder.

Federal Deposit Insurance Corporation (FDIC).   A federal agency established in 1934 to insure deposits held by national and state-chartered banks and mutual savings banks.

Federal funds rate.   The rate of interest established in the federal funds market, which brings together depository institutions with excess reserves and depository institutions in need of reserves. The transfer of funds is usually conducted electronically through the facilities of the Federal Reserve.

Federal Home Loan Bank Board (FHLBB).   A federal agency established in 1934 to charter, regulate, and supervise federal S&Ls.

Federal Open Market Committee (FOMC).   A twelve-member committee of the Federal Reserve responsible for formulating and conducting open market operations. Seven of the twelve members are composed of the Board, and the chair of the Board is the chair of the FOMC. The remaining five members are the president of the Federal Reserve Bank of New York and four other presidents of regional Federal Reserve Banks on a rotating basis.

Federal Reserve Act of 1913.   Legislation that established the first truly central monetary authority in the United States, the Federal Reserve System.

Federal Reserve notes.   Currency issued by the Federal Reserve Banks.

Federal Savings and Loan Insurance Corporation (FSLIC).   Established in 1934 as part of the FHLBB to insure deposits of federal and state-chartered S&Ls.

Fiat.   See Fiduciary.

Fiduciary.   In reference to monetary standards, fiduciary implies trust or confidence that the promises to pay issued by banks or government will be honored by the issuer despite the lack of a 100 percent reserve of some commodity money such as gold or silver. Any fractional reserve monetary system contains significant fiduciary elements. The term *fiat* is also used in the same manner to describe public trust and confidence in promises to pay.

Financial innovation, regulator-induced.   The process of introducing new financial assets, services, or institutions initiated by legislation or regulatory decree.

Financial innovation, market-induced.   The process of introducing new financial assets, services, or institutions initiated by the market in response to binding constraints that limit profit opportunities, or to technical progress.

Financial reform.   Changes in the structure of the financial system or in the conduct of the monetary authority, initiated by either government or the market.

Financial system.   A collection of markets where funds are transferred between lenders and borrowers or, more formally, between surplus and deficit units. The financial system channels funds between these two groups through direct and intermediary financial markets. Direct financial markets consist of the direct exchange of obligations and funds between deficit and surplus units, and, as a result, the surplus unit assumes the default risk of the deficit unit. Intermediary or indirect financial markets consist of an intermediary or financial institution that stands between the surplus and deficit unit. The institution exchanges its own obligations for the funds from the surplus unit and uses the accumulated funds to make loans to deficit units. In this way, the surplus unit assumes only the generally lower risk of the financial institution rather than the generally higher risk of the deficit unit. See also Deficit unit, Surplus unit, Direct finance, and Intermediation or indirect finance.

FINE Study.   The 1975 *Financial Institutions and the Nation's Economy* study, which supported many of the recommendations of the Hunt Report.

Fisherian mechanism.   A description of how inflationary expectations are incorporated into market-determined interest rates; named after Irving Fisher, a famous American economist of the past. Also referred to as the Fisher effect on interest rates.

Float (Federal Reserve float).   Additional reserves created by time lags in the check-clearing process in which a bank retains access to reserves that are passed on to other banks in settlement for outstanding checks; during these time lags the checks have not yet cleared through the Federal Reserve's check-clearing facility.

Free banking.   A concept, first introduced by New York in 1838, that allowed any business to engage in banking once a minimum set of standards were satisfied.

Geographic constraints.   Restrictions imposed by federal or state government that constrain interstate or intrastate activities of depository institutions.

Great Depression.   The most significant decline in the United States economy, which started officially in August 1929 and did not end until the U.S. entry into World War II.

Humphrey-Hawkins Act of 1978.   Also known as the Full Employment and Balanced Growth Act of 1978. This legislation established specific, though somewhat unrealistic, goals of stabilization; however, it did establish the current reporting framework for the Federal Reserve regarding monetary aggregate targets. Preliminary targets for the coming year are announced in July of the current year with final targets announced in February of the target year.

Hunt Report.   Also known as the *1971 Report of the President's Commission on Financial Structure and Regulation.* Many of the recommendations of the Hunt Report were incorporated into the 1980 and 1982 acts.

Implicit interest payment.   Nonmonetary return to a deposit holder in the form of free or reduced-priced services.

Interest rate risk.   The risk that interest rates will increase (or fall) more than expected, requiring an institution to pay a higher (or lower) rate than it earns on the asset portfolio in order to attract and maintain deposits. Institutions that mismatch the maturity or duration of their assets and liabilities (those that borrow short and lend long, or conversely) are particularly subject to interest rate risk.

Intermediate targets. A set of targets placed between the instruments controlled directly by the Federal Reserve and the final policy targets. Intermediate targets are used to help the monetary authority guide its instruments to better achieve the final policy targets.

Intermediation or indirect finance. The segment of the financial system characterized by financial institutions that intermediate between the surplus and deficit unit. By offering its own debt obligations such as deposits to the surplus unit, the financial institution or intermediary accumulates the funds to lend to the deficit unit.

Investment banking. As opposed to commercial banking, an investment bank can underwrite or otherwise hold a wide range of public and private obligations but cannot offer demand deposit services.

IS function. A function showing all combinations of the level of income and the interest rate that determines equilibrium between aggregate demand and supply for goods and services.

Lagged reserve accounting (LRA). A system that computes current reserve requirements for depository institutions based on deposit levels some time (for example, two weeks) in the past.

Lender of last resort. An entity designed to provide liquidity to the financial system in order to maintain stable markets and institutions.

Liability management. A strategy for operating a depository institution that regards the sources of funds as manageable.

Liquidity (L). A broad measure of liquidity in the United States published by the Federal Reserve and defined as the sum of the following components: M3 plus public holdings of U.S. savings bonds, plus short-term Treasury securities, plus banker's acceptances, plus commercial paper.

LM function. A function that shows all combinations of the level of income and the interest rate that determines equilibrium between the demand and supply for money.

M1. Basic measure of the U.S. money supply defined as coin, currency in circulation, traveler's checks of nonbank issuers, demand deposits, and other checkable (or transaction) accounts. (It excludes, however, MMDAs.)

M2. A broad measure of the U.S. money supply, defined as the sum of M1, plus overnight Eurodollar deposits (issued to U.S. residents by foreign branches of U.S. banks worldwide), plus overnight and continuing contract repurchase agreements, plus Money Market Mutual Fund shares held by individuals, plus Money Market Deposit Accounts, plus savings accounts, plus small time-deposit accounts (less than $100,000). Excludes IRA and Keogh accounts.

M3.   A broad measure of the U.S. money supply defined as M2 plus large CDs ($100,000 or larger), plus long-term Eurodollar deposits and repurchase agreements, plus Money Market Mutual Funds held by institutions.

Manager of the system account.   The officer of the Federal Reserve Bank of New York who implements open market operations by buying and selling government securities from the Federal Reserve's portfolio on the money markets.

Margin requirements.   Requirements imposed by the Federal Reserve's Board of Governors and specifying the percentage of the value of stock that must be paid in cash in order to regulate the amount of credit used to purchase stock.

McFadden Act of 1927.   Legislation stipulating geographic constraints that defined state boundaries as the limit beyond which banks could not branch.

Monetary aggregates.   Term used to describe various measures of the money supply.

Monetary authority.   The entity responsible for controlling the money supply and providing other central banking functions. The Federal Reserve System is the monetary authority in the United States.

Money market certificate (MMC).   Six-month time certificates authorized in 1978 that were not subject to Regulation Q ceilings. Until October 1, 1983, MMCs earned a market return tied to the six-month Treasury bill rate and had a minimum balance requirement of $10,000.

Money Market Deposit Account (MMDA).   A deposit account introduced by the Garn– St Germain Act of 1982 in order to be directly competitive with Money Market Mutual Fund shares. MMDAs earn a market interest rate, are federally insured, are subject to a minimum balance of $2,500, and possess limited transaction features. On January 1, 1985, the minimum balance falls to $1,000 to $0 a year later.

Money Market Mutual Fund (MMMF).   Certain institutions sell shares and use these accumulated funds to purchase money market instruments such as large CDs, Eurodollar deposits, Treasury bills, commercial paper, and so forth. MMMF shares earn a market interest rate, are offered in large or small minimum amounts, possess limited transaction features; however, MMMFs are not federally insured.

Money multiplier.   A framework that shows the relationship between changes in reserves of depository institutions and the money supply. The money multiplier is greater than one in a fractional reserve banking system.

Moral hazard.   In the context of insurance, behavior that is induced by the presence of
insurance.

Mutual savings bank.   A financial institution that specializes in mortgage lending and is
located primarily in the northeastern part of the United States. Mutual
savings banks are similar to S&Ls in a number of respects.

National Bank Act of 1863.   Legislation that established the national banking system
and the Office of the Comptroller of the Currency.

National bank notes.   Bank notes that could be issued only by nationally chartered
banks. National bank notes were replaced by Federal Reserve notes as the
nation's currency.

National Credit Union Administration (NCUA).   Federal agency responsible for
chartering, regulating, and supervising federal credit unions.

Negotiable Order of Withdrawal (NOW) *Account.*   Savings deposit subject to transfer
by check. Until the phase-out of Regulation Q, NOW accounts are subject
to an interest rate ceiling. SNOW accounts, although not subject to
interest rate ceilings, must have a maintained balance of $2,500 or more.
The minimum balance falls to $1,000 on January 1, 1985 and to $0 one year
later.

Net worth certificate.   Established by the 1982 Garn–St Germain Act as one method
available to federal regulators to aid troubled depository institutions. Net
worth certificates are purchased from the depository institution by the
regulatory agency to artificially raise net worth.

Nonbank bank.   A business that offers banking services but does not meet the legal
definition of a commercial bank in that it does not both make commercial
loans and accept demand deposits.

Nonborrowered reserves.   Reserves of depository institutions minus borrowings from
the Federal Reserve.

Nondepository financial institution.   A financial institution or intermediary that obtains
the major source of funds from nondeposit liabilities such as life insurance
companies or mutual fund investment companies.

Nonpersonal deposit.   A category of deposits subject to reserve requirements and currently defined to include large CDs, Eurodollars, and business savings deposits.

Numeraire.   A standard to which dissimilar things can be compared. The dollar is the numeraire in the United States, and thus the relative value of everything else can be expressed in terms of dollars.

Open market operations.   The major instrument of monetary policy. The purchasing and selling of Treasury securities and other money market instruments in the open market by the Federal Reserve through the Federal Open Market Committee (FOMC). Purchases of securities increase reserves available to depository institutions, whereas sales of securities decrease reserves available to depository institutions.

Passbook savings deposit.   See Savings deposit.

Phillips curve.   A relationship that describes a trade-off between levels of inflation and unemployment.

Portfolio.   Term used to describe a collection of assets or liabilities held by any entity.

Potential competition.   Competition that already exists is recognized as restraining firms to behave fairly and efficiently. Modern microeconomic theory argues that the threat of potential competition from firms ready or able to enter an industry accomplishes the same goals.

Proviso clause.   Part of the instructions used to carry out monetary policy, primarily by open market operations. Loosely means that open market operations should achieve certain objectives "provided" that other conditions are satisfied.

Public choice theory of regulation.   The argument that regulation is influenced by the structure of the regulatory framework and the objectives of the regulators.

Public interest or welfare theory of regulation.   The argument that regulation occurs to combat market failure and is designed to enhance the public interest or welfare.

Regulation Q.   Nonzero interest rate ceilings imposed on federally insured savings and time deposits of depository institutions.

Regulatory dialectic.   Term introduced by Edward J. Kane to describe the introduction of financial regulation, followed by financial innovation to circumvent binding regulation, followed by re-regulation, and so on.

Repurchase agreement (RP).   An agreement to sell and then repurchase securities at a stated price. Frequently used by banks as a source of funds by purchasing a demand deposit account "overnight" with Treasury securities as collateral and than repurchasing the Treasury securities the "next day."

Reserve aggregates. Various measures of reserves available to depository institutions.

Savings and loan association (S&L). Financial institution that specializes in mortgage lending. Similar to mutual savings banks; however, S&Ls are relatively more specialized mortgage lenders.

Savings bank. Similar to S&Ls; the Garn–St Germain Act permits S&Ls to readily convert to savings bank designation.

Savings deposit. A deposit not subject to transfer by check and subject to Regulation Q ceilings.

Savings institution. Depository institution that relies on deposits other than demand deposits as its major source of funds, presently defined to include S&Ls, mutual savings banks, and credit unions.

Scale economies. A firm said to possess scale economies becomes more efficient as it increases in size, while conducting the same set of operations.

Scope economies. A firm said to benefit from scope economies becomes more efficient as it increases the range of its (usually related) activities.

Secondary market. Financial market that provides for the sale and resale of obligations before they reach maturity.

Securities and Exchange Commission (SEC). Federal agency established in 1934 to regulate and supervise money and capital markets.

Social contract and housing. The implicit and explicit contract among government, mortgage lenders, housing industry, and purchasers of housing that is designed to channel large amounts of funds into housing.

Special interest theory of regulation. The argument that regulation is designed to enhance the profit opportunities of one or more special interests.

Suffolk System. An example of financial innovation in the 1820s in which Boston banks imposed conservative banking practices on so-called country banks that had a propensity to overissue bank notes.

Super Negotiable Order of Withdrawal (SNOW) *Account.* Savings deposit subject to transfer by check and not subject to any interest rate ceiling (on deposits over $2,500).

Surplus unit.   Any economic unit (government, business, or household) whose total nonfinancial receipts exceed its total expenditures. Surplus units are net suppliers of funds to the financial system. Their lending exceeds their borrowing activities.

Thrift institution.   Depository institution that allocates a major portion of its loan portfolios to mortgages; presently defined to include S&Ls and mutual savings banks.

Time deposit.   A deposit, not subject to transfer by check, that has a stated maturity period. Regular time deposits are issued in amounts less than $100,000, and large certificates of deposits or CDs are issued in amounts of $100,000 or more.

Total Domestic Nonfinancial Credit.   The credit variable used by the Federal Reserve. See Debt.

Transaction deposits.   A major part of the money supply, defined by the Federal Reserve as "all deposits on which the account holder is permitted to make withdrawals by negotiable or transferable instruments, payment orders of withdrawal, telephone and preauthorized transfers (in excess of three per month), for the purpose of making payments to third persons or others." Transaction deposits include demand deposits, NOW and SNOW accounts, and credit union shares drafts.

Variable Rate Mortgages (VRMs).   Mortgages whose interest rates change in line with market interest rates. They are also called adjustable rate mortgages (ARMs).

Variance.   A measure of the variability about the average of a set of data.

Velocity of money.   The number of times per period money turns over to support a given level of economic activity. Income velocity of M1 is measured as the ratio of M1 to the level of GNP.

REFERENCES

Acheson, Keith, and Chant, John F. "Bureaucratic Theory and the Choice of Central Bank Goals." *Journal of Money, Credit and Banking* 5 (May 1973): 637–55.

Arrow, Kenneth J. *Social Choice and Individual Values.* Cowles Foundation, Monograph no. 12. New York: John Wiley and Sons, 1951; 2nd ed., 1963.

Avery, Robert B., and Kwast, Myron L. "An Analysis of the Short-Run Money Supply Mechanism." Research Papers in Banking and Financial Economics. Board of Governors of the Federal Reserve, May 1983.

Baer, Herbert. "Thrift Dominance and Specialization in Housing Finance: The Role of Taxation." *Housing Finance Review* 2 (October 1983): 353–67.

Bailey, Elizabeth, "Contestability and the Design of Regulatory and Anti-Trust Policy." *American Economic Review* 71 (May 1981): 178–83.

Bailey, Elizabeth, and Panzar, John C. "The Contestability of Airline Markets During the Transition to Deregulation." *Law and Contemporary Problems* 44 (December 1980): 125–46.

Batten, Dallas S., and Stone, Courtenay C. "Are Monetarists an Endangered Species?" *Review* (Federal Reserve Bank of St. Louis), 65 (May 1983): 5–16.

Beck, Lowell R. "Insurance Business Could Be a Risky Policy for Banks." *Wall Street Journal*, February 21, 1984, p. 28.

Benston, George J. "Interest Payments on Demand Deposits and Bank Investment Behavior." *Journal of Political Economy* 72 (October 1964): 431–49.

———. "Federal Regulation of Banking: Analysis and Policy Recommendations." *Journal of Bank Research*, Winter 1983, pp. 216–44.

Benston, George; Berger, Allen N.; Hanweck, Gerald A.; and Humphrey, David B. "Economies of Scale and Scope in Banking." In *Proceedings of the Conference on*

Bank Structure and Competition. Federal Reserve Bank of Chicago, May 1983, pp. 432–55.

Bernanke, Ben S. "Nonmonetary Effects of the Financial Crisis in the Propagation of the Great Depression." *American Economic Review* 73 (June 1983): 257–76.

Bierwag, G. D., and Kaufman, George G. "A Proposal for Deposit Insurance with Risk-Sensitive Premiums." In *Proceedings of the Conference on Bank Structure and Competition*. Federal Reserve Bank of Chicago, May 1983, pp. 223–42.

Board of Governors of the Federal Reserve. *New Monetary Control Procedures*. Federal Reserve Staff Study. 2 vols. Washington, D.C., February 1981.

———. *Federal Reserve Bulletin*. August 1983 and various issues.

———. *Country Exposure Lending Survey*. Washington, D.C., 1983; 1984.

Brewer, Elijah. "Treasury to Invest Surplus Tax and Loan Balances." *Economic Perspectives* (Federal Reserve Bank of Chicago), November/December 1977, pp. 14–20.

Brewer, Elijah, and Garcia, Gillian G. "A Discriminant Analysis of S&L Accounting Profits, 1976–1981." Federal Home Loan Bank Board, Invited Working Paper no. 50, September 1984.

Bryant, Ralph C. *Controlling Money: The Federal Reserve and Its Critics*. Washington, D.C.: Brookings Institution, 1983.

Burns, Arthur. "The Role of the Money Supply in the Conduct of Monetary Policy." *Monthly Review* (Federal Reserve Bank of Richmond), 59 (December 1973): 2–8.

Buser, Stephan A.; Chen, Andrew H.; and Kane, Edward J. "Federal Deposit Insurance, Regulatory Policy, and Optimal Bank Capital." *Journal of Finance* 35 (March 1981): 51–60.

Campbell, Tim S., and Glenn, David. "Deposit Insurance in a Deregulated Environment." *Journal of Finance* 39 (July 1984): 775–85.

Cargill, Thomas F. "Clark Warburton and the Development of Monetarism Since the Great Depression." *History of Political Economy* 11 (1979): 425–49.

———. "The Institutional Framework of Monetary Policy." *Social Science Journal* 17 (January 1980): 79–88.

———. "A Tribute to Clark Warburton, 1896–1979." *Journal of Money, Credit and Banking* 13 (February 1981): 89–93.

———. *Money, the Financial System, and Monetary Policy*. Englewood Cliffs, N.J.: Prentice-Hall, 1983.

Cargill, Thomas F., and Garcia, Gillian G. *Financial Deregulation and Monetary Control*. Stanford: Hoover Institution Press, 1982.

———. *A Supplement on the Garn–St Germain Depository Institutions Act of 1982: Progress Toward Deregulation*. Englewood Cliffs, N.J.: Prentice-Hall, 1983.

Cargill, Thomas F., and Meyer, Robert A. "The Term Structure of Inflationary Expectations and Market Efficiency." *Journal of Finance* 35 (March 1980): 57–70.

Carron, Andrew S. *The Plight of the Thrift Institutions*. Washington, D.C.: Brookings Institution, 1982.

————. *The Rescue of the Thrift Industry*. Washington, D.C.: Brookings Institution, 1983.

Cheng, Hang-Sheng. "Financial Reform in Australia and New Zealand." *Economic Review* (Federal Reserve Bank of San Francisco), (Winter 1983): 9–24.

Christelow, Dorothy. "Financial Innovation and Monetary Indicators in Japan." *Quarterly Review* (Federal Reserve Bank of New York), 6 (Spring 1981): 42–53.

Cone, Kenneth Robert. "Regulation of Depository Financial Institutions." Ph.D. Dissertation, Stanford University, 1982.

Conference of State Bank Supervisors. *A Profile of State-Chartered Banking*. Washington, D.C., 1979 and 1984.

Cook, Timothy Q., and Duffield, Jeremy A. "Money Market Mutual Funds." *Economic Review* (Federal Reserve Bank of Richmond), 65 (July/August 1979): 15–31.

Cook, Timothy Q., and Summers, Bruce, eds. *Instruments of the Money Market*. 5th ed. Richmond, Va.: Federal Reserve Bank of Richmond, 1981.

Craine, Roger; Havenner, Arthur; and Berry, James. "Fixed Rules vs. Activism in the Conduct of Monetary Policy." *American Economic Review* 68 (December 1978): 769–83.

Crockett, John, and King, A. Thomas. "The Contribution of New Asset Powers to S&L Earnings: A Comparison of Federal-and-State-Chartered Associations in Texas." Federal Home Loan Bank Board, Research Working Paper no. 110, July 1982.

Cumming, Christine, and Miners, Cathy. "Targeting the Real Interest Rate: Does the Measure Matter?" Federal Reserve Bank of New York, Research Working Paper no. 82–34, October 1982.

Dunham, Constance. "The Growth of Money Market Mutual Funds." *New England Economic Review* (Federal Reserve Bank of Boston), September/October 1980, pp. 20–34.

Dunham, Constance, and Guerin-Calvert, Margaret. "How Quickly Can Thrifts Move into Commercial Lending?" *New England Economic Review* (Federal Reserve Bank of Boston), November/December 1983, pp. 42–54.

Eisenbeis, Robert A. "New Investment Powers for S&Ls: Diversification or Specialization." *Economic Review* (Federal Reserve Bank of Atlanta), 68 (July 1983): 53–62.

Fama, Eugene E. "Banking Regulation in the Theory of Finance." *Journal of Monetary Economics* 6 (January 1980): 39–58.

Federal Deposit Insurance Corporation. *Annual Report*, Various issues.

Federal Home Loan Bank Board. *Savings and Home Financing Source Book*. 1975, 1978, and 1982.

————. *Combined Financial Statements*. 1975, 1978, and 1982.

————. *News*, February 1, 1984.

————. *Journal* 17, no. 3 (April 1984).

Federal Reserve Bank of Atlanta. "Interstate Banking." *Economic Review*, May 1983, pp. 2–71.

Federal Reserve Bank of Chicago. "The Garn–St Germain Depository Institutions Act of 1982." *Economic Perspectives* 7 (March/April 1983).

Federal Reserve Bank of New York. "Depository Institutions and Their Regulators." Public Information Department, February 1984.

Fieleke, Norman S. "International Lending on Trial." *New England Economic Review* (Federal Reserve Bank of Boston), May/June 1983, pp. 5–13.

Fitton, Michael P. "Bank Credit Cards and the Checkless Society." Ph.D. Dissertation, The Stonier Graduate School of Banking, Rutgers–The State University, 1969.

Freedman, Charles. "Financial Innovation in Canada: Causes and Consequences." In *Conference on Interest Rate Deregulation and Monetary Policy.* Federal Reserve Bank of San Francisco, November 28–30, 1982, pp. 191–200.

Fried, Joel. "Government Loan and Guarantee Programs." *Review* (Federal Reserve Bank of St. Louis), 10 (December 1983): 22–30.

Friedman, Benjamin M. "The Inefficiency of Short-Run Monetary Targets for Monetary Policy." *Brookings Papers on Economic Activity* 2 (1977): 293–346.

———. "Monetary Policy with Credit Aggregate Target." National Bureau of Economic Research Working Paper no. 980, September 1982.

Friedman, Milton. *A Program for Monetary Stability.* New York: Fordham University Press, 1959.

———. "Should There Be an Independent Monetary Authority?" In Leland B. Yeager, ed., *In Search of a Monetary Constitution.* Cambridge, Mass.: Harvard University Press, 1962, pp. 219–43.

———. "The Role of Monetary Policy." *American Economic Review* 58 (March 1968): 1–17.

———. "Letter on Monetary Policy." *Monthly Review* (Federal Reserve Bank of Richmond), 60 (May/June, 1974): 20–23.

———. "Monetary Policy: Theory and Practice." *Journal of Money, Credit and Banking* 14, Part 2 (November 1982): 98–118.

Friedman, Milton, and Schwartz, Anna J. *A Monetary History of the United States, 1867–1960.* Princeton, N.J. : Princeton University Press, 1963.

Gambs, Carl M. "State Reserve Requirements and Bank Cash Assets." *Journal of Money, Credit and Banking* 12 (November 1980): 462–70.

Garcia, Gillian G. "Credit Cards: An Interdisciplinary Survey." *Journal of Consumer Research* 6 (March 1980): 327–37.

———. "Some Implications of the Deregulation of Interest Rates for Monetary Control." Federal Reserve Bank of Chicago, Internal Memorandum, 1983.

———. "The Right Rabbit: Which Intermediate Target Should the Fed Pursue?" *Economic Perspectives* (Federal Reserve Bank of Chicago), May–June 1984, pp. 15–31.

Garcia, Gillian G., and McMahon, Annie. "Regulatory Innovation: The New Bank Accounts." *Economic Perspectives* (Federal Reserve Bank of Chicago), April 1984, pp. 12–23.

Garcia, Gillian G., and Pak, Simon. "The Ratio of Currency to Demand Deposits in the United States." *Journal of Finance* 34 (June 1979): 703–15.

Garcia, Gillian G., et al. "Financial Deregulation: Historical Perspective and Impact of the Garn–St Germain Depository Institutions Act of 1982." Federal Reserve Bank of Chicago, Staff Study 83–2, March 1983.

Gilbert, R. Alton, "Bank Market Structure and Competition: A Survey," *Journal of Money, Credit and Banking*, 16 (November 1984), 617–644.

Goldenweiser, Emanuel. *American Monetary Policy*. New York: McGraw-Hill, 1951.

Golembe, Carter H., and Holland, David S. *Federal Regulation of Banking, 1983–84*. Washington, D.C.: Golembe Associates, 1983.

Goodhart, Charles. *Monetary Theory and Practice: The U.K. Experience*. London: Macmillan, 1984.

Gordon, Robert J. "Beyond Monetarism." Testimony Prepared for the Subcommittee on Domestic Monetary Policy of the House Committee on Banking, Finance and Urban Affairs, U.S. House of Representatives, Hearings on Alternative Anti-Inflation Policies, December 1, 1982.

———. "Using Monetary Control to Dampen the Business Cycle: A New Set of First Principles." National Bureau of Economic Research Working Paper no. 1210, October 1983.

Gordon, Robert J., and Wilcox, James A. "Monetarist Interpretations of the Great Depression: An Evaluation and Critique." In Karl Brunner, ed., *The Great Depression Revisited*. Boston: Martinus Nijhoff Publishing, 1981, pp. 49–107.

Greider, William. "The Education of David Stockman." *Atlantic Monthly*, December 1981, pp. 27–54.

Grossman, Jacob. "The 'Rationality' of Money Supply Expectations and the Short-Run Response of Interest Rates to Monetary Surprises." *Journal of Money, Credit and Banking* 13 (November 1981): 409–24.

Gurley, John G., and Shaw, Edward S. *Money in a Theory of Finance*. Washington, D.C.: Brookings Institution, 1960.

Hafer, R. W. "Inflation: Assessing Its Recent Behavior and Future Prospects." *Review* (Federal Reserve Bank of St. Louis), 65 (August/September 1983): 38–41.

Hafer, R. W., and Hein, Scott E. "The Wayward Money Supply: A Post-Mortem of 1982." *Review* (Federal Reserve Bank of St. Louis), 65 (March 1983): 17–25.

Hall, Robert E. "Optimal Fiduciary Monetary Systems." *Journal of Monetary Economics* 12 (March 1983): 333–50.

Hamburger, Michael. "Recent Velocity Behavior, the Demand for Money and Monetary Policy." In *Proceedings of the Conference on Monetary Targeting and Velocity*. Federal Reserve Bank of San Francisco, December 1983, pp. 108–28.

Hammond, Bray. *Banks and Politics in America from the Revolution to the Civil War*. Princeton, N.J.: Princeton University Press, 1957.

Hansen, Alvin H. *Fiscal Policy and Business Cycles*. New York: W. W. Norton & Company, 1941.

Heggestad, Arnold A. "A Survey of Studies on Banking Competition: A Review and Evaluation." In Franklin R. Edwards, ed., *Issues in Financial Regulation*. New York: McGraw-Hill, 1979, pp. 449–90.

Hendershott, Patric H. "Governmental Policy and the Allocation of Capital Between Residential and Industrial Uses." *Financial Analysts Journal* 39 (July/August 1983): 37–42.

Hetzel, Robert L. "The October 1979 Regime of Monetary Control and the Behavior of the Money Supply in 1980." *Journal of Money, Credit and Banking* 14 (May 1982): 234–51.

Horovitz, Paul M. "The Case Against Risk-Related Deposit Insurance Premiums." *Housing Finance Review* 2 (July 1983): 253–63.

The Housing Act of 1949. Chapter 338, 63 stat (1949). 81st Cong., 1st sess.

Howard, David H., and Johnson, Karen H. "Financial Innovation, Deregulation, and Monetary Policy: The Foreign Experience." In *Conference on Interest Rate Deregulation and Monetary Policy*. Federal Reserve Bank of San Francisco, November 28–30, 1982, pp. 139–84.

Hughes, Jonathan. *American Economic History*. Glenview, Ill.: Scott, Foresman and Company, 1983.

Irvine, Owen F., Jr. "The Real Rate of Interest, for Whom?" *Applied Economics* 15 (1983): 635–48.

Johannes, James M., and Robert H. Rasche. "Can the Reserves Approach to Monetary Control Really Work?" *Journal of Money, Credit and Banking* 13 (August 1981): 298–313.

Johnson, Harry G. "Problems of Efficiency in Monetary Management." *Journal of Political Economy* 76 (September/October 1968): 971–90.

Johnston, Verle B. "The McFadden Act: A Look Back." *Weekly Letter* (Federal Reserve Bank of San Francisco), August 19, 1983.

Jones, Sidney L. *The Development of Economic Policy: Financial Institutions Reform*. Ann Arbor: University of Michigan Press, 1979.

Judd, John P. "Where Do We Go from Here?" In *Proceedings of the Conference on Monetary Targeting and Velocity*. Federal Reserve Bank of San Francisco, December 1983, pp. 139–44.

Judd, John P., and Scadding, John L. "The Search for a Stable Money Demand Function." *Journal of Economic Literature* 20 (September 1982a): 993–1023.

———. "What Do Money Market Models Tell Us About How to Use Monetary Policy?" *Journal of Money, Credit and Banking* 14, Part 2 (November 1982b): 868–77.

Judd, John P., and Throop, Adrian W. "Penalty Discount Rate?" *Weekly Letter* (Federal Reserve Bank of San Francisco), October 30, 1981.

Kaldor, Nicholas. *The Scourge of Monetarism*. Oxford, Eng.: Oxford University Press, 1982.

Kaminow, Ira. "Required Reserve Ratios, Policy Instruments and Money Stock Control." *Journal of Monetary Economics* 3 (1977): 389–408.

Kanatas, George. "Deposit Insurance and the Discount Window: Pricing Under Asymmetric Information." Evanston, Ill.: Northwestern University, Kellogg Graduate School of Management, Working Paper, August 1984.

Kanatas, George, and Greenbaum, Stuart I. "Bank Reserve Requirements and Monetary Aggregates." *Journal of Banking and Finance* 6 (1982): 507–20.

Kane, Edward J. "Short-Changing the Small Saver During the Vietnam War." *Journal of Money, Credit and Banking* 2 (November 1970): 513–22.

———. "Good Intentions and Unintended Evil: The Case Against Selective Credit Allocation." *Journal of Money, Credit and Banking* 9 (February 1977): 55–69.

———. "Accelerating Inflation, Technological Innovation, and the Decreasing Effectiveness of Banking Regulation." *Journal of Finance* 36 (May 1981): 355–67.

———. "S&Ls and Interest Rate Regulation: The FSLIC as an In-Place Bailout Program." *Housing Finance Review* 1 (July 1982): 219–43.

———. "The Role of Government in the Thrift Industry's Net-Worth Crisis." *Financial Services: The Changing Institutions and Government Policy*. Englewood Cliffs, N.J.: Prentice-Hall, 1983a.

———. "A Six-Point Program for Deposit Insurance Reform." *Housing Finance Review* 2 (July 1983b): 269–78.

———. "Strategic Planning in a World of Reregulation and Rapid Technological Change." Ohio State University, College of Administrative Sciences, Working Paper no. 83–46, August 1983c.

———. "Technological and Regulatory Forces in the Developing Fusion of Financial Services Competition." Ohio State University, College of Administrative Sciences, Working Paper no. 84–4, January 1984.

Kaplan, Marshall A. "Deregulation and New Powers in the Savings and Loan Industry: What This Portends." *Housing Finance Review* 2 (April 1983): 145–56.

Kaufman, George G. "The Thrift Institution Problem Reconsidered." *Journal of Bank Research* 3 (Spring 1972): 26–33.

———. "The Fed's Post–October 1979 Technical Operating Procedures Under Lagged Reserve Requirements: Reduced Ability to Control Money?" *Financial Review* 17 (November 1982): 279–94.

Keir, Peter. "Impact of Discount Policy Procedures on the Effectiveness of Reserve Targeting." In *New Monetary Control Procedures*. Board of Governors of the Federal Reserve, Staff Study. Vol. 1, 1981.

Klebaner, Benjamin J. *Commercial Banking in the United States: A History*. Hinsdale, Ill.: Dryden Press, 1974.

Klitgaard, Thomas. "Space Age Monetary Theory." *Weekly Letter* (Federal Reserve Bank of San Francisco), October 28, 1983.

Kopcke, Richard W. "The Condition of Massachusetts Savings Banks and California Savings and Loan Associations." *The Future of the Thrift Industry*. Federal Reserve Bank of Boston Conference Series no. 24, 1981.

Lang, Richard W. "TTL Note Accounts and the Money Supply Process." *Review* (Federal Reserve Bank of St. Louis), 61 (October 1979): 3–14.

Laurent, Robert L. "Reserve Requirements, Deposit Insurance and Monetary Control." *Journal of Money, Credit and Banking* 13 (August 1981): 314–24.

——. "Lagged Reserve Accounting and the Fed's New Operating Procedure." *Economic Perspectives* (Federal Reserve Bank of Chicago), 6 (Midyear 1982): 32–43.

——. "Quasi-Contemporaneous Reserves: Monetary Policy's Newest Pig-in-a-Poke." Federal Reserve Bank of Chicago, Staff Memoranda no. 84–5, November 1984.

Levin, Fred J., and Meek, Paul. "Implementing the New Operating Procedures: The View from the Trading Desk." In *New Monetary Control Procedures*. Board of Governors of the Federal Reserve, Staff Study. Vol. 1, 1981.

Lindsey, David E. "Nonborrowed Reserve Targeting and Monetary Control." In Lawrence H. Meyer, ed., *Improving Money Stock Control: Problems, Solutions, and Consequences*. Boston: Kluwer-Nijhoff Publishing, 1983, pp. 3–41.

Mackay, Robert J., and Reid, Joseph D., Jr. "On Understanding The Birth And Evolution of the Securities and Exchange Commission: Where Are We in the Theory of Regulation?" In Gary M. Walton, ed., *Regulatory Change in an Atmosphere of Crisis: Current Implications of the Roosevelt Years*. New York: Academic Press, 1979, pp. 101–21.

Maisel, Sherman J. *Managing the Dollar*. New York: W. W. Norton & Company, 1973.

Mascaro, Angelo, and Meltzer, Allan H. "Long-and-Short-Term Interest Rates in a Risky World." *Journal of Monetary Economics* 12 (1983): 485–518.

Mayer, Thomas. *Monetary Policy in the United States*. New York: Random House, 1968.

——. "Money and the Great Depression: A Critique of Professor Temin's Thesis." *Explorations in Economic History* 15 (April 1978a): 127–45.

Mayer, Thomas, et al. *The Structure of Monetarism*. New York: W. W. Norton & Company, 1978b.

Meek, Paul. "Comment on Papers Presented by Messrs. Fforde and Coleby." In Paul Meek, ed., *Central Bank Views of Monetary Targeting*. Federal Reserve Bank of New York, May 1982, pp. 70–71.

Meulendyke, Ann-Marie. "Reserve Targeting Under CRR." Paper Presented at the Financial Analysis Committee Meeting at the Federal Reserve Bank of Cleveland, October 1983.

Mishkin, Frederic S. "Does Anticipated Monetary Policy Matter? An Economic Investigation." *Journal of Political Economy* 90 (February 1982): 22–51.

Modigliani, Franco, and Papademos, Lucas D. "The Structure of Financial Markets and the Monetary Mechanism." In *Controlling the Monetary Aggregates, III*. Federal Reserve Bank of Boston, Conference Series no. 23, October 1980, pp. 111–55.

Monti, Mario; Cesarini, Francesco; and Scognamiglio, Carlo. "Report on the Italian Credit and Financial System." *Banco Nazionale Del Lavoro Quarterly Review*, June 1983.

Nathan, Harold C. "Economic Analysis of Usury Laws." *Journal of Bank Research* 10 (Winter 1980): 200–11.

North, Douglas C. *American Economic Growth, 1790–1860.* New York: W. W. Norton & Company, 1966.

Offenbacher, Edward K., and Porter, Richard D. "Empirical Comparisons of Credit and Monetary Aggregates Using Vector Autogression Methods." Board of Governors of the Federal Reserve, Special Studies Paper no. 181, August 1983.

Panzar, John C., and Willig, Robert D. "Economies of Scope." *American Economic Review* 71 (May 1981): 268–72.

Patinkin, Don. "Financial Intermediaries and the Logical Structure of Monetary Theory." *American Economic Review* 51 (March 1961): 95–116.

Peltzman, Sam. "Toward a More General Theory of Regulation." *Journal of Law and Economics* 19 (August 1976): 211–40.

Pesek, Boris, and Saving, Thomas R. *Money, Wealth, and Economic Theory.* New York: Macmillan, 1967.

Pierce, David A.; Grupe, Michael R.; and Cleveland, William P. "Seasonal Adjustment of the Weekly Monetary Aggregates: A Model-Based Approach." Board of Governors of the Federal Reserve, Staff Study, August 1983.

Pierce, James L. "The Myth of Congressional Supervision of Monetary Policy." *Journal of Monetary Economics* 4 (April 1978): 63–70.

————. "Some Public Policy Issues Raised by the Deregulation of Financial Institutions." *Contemporary Policy Issues* 2 (January 1983): 33–48.

Pigott, Charles. "Financial Reform in Japan." *Economic Review* (Federal Reserve Bank of San Francisco), Winter 1983, pp. 25–46.

Poole, William. "Federal Reserve Operating Procedures: Survey and Evaluation of the Historical Record Since October 1979." *Journal of Money, Credit and Banking* 14, Part 2 (November 1982): 575–96.

Poole, William, and Lieberman, Charles. "Improving Monetary Control." *Brookings Papers on Economic Activity* 1 (1972): 293–334.

Posner, Richard A. "Theories of Economic Regulation." *Bell Journal of Economics and Management Science* 5, no. 2 (Autumn 1974): 335–58.

Prestopino, Chris J. "Do Higher Requirements Discourage Federal Reserve Membership?" *Journal of Finance* 31 (December 1976): 1471–480.

Pyle, David H. "The Losses on Savings Deposits from Interest Rate Regulation." *Bell Journal of Economics and Management* 5, no. 2 (Autumn 1978): 614–22.

Report of the President's Commission on Financial Structure and Regulation. Washington, D.C.: Government Printing Office, December 1971.

Rhoades, Stephen A. "The Competitive Effects of Interstate Banking." *Federal Reserve Bulletin* 66 (January 1980): 1–8.

Rockoff, Hugh. "Money, Prices, and Banks in the Jacksonian Era." In Robert W. Fogel and Stanley L. Engerman, eds., *The Reinterpretation of American Economic History.* New York: Harper & Row, 1971, pp. 448–58.

Rosenblum, Harvey, and Siegel, Diane. "Competition in Financial Services: The Impact of Nonbank Entry." Federal Reserve Bank of Chicago, Staff Study, 83–1, 1983.

Sheffrin, Steven M. *Rational Expectations*. Cambridge, Eng.: Cambridge University Press, 1983.

Spindt, Paul A. "Money Is What Money Does: A Revealed Production Function Approach to Monetary Aggregation." Board of Governors of the Federal Reserve, Special Studies Paper no. 177, June 1983.

Starr, Ross. "Variation in Monetary Composition of Debt and Behavior of the Monetary Aggregates: The Maturity Shift Hypothesis." In *Proceedings of the Sixth West Coast Academic/Federal Reserve Economic Research Seminar*. Federal Reserve Bank of San Francisco, October 1982, 202–33.

Stigler, George J. "The Theory of Economic Regulation." *Bell Journal of Economics and Management Science* 2 (Spring 1971): 3–21.

Taggart, Robert A., Jr. "Effects of Deposit Rate Ceilings: The Evidence from Massachusetts Savings Banks." *Journal of Money, Credit and Banking* 10 (May 1978): 139–57.

Tatom, John A. "Alternative Explanations of the 1982–3 Decline in Velocity." In *Proceedings of the Conference on Monetary Targeting and Velocity*. Federal Reserve Bank of San Francisco, December 1983, pp. 22–56.

Temin, Peter. *The Jacksonian Economy*. New York: W. W. Norton & Company, 1969.

Thornton, Daniel L. *Monetary Trends*. Federal Reserve Bank of St. Louis, October 1983.

Thygerson, Kenneth J. "Financial Restructuring: Impact on Housing." In *Contemporary Policy Issues*. Long Beach, Calif.: Western Economic Association, January 1983, 18–32.

Tobin, James. "Commercial Banks as Creators of 'Money.' " In Dean Carson, ed., *Banking and Monetary Studies*. Homewood, Ill.: Irwin, 1963, pp. 408–19.

U.S. Congress, House, Committee on Banking, Currency and Housing. *The Financial Institutions and the Nation's Economy*. Washington, D.C.: Government Printing Office, 1975.

U.S. Department of Commerce, Bureau of the Census. *Historical Statistics of the United States: Colonial Times to 1970, Part 2*. Washington, D.C.: Government Printing Office, 1975.

U.S. Department of Commerce, Bureau of Economic Analysis. *National Income and Product Accounts*. August 1983.

U.S. Department of the Treasury. *Report of the Interagency Task Force on Thrift Institutions*. June 1980.

U.S. League of Savings Associations. *Savings and Loan '78 Fact Book*. Chicago, 1978.

———. *'84 Savings and Loan Source Book*.

Van Horne, James C. *Financial Market Rates and Flows*. Englewood Cliffs, N.J.: Prentice-Hall, 1984.

Volcker, Paul A. "Monetary Policy Report to Congress." *Federal Reserve Bulletin* 69 (March 1983): 127–40.

Wallich, Henry C., and Keir, Peter M. "The Role of Operating Guides in U.S.

Monetary Policy: A Historical Review." *Federal Reserve Bulletin* 65 (September 1979): 679–91.

Warburton, Clark. *Depression, Inflation, and Monetary Policy: Selected Papers, 1945–1953.* Baltimore, Md.: Johns Hopkins University Press, 1966.

Weintraub, Robert E. "Congressional Supervision of Monetary Policy." *Journal of Monetary Economics* 4 (April 1978): 341–62.

West, Robert Craig, *Banking Reform and the Federal Reserve, 1863–1923.* Ithaca, N.Y.: Cornell University Press, 1977.

Whitehead, David D. "Interstate Banking: Taking Inventory." *Economic Review* (Federal Reserve Bank of Atlanta), 68 (May 1983a): 4–20.

———. *A Guide to Interstate Banking.* Federal Reserve Bank of Atlanta, 1983b.

Willis, Parker B. *The Federal Funds Market: Its Origin and Development.* 5th ed. Federal Reserve Bank of Boston, 1972.

Wojnilower, Albert M. "The Central Role of Credit Crunches in Recent Financial History." *Brookings Papers on Economic Activity* 2 (1980): 277–326.

Wolkowitz, Benjamin, and Lloyd-Davies, Peter R. "Reducing Federal Reserve Float." *Federal Reserve Bulletin* 65 (December 1979): 945–50.

Wood, John. "Financial Intermediaries and Monetary Control: An Example." *Journal of Monetary Economics* 8 (September 1981): 145–63.

INDEX